The Learning and Teaching of Phonological Decoding in Chinese EFL Children

Keren Hua

The Learning and Teaching of Phonological Decoding in Chinese EFL Children

 Springer

Keren Hua
Shanghai Sanda University
Shanghai, China

ISBN 978-981-97-6890-5   ISBN 978-981-97-6891-2   (eBook)
https://doi.org/10.1007/978-981-97-6891-2

This Springer imprint is published by the registered company Springer Nature Singapore Pte Ltd.
The registered company address is: 152 Beach Road, #21-01/04 Gateway East, Singapore 189721,
Singapore

If disposing of this product, please recycle the paper.

Acknowledgements

I would like to take this opportunity to thank all the people who have offered their generous support to my Ph.D. project, on which this book is based.

First and foremost, I would like to express my sincere gratitude to Prof. Florence Myles, my supervisor, for her immense support, constant encouragement, invaluable input and insightful comments. Without her, this thesis would not have been completed. Doing a Ph.D. with Florence is such a blissful journey. Her humour always kept me cheerful on the bumpy road and her wisdom steered me in the right direction.

In addition, I extend my gratitude to Dr. Helen Emery for generously sharing her expertise in the research area of early literacy development. My sincere thanks also go to Dr. Philip Hofmeister for his professional assistance with the statistics.

My special thanks are due to the primary school teachers, students and the textbook writer who participated in my study. Without their invaluable assistance and cooperation, this book would not have been possible.

I am also grateful to the wonderful faculty and staff at the University of Essex, my beloved friends and fellow Ph.D. colleagues, who have shown me their support, care and encouragement throughout the process.

My thanks also go to Shanghai Sanda University for the contribution towards the costs of this Ph.D. study.

Finally, but most importantly, I would like to express my gratitude to my parents, who are always there for me. Their unconditional love, constant support and warm encouragement gave me the strength to complete this research work. To them, I dedicate this book.

Contents

Chapter 1
Introduction

Phonological decoding is a crucial skill in the process of learning to read in English. The present study investigates the English phonological decoding ability of Chinese children learning English as a foreign language (EFL) in the context of mainland China. As classroom instruction is the major source of English input for Chinese EFL children and influences their learning of phonological decoding, this study also aims to describe, interpret and evaluate the teaching of phonological decoding to Chinese EFL children, and to a certain extent explore the relationship between their phonological decoding ability and the instructional practice. This chapter starts with the description of the background and rationale of the research before introducing the context for the study. Then the focus and significance of the study are given, followed by the organisation of the book. After this, key terminological terms are defined and specific text conventions are explained.

1.1 Background and Rationale of the Study

Learning to read in English is an enormously complex activity which involves the acquisition of many different abilities, such as word recognition abilities (e.g. sight word reading, namely reading words by accessing them in memory, and phonological decoding, namely transforming printed words into sound representations with reliance on spelling-sound correspondences), language comprehension abilities (e.g. oral vocabulary, the abilities to process semantic and syntactic information), cognitive ability (e.g. working memory), and the ability to apply the real-world background knowledge (Lesaux and Geva 2006; Stuart et al. 2008). This study focuses on one of these abilities, phonological decoding, which is a crucial skill for all aspects of English language learning. There is evidence that the development of phonological decoding skills is the vital component throughout the process of L1/L2/FL word-level reading development (Chu 2002; Ehri 2005b, 2020; Hamada and Koda 2008, 2011;

Hu 2003; Segalowitz et al. 1998; Yin et al. 2007). For L1 children, the extraction of the sound representation of a word via the phonological decoding route can enable them to locate the word in their mental lexicon and then retrieve its meaning. Although for L2/FL children, learning to read words is not a simple phonological issue, involving not only extracting the phonological information from individual words but also associating the sound with the concepts, the establishment of a complete and solid sound representation for a word is believed to be the first and foremost springboard to success in young L2/FL children's learning to read words (Hu 2003; Segalowitz et al. 1998). As Woore (2009) argued, the facilitative role of phonological decoding in learning to read words applies not only to "conscious memorisation (e.g. when learning a list of words) but also to incidental acquisition of new words when reading" (p. 5). Such facilitative function of phonological decoding in learning to read words is also supported by Ehri (2005a), who indicated that for the word already existing in the oral vocabulary, learners can directly get access to its meaning though the phonological decoding route and thereby recognise the word in its printed form. And for a new word, more than one complete graphophonic analysis is needed to secure the word in memory and the word is thereby given a unique address that eliminates confusion among similarly spelled words, which is particularly vital at higher levels, when reading becomes a principal source of vocabulary expansion.

There is also evidence that the lower level phonological decoding processes are integral components of L1/L2/FL reading comprehension and a strong predictor of reading success (Nassaji 2003; Rayner et al. 2001; Wang et al. 2002). Although reading comprehension as a meaning construction process also involves higher–level syntactic and semantic processes, the role of efficient phonological decoding processes cannot be ignored. With the accurate and expeditious word-level reading skill, the L1/L2/FL readers can free up their cognitive resources that are intended for decoding the constituent letters within words and devote their active attention to more sophisticated comprehension tasks such as making inferences and summarising main ideas (Adams 1990; Anderson 1999; Grabe 1991; Samuels 1994; Schwanenflugel et al. 2006; Stanovich 1992).

However, phonological decoding is not an easy task for L1 children, and this is also true for children learning English as a second or foreign language, particularly those whose L1 orthographic and phonological systems are substantially different from English. A spate of research has been conducted on L1 children's acquisition of phonological decoding in English (Ehri 1992, 2005a; Frith 1985; Gough et al. 1992; Marsh et al. 1981). In the past decade, there has been growing interest in the nature of this skill and its acquisition in the L2/FL context (e.g. Chiappe and Siegel 1999; McBride-Chang and Treiman 2003; Yin et al. 2007). However, in the L2 reading research within the context of Chinese L1-English L2, the studies on the issues of phonological decoding development are seriously lacking (e.g. McBride-Chang and Treiman 2003; Yin et al. 2007). Therefore, it is essential to explore Chinese children's phonological decoding ability, which is an important process we still know little about.

Considering that classroom instruction constitutes the main source of input in English for FL children, it would be interesting to investigate the teaching of phonological decoding to Chinese children. Much L1 research has shown the necessity of providing beginning readers with explicit and systematic phonics instruction in helping them to acquire the knowledge and skills required for phonological decoding (Adams 1990; National Reading Panel 2000; Rose 2006; Torgerson et al. 2006). ESL/EFL studies have also revealed the effects of phonics instruction on learners' phonological decoding development (Chen 2003; Qiu 2007; Stuart 1999). Findings from the present study aim to provide a better understanding of Chinese EFL children's phonological decoding ability, of the instructional practice of phonological decoding, and a tentative exploration of the relationship between their phonological decoding ability and the instructional practice.

1.2 The Context for the Study

1.2.1 Teaching English to Young Learners in China

Over the last two decades, there has been a rapid worldwide expansion of programmes in Teaching English to Young Learners (TEYL), mainly as a response to the pressing demand for improving proficiency in English, given its status as a global communication tool. In 2000, the British Council held a worldwide survey on teaching English as a foreign language to young learners (age below 11) at primary level and its results confirmed the increasing global trend of TEYL. Although mainland China was not included in the survey, probably because when the survey was carried out English had not been standardised as a compulsory subject in primary schools across China, it should be pointed out that some large cities in China had started to offer English at grade 4 or 5 (age 9–11) in key schools from the early 1990s. Moreover, as early as in 1988, Shanghai was entrusted by the Ministry of Education (MoE) of the People's Republic of China with the task of pioneering curricular changes in basic education and providing relevant experience for other parts of China. The motive behind this move was to tackle the growing nationwide dissatisfaction since the 1970s with the outdated curriculum on one hand, and on the other hand, to expand TEYL into the regions whose rapid socioeconomic development required personnel proficient in English (Hu 2002, 2005). After 10 years of trials, Shanghai Curriculum and Teaching Materials Reform Commission, in 1998, finalised the new curriculum for nine-year compulsory education.[1] The new curriculum required that English instruction start at grade 3 (age 8–9). However, the primary English teaching developed so fast in

---

[1] Nine-year compulsory education comprises compulsory primary and junior secondary schooling. In some areas, five years of primary schooling is followed by four years of junior-secondary education, while in the other areas, six years and three years are allocated respectively for primary and junior secondary education (Hu 2002).

Shanghai that in 2001 all the primary schools in Shanghai had already started to offer English classes at grade one (age 6–7).

Encouraged by the success of Shanghai in TEYL and realising the need to upgrade the English level of all Chinese citizens, on January 18, 2001, China's Ministry of Education issued a policy statement entitled *The Ministry of Education Guidelines for Vigorously Promoting the Teaching of English in Primary Schools*, requiring that English should be offered as a compulsory subject in grade 3 (age 8–9), first in cities and counties, starting in autumn 2001, generally moving to towns and villages, starting in autumn 2002, with a minimum of 80 min a week. It was estimated that in 2001 when the policy was implemented, there were 130 million primary school pupils in China. Such a large-scale initiative is ambitious and daunting. Moreover, knowledge about the teaching of English at primary level in China is still limited. With a view to ensuring the successful expansion of TEYL into primary schools, more studies at this level are needed. This provides one of the motivations for this study. Additionally, considering the long history of Shanghai in TEYL at primary level and its pioneering role, this research chose its teachers and pupils as the participants. The English teaching context in China is described in more details in the next sections.

1.2.2   The General Educational System in Mainland China

In this section, the Chinese educational system is firstly discussed briefly and then the relation between national government and provincial government in the primary educational system is described.

The Chinese educational system consists of five tiers: kindergarten, primary school, junior secondary school, senior secondary school, and post-secondary or university/college (see Fig. 1.1).

Basically, the educational system in China is centralised. At the primary level, the national government has the responsibility for making national educational policies, designing curriculum objectives, allocating time and content requirements, reviewing and approving textbooks to be used in schools, and producing guidelines for curriculum implementation across the national educational system as a whole. The national English curriculum related to primary level will be more fully described in the next section. In line with the national educational policies and guidelines, each provincial government works out its own strategic plans for the provision of primary English, manages teacher training, choosing textbooks from the list of approved textbooks. Although there is no national system of assessment for primary schools, the district educational department is required to design the assessment and monitor the progress and quality of its local primary school education for each core subject including English.

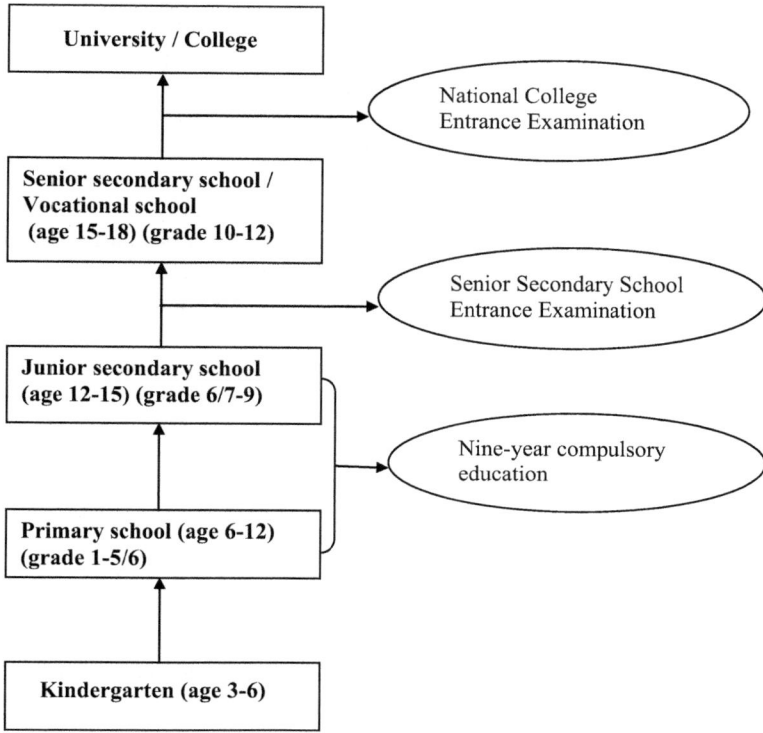

Fig. 1.1 China's educational system

1.2.3   National Primary School English Curriculum

Along with the national policy (Ministry of Education 2001a) to promote the provision of English in primary schools, Chinese MoE (2001b) promulgated *National English Curriculum Standards for Nine-year Compulsory Education and Senior High Schools (Piloting Edition)* to guide the teaching of English as a foreign language in primary schools, junior and senior secondary schools. In 2011, Chinese MoE issued the slightly revised version of *English Curriculum Standards for Compulsory Education* (hereafter ECS), which exclusively targets the curriculum standards pertinent to grades 1–9. The fundamental objective of the 2011 ECS is to develop students' language proficiency, which is based not only on language skills and linguistic knowledge, but also on attitudes to learning, learning strategies and cultural awareness. With the increasing emphasis on developing students' sense of value and building their characters, the 2022 ECS (Ministry of Education 2022) sets its objective as the development of core competencies, in which cultural awareness, thinking skills, and learning strategies are given the same weight as language skills and linguistic knowledge.

Despite the revisions, the 2011 and 2022 ECS share the same ultimate goal for phonological decoding upon completion of English learning in primary schools, that is, decoding English words by drawing on phonics rules. In addition, the goals for word reading instruction remain the same in the 2011 and 2022 ECS, although the descriptors for word reading are included in the different lists. The 2011 ECS lists the goals for word reading under the development of reading skills while the 2022 version separates them under the lists of goals for vocabulary and pronunciation learning. As regards text reading, the teaching goals remain primarily the same in the two versions of ECS, except that the 2022 ECS suggests a more diverse range of text types to develop text reading skills. Throughout the present study, the teaching of primary school English is guided by the 2011 ECS. Therefore, this section will further elaborate on what the 2011 ECS states about the knowledge and skills that are taken into account in this study, such as phonological decoding, word reading and text reading.

1.2.3.1 Curriculum Objectives

The 2011 ECS puts forward the objectives for language skills, including word and text reading skills, at two ability levels (Level 1 and Level 2) with descriptors for each level. For linguistic knowledge, attitudes to learning, learning strategies and cultural awareness, the objectives and corresponding descriptors are provided at the end of primary schooling, i.e. Level 2. The correspondence between the level system and the grade system in the 2011 ECS is shown in Table 1.1. Grades 3 and 4 should work towards Level 1 while grades 5 and 6 towards Level 2. But it should be noted that the curriculum is designed based on the national policy (Ministry of Education 2001a), which requires English instruction to start from grade 3. Yet some schools in large cities such as Shanghai start teaching English from grade 1. To address this difference, the 2011 curriculum guidelines state that for schools starting English teaching from grade 1, Level 1 can be applied to lower primary grades such as grades 1 and 2, and Level 2 is the minimum objective for higher primary grades such as grades 4 and 5 to work towards. In other words, Level 1 represents the required standard for lower primary grades, and Level 2 represents the required standard for the end of primary school.

The 2011 ECS requires English instruction in the lower grades to focus on listening and speaking skills while the higher primary grades will further strengthen those two skills and at the same time develop pupils' reading and writing skills. Here, we will discuss the requirement for the reading skills at Levels 1 and 2, because reading is always placed in a central position for English language teaching and learning in China, and is also the central research area for the present study.

Three objectives are provided for English reading instruction in lower primary grades, i.e. Level 1, and six objectives in higher primary grades, i.e. Level 2. Students in the lower grades are required to be able to (1) recognise words printed with pictures; (2) recognise objects first and then understand words describing them; (3) read and understand short and simple stories with the aid of pictures. For the higher grades,

Table 1.1 The levels and grades in primary school English curriculum standards (Ministry of Education 2011)

Primary school grades	English Curriculum Standards (2011) Work towards:	Notes
Grade 1	/	No specifications for this level; Instruction is mainly in the form of viewing, listening and speaking
Grade 2		
Grade 3	Level 1	Students should start studying English in Grade 3
Grade 4		
Grade 5	Level 2	The required standard for the end of primary school
Grade 6		

the students are required to be able to (1) read and recognise learned words; (2) read aloud simple words by drawing on phonics rules; (3) read and understand short and simple instructions in textbooks; (4) read and understand simple information expressed in texts like greeting cards; (5) read and understand simple stories or short texts with the aid of pictures and form the habit of reading for overall comprehension; (6) read aloud accurately the learned stories and texts (Ministry of Education 2011, pp. 13–14). In addition, the 2011 ECS provides the objectives for the knowledge of phonics rules at Level 2, that is, grasping the knowledge of 26 letter names and simple phonics rules.

It is evident from the 2011 ECS that attention is attached to phonological decoding, word recognition and text reading at the primary school level of English instruction. In terms of word recognition, pupils in lower grades are required to read and recognise words with visual aids such as pictures and objects, while requirement for pupils in higher grades is increased. They are supposed to read and recognise taught words without any visual help. Meanwhile, they are also expected to grasp simple phonics rules and apply these rules to read aloud simple words. With regard to the reading at text level, besides the ability to understand simple stories accompanied by pictures as visual support, which is the requirement for both lower and higher grades, pupils in higher graders are also expected to read aloud the learned texts. It can also be inferred from the objectives listed in the curriculum standards that simple stories with illustration of pictures are suggested as the major source of reading materials in primary school English textbook.

1.2.3.2 Implementation Guidelines

The 2011 ECS provides guidelines for teaching and learning, assessment and evaluation, materials design, and development and use of curricular resources. This section will summarise the points related to this research in the following aspects.

Teaching and Learning

The guidelines advocate the adoption of task-based teaching and learning as much as possible in order that students can use the language for real communication. Teachers are required to creatively design learning activities that are relevant to the students' real life, according to the overall curriculum objectives and content. It is also required to engage students' interest in the activity and organise them effectively so that they participate actively and complete the tasks.

It is interesting to note that although example lesson plans are provided in the ECS for teaching listening, speaking, listening and reading skills, there is no example lesson plan for phonics instruction. And no modelling of using phonological decoding in vocabulary and reading instruction was found in the example lessons.

Assessment and Evaluation

It is suggested in the guidelines to use formative assessment as the major method of assessing pupils' achievement in English, in order to encourage students, and motivate them to participate actively in learning English. The types of formative assessment for different levels of primary grades are listed as below:

(1) For lower grades, assessment should use activities similar to normal teaching and learning activities. Through observing students' behaviour and discussing their progress with them teachers should assess their ability to use English to do things.
(2) For higher grades, a combination of oral and written tests can be used. Oral tests should check students' ability to use language to communicate about content close to their real lives. Written tests should focus on checking their listening and reading skills, using methods that are as active and lively as possible.

Materials Design

When dealing with writing materials for primary school children, the ECS states:

(1) The teaching content should follow the principle from simple to complex, from easy to difficult.
(2) Important language points should be repeated regularly.
(3) Materials should be as interesting as possible in order to stimulate students' interest and motivate them to learn the language.
(4) Content for the lower grades of primary school should focus mainly on listening and speaking abilities.
(5) Materials should provide real-life situations to nurture students' communicative ability.
(6) Materials should include audio-visual materials.

Development and Use of Curricular Resources

The 2011 ECS indicates that English curricular resources include the textbook, supplementary teaching materials and teaching environment, such as audio-visual materials, visual aids, multimedia materials, radio/television programmes, internet resources, newspaper, magazines, and the teaching facilities in classrooms, etc. Some relevant suggestions are stated in the ECS as below:

(1) Teachers need to understand and be familiar with the design of the textbook in order to use the textbook effectively.
(2) Teachers should take advantage of school facilities such as televisions, multi-media computers, VCD or DVD players, and projectors, etc., to enrich both the teaching and learning process.
(3) Teachers should create ample opportunities for students to use computer and internet resources and thereby promote autonomous learning.

1.3 Focus of the Study

The central topic of the study focuses on Chinese EFL children's phonological decoding ability and the teaching of phonological decoding to the participants. The study firstly explores (1) children's ability to decode different types of orthographic units, (2) the strategies children at different levels of reading ability employ in sounding out vowel graphemes, (3) children's phonological decoding ability in relation to their reading ability. Then the study explores the textbook materials used to teach phonological decoding to the children and the classroom instructional practices. The issues relevant to the phonological decoding materials and classroom instruction can be summarised as follows: the scope and sequence of the component knowledge and skills of phonological decoding, the practice provided in the teaching materials, the extent to which the letter-sound relations are taught for sounding out the words in the phonics section and the textbook vocabulary, the classroom instruction of phonics, the application of phonological decoding in in vocabulary teaching, and the text-level reading activities used in the classroom. All these issues are referred to in detail in the study's research questions (see Sect. 3.1). The relationships between those different elements will also be investigated.

1.4 Significance of the Study

The investigation of Chinese children's phonological decoding ability adds more understanding to the research field of phonological decoding in the L2/FL context. Findings obtained from the current study provide insights into Chinese children's phonological decoding profile, including performance in decoding different types of orthographic units, the strategies children at different levels of reading ability use to sound out vowel graphemes, and their decoding ability in relation to reading ability. These findings also provide valuable information for EFL teachers in Chinese primary schools to better understand their students' lower level word decoding processes in order to plan instruction that best suits their students' capacities and needs.

The investigation of the teaching materials and classroom instruction pertaining to phonological decoding enriches our understanding of how the decoding instruction is designed, developed and delivered to primary students in the context, and thereby informs the interplay between the classroom instruction and children's development of phonological decoding skills.

Moreover, to the best of my knowledge, since phonological decoding was included in Chinese primary English curriculum, there has not been any previous study exploring students' decoding performance and evaluating the effectiveness of the teaching programme. The present study is therefore significant and timely in the context as its implications could contribute to the design, development, delivery, and evaluation of the phonological decoding programme.

1.5 Organisation of the Book

This book consists of six chapters. This introduction chapter has presented the background and rationale, the context, the focus, and the significance of the study. Chapter 2 provides a more detailed review of the literature relevant to this study, covering the definitions and components of phonological decoding, previous research findings on the acquisition of phonological decoding in L1 and FL/L2 contexts, and on the factors affecting Chinese EFL children's decoding acquisition, such as L1 orthography, literacy experience, English phonology, and classroom instruction of phonological decoding. In addition, the research issues addressed in this study are discussed. Chapter 3 presents the research purpose and questions, research paradigm, data sources and instruments. This chapter also includes results gained from a pilot study assessing the research instruments. Chapter 4 presents the results of both quantitative and qualitative analyses of the data generated from the battery of tests. The results are usually discussed as they are presented in order to answer the research questions relevant to children's phonological decoding ability. Chapter 5 presents the results of both quantitative and qualitative analyses of the data generated from the teaching materials and classroom observations. The results are usually discussed as they are presented in order to answer the research questions relevant to the teaching of phonological decoding. Chapter 6, the last chapter of the book, aims to summarise the main findings and to discuss the links between children's phonological decoding ability and the instruction they receive. Finally, the contribution of the study, its pedagogical implications, its limitations and suggestions for further research are provided as conclusion.

1.6 Definition of the Terminological Terms

Terminological terms used in this study are defined below.

Analytic approach of phonics instruction: children are taught to analyse letter-sound relations once the word is identified.

Body: the orthographic equivalent of the rime of a monosyllabic word.

A **digraph** is a two-letter grapheme where two letters represent one sound such as <ea> in *seat* and <sh> in *ship*.

Grapheme: is an individual letter or letter chunk that represents a single sound (phoneme) in a word. In English, graphemes can be made up from one letter e.g. *p*, two letters e.g. *sh*, or three letters e.g. *tch*.

Minimal pair: two words whose pronunciation is different only by one sound segment that occurs in the same position, like *sheep* and *ship*.

Nursery rhyme: a short poem having a regular correspondence of sounds, especially at the ends of lines.

Phoneme: the smallest and perceptually distinct segment of speech that signals meaningful differences in words, like /p/, /b/, /d/, and /t/ in the words *pad*, *pat*, *bad*, and *bat*.

Phonics instruction in the present study refers to the approach in which the teacher helps children learn how to decode words with reliance on their knowledge of spelling-sound relations.

The term **phonological decoding** is used interchangeably with **decoding** in this study. It refers to deriving the phonological representation of a printed word by mapping sounds to the constituent letters and blending the sounds together. The size of the letter units can be individual graphemes or larger sub-word units, i.e. rime patterns.

Rime: the end of a monosyllabic word, comprising the central vowel plus final consonant(s) in a monosyllabic word, e.g. *<op>*, *<at>*, *<ight>*, *<ump>* .

A **split digraph** has a letter that splits, i.e. comes between, the two letters in the digraph, as in *make* and *gate*, where <k> separates the digraph <a-e> which in both words represents the phoneme /eɪ/. There are six split digraphs in English spelling: <a-e>, <e-e>, <i-e>, <o-e>, <u-e>, <y-e>, as in *make, scene, like, bone, cube, type.*

Synthetic approach of phonics instruction: children are taught to convert letters into sounds or phonemes and then blend the sounds to form word sound.

A **trigraph** is a three-letter grapheme where three letters represent one sound, e.g. <igh> in *night*.

1.7 Some Text Conventions

< > : is used to signify the sub-word units, e.g. <at> and <b> in *bat*.

Italics: indicates the printed form of words or nonwords, e.g. *bat, yat*.

/ /: is used to represent the phonemic transcription adopting the International Phonetic Alphabetic system, e.g. /æ/.

[ ]: is used to represent the Roman alphabet letters in the Pinyin system.

References

Adams, M. J. (1990). *Beginning to read: Thinking and learning about print*. Urbana-Champaign, IL: Center for the Study of Reading.

Anderson, N. J. (1999). *Exploring second language reading: Issues and strategies*. Boston, MA: Heinle & Heinle.

Chen, Y. (2003). *The effects of phonological decoding training on English word recognition skills in Taiwanese EFL children*. (Unpublished Master dissertaion). National Taipei University of Education.

Chiappe, P., & Siegel, L. S. (1999). Phonological awareness and reading acquisition in English- and Punjabi-speaking Canadian children. *Journal of Educational Psychology, 91*(1), 20–28.

Chu, H. (2002). Beginning EFL learners' decoding skill and word reading ability. *Taipei Municipal Teachers College Journal, 33*, 471–484.

Ehri, L. C. (1992). Reconceptualizing the development of sight word reading and its relationship to recoding. In P. Gough, L. Ehri, & R. Treiman (Eds.), *Reading acquisition* (pp. 107–143). Hillsdale, NJ: Lawrence Erlbaum Associates.

Ehri, L. C. (2005a). *Development of sight word reading: Phases and findings*. Oxford: Blackwell Publishing Ltd.

Ehri, L. C. (2005b). Learning to read words: Theory, findings, and issues. *Scientific Studies of Reading, 9*(2), 167–188.

Ehri, L. C. (2020). The science of learning to read words: A case for systematic phonics instruction. *Reading Research Quarterly, 55*(S1), S45–S60.

Frith, U. (1985). Beneath the surface of developmental dyslexia. In K. Patterson, J. C. Marshall, & M. Coltheart (Eds.), *Surface Dyslexia: Cognitive and Neuro-Psychological Studies of Phonological Reading* (pp. 301–330). London: Lawrence Erlbaum Associates.

Gough, P. B., Juel, C., & Griffith, P. L. (1992). Reading, spelling, and the orthographic cipher. In P. B. Gough, L. C. Ehri, & R. Treiman (Eds.), *Reading acquisition* (pp. 35–48). Hillsdale, NJ: Lawrence Erlbaum Associates.

Grabe, W. (1991). Current developments in second language reading research. *TESOL Quarterly, 25*(3), 375–406.

Hamada, M., & Koda, K. (2008). Influence of first language orthographic experience on second language decoding and word learning. *Language Learning, 58*(1), 1–31.

Hamada, M., & Koda, K. (2011). The role of the phonological loop in English word learning: A comparison of Chinese ESL learners and native speakers. *Journal of Psycholinguistic Research, 40*(2), 75–92.

Hu, G. (2002). Recent important developments in secondary English-language teaching in the People's Republic of China. *Language, Culture and Curriculum, 15*(1), 30–49.

Hu, C. F. (2003). Phonological memory, phonological awareness, and foreign language word learning. *Language Learning, 53*(3), 429–462.

Hu, G. (2005). English language education in China: Policies, progress, and problems. *Language Policy, 4*(1), 5–24.

Lesaux, N. K., & Geva, E. (2006). Synthesis: Development of literacy in language-minority students. In D. August & T. Shanahan (Eds.), *Developing literacy in second-language learners: Report of the National Literacy Panel on language-minority children and youth* (pp. 53–74). Mahwah, NJ, US: Lawrence Erlbaum Associates Publishers.

Marsh, G., Friedman, M., Welch, V., & Desberg, P. (1981). A cognitive-developmental theory of reading acquisition. In G. E. McKinnon & T. G. Waller (Eds.), *Reading research: Advances in theory and practice* (Vol. 3, pp. 199–221). New York: Academic Press.

McBride-Chang, C., & Treiman, R. (2003). Hong Kong Chinese kindergartners learn to read English analytically. *Psychological Science, 14*(2), 138–143.

Ministry of Education, China. (2001a). *Guidelines for vigorously promoting the teaching of English in primary schools.* Beijing: Beijing Normal University Press.

Ministry of Education, China. (2001b). *National English curriculum standards for nine-year compulsory education and senior high schools (Piloting Edition).* Beijing: Beijing Normal University Press.

Ministry of Education, China. (2011). *English curriculum standards for compulsory education.* Beijing: Beijing Normal University Press.

Ministry of Education, China. (2022). *English curriculum standards for compulsory education.* Beijing: Beijing Normal University Press.

Nassaji, H. (2003). Higher–level and lower–level text processing skills in advanced ESL reading comprehension. *The Modern Language Journal, 87*(2), 261–276.

National Reading Panel. (2000). *Teaching children to read: An evidence-based assessment of the scientific research literature on reading and its implications for reading instruction.* Retrieved November 16, 2010, from https://www.nichd.nih.gov/publications/pubs/nrp/Pages/smallbook.aspx

Qiu, J. (2007). An experimental study on phonics instruction. *Journal of Basic English Education, 9*(1), 29–33.

Rayner, K., Foorman, B. R., Perfetti, C. A., Pesetsky, D., & Seidenberg, M. S. (2001). How psychological science informs the teaching of reading. *Psychological Science in the Public Interest, 2*(2), 31–74.

Rose, J. (2006). *Independent review of the teaching of early reading: Final report.* London: Department for Education and Skills Publications.

Samuels, S. J. (1994). Word recognition. In R. B. Ruddell, M. R. Ruddell, & H. Singer (Eds.), *Theoretical models and processes of reading* (pp. 359–380). Newark, Delaware: International Reading Association.

Schwanenflugel, P. J., Meisinger, E. B., Wisenbaker, J. M., Kuhn, M. R., Strauss, G. P., & Morris, R. D. (2006). Becoming a fluent and automatic reader in the early elementary school years. *Reading Research Quarterly, 41*(4), 496–522.

Segalowitz, S. J., Segalowitz, N. S., & Wood, A. G. (1998). Assessing the development of automaticity in second language word recognition. *Applied Psycholinguistics, 19*(1), 53–67.

Stanovich, K. E. (1992). The psychology of reading: Evolutionary and revolutionary developments. *Annual Review of Applied Linguistics, 12*(1), 3–30.

Stuart, M., Stainthorp, R., & Snowling, M. (2008). Literacy as a complex activity: Deconstructing the simple view of reading. *Literacy, 42*(2), 59–66.

Stuart, M. (1999). Getting ready for reading: Early phoneme awareness and phonics teaching improves reading and spelling in inner-city second language learners. *British Journal of Educational Psychology, 69*(4), 587–605.

Torgerson, C., Brooks, G., & Hall, J. (2006). *A systematic review of the research literature on the use of phonics in the teaching of reading and spelling.* London: Department for Education and Skills.

Wang, Y., Lin, C., & Yu, G. (2002). Relationship between phonological skill and reading comprehension ability among poor English learners. *Acta Psychologica Sincia, 34*(3), 279–283.

Woore, R. (2009). Beginners' progress in decoding L2 French: Some longitudinal evidence from English modern foreign languages classrooms. *The Language Learning Journal, 37*(1), 3–18.

Yin, L., Anderson, R. C., & Zhu, J. (2007). Stages in Chinese children's reading of English words. *Journal of Educational Psychology, 99*(4), 852–866.

Chapter 2
Theory and Research on Phonological Decoding

This chapter provides a review of literature on the notion of phonological decoding, the learning and the teaching of phonological decoding in L1 and L2 contexts, with the aim of establishing an understanding of the theoretical background and empirical research that underpin the present study.

Section 2.1 clarifies the definitions of phonological decoding and Sect. 2.2 presents the component knowledge and skills of phonological decoding. Section 2.3 describes the important role of phonological decoding in learning to read in English. Section 2.4 reviews the theories and studies on the developmental phases of English phonological decoding in L1 and L2/FL contexts. Section 2.5 presents and discusses the factors influencing Chinese EFL children's development of phonological decoding skills, such as the difference between English and Chinese writing system, Chinese literacy experience, English phonology, Classroom teaching of phonological decoding.

2.1 Defining Phonological Decoding

Definitions of phonological decoding, as a critical component skill in learning to read English, have been offered by researchers in the field of literacy acquisition and educational psychology, e.g. Lipka et al. (2005) for the former and Ehri (1992, 1994, 1999, 2005a, 2020) for the latter, as well as cognitive psychology, e.g. Harley (2008) and Share (1995). The core concept of phonological decoding is the extraction of phonological information from printed words.

There are different terms that have been used to specify the process of print-to-sound translation, such as phonological recoding (Ehri 2005b; Share 1995), or sub-lexical recoding (Harley 2008). Although they are often used interchangeably with phonological decoding, they embody somewhat different assumptions. Phonological recoding implicates the process of recoding the printed word back to its oral representation in the mental lexicon (Share 1995). In other words, the pronunciation of a word

© The Author(s), under exclusive license to Springer Nature Singapore Pte Ltd. 2024
K. Hua, *The Learning and Teaching of Phonological Decoding in Chinese EFL Children*, https://doi.org/10.1007/978-981-97-6891-2_2

is retrieved when it is newly encountered in print through systematic relationships between letters and sounds, and the sound representation of the word is then used to match with one in the oral vocabulary repertoire. Sub-lexical recoding suggests not only the use of spelling-sound correspondences at the level of graphemes but also the influence of the larger orthographic units, namely bodies (see definition in Sect. 1.6) on the decoding process of words (Harley 2008). In the present study, phonological decoding, rather than phonological/sub-lexical recoding, is operationalised because the study investigates children's ability to derive the speech-based information from the printed letters and assemble the segment sounds, regardless of whether the sound representations are in their oral vocabulary or not.

In some studies (e.g. Lipka et al. 2005), phonological decoding only involves the application of spelling-sound correspondences at the level of graphemes (single letter or letter combinations that represent single sounds/phonemes, e.g. <sh>, <o>, <p>), and phonemes (the smallest individual sounds, e.g. /ʃ/, /ɒ/, /p/). However, in some models (e.g. Ehri 2005b; Harley 2008), the correspondences can be at the level of the smallest sub-word units, namely between graphemes and phonemes, or at the level of larger sub-word units, namely between orthographic bodies and phonological rimes.

In the present study, the process of phonological decoding does not limit itself to the mapping of phonemes onto graphemes. Here, phonological decoding is operationalised as the ability to map the phonological representations onto the sub-word units (graphemes and orthographic rimes), and blend the derived constituent sounds (Harley 2008; Iversen and Tunmer 1993). The phonological decoding route consists of two subsystems (sub-word units), namely a standard grapheme–phoneme conversion mechanism supplemented with a rime subsystem that makes use of information about correspondences between orthographic and phonological rimes (e.g. <op> in *shop*) (Harley 2008). The rime subsystem reflects the influence of larger orthographic units on word pronunciation. It should be noted that phonological decoding does not necessarily guarantee the direct access to the exact phonological representation of a word, due to the lack of straightforward grapheme-phoneme relations in English orthography. When decoding a word, children may generate more than one candidate phonological representations of a word until the phonological representation is matched with a spoken word in the mental lexicon. However, when there is no prior experience with the spoken word for children, especially L2 children, to refer to, there may be ambiguity or uncertainty in choosing the correct phonological forms, and children may therefore need external help (e.g. teachers, dictionary) in locating its exact spoken form. Despite this, the decoding mechanism is undoubtedly conducive to securing the spelling-sound connections of the word in memory (Ehri 2005a, b; Hamada and Koda 2011).

To recapitulate, the present study will focus on phonological decoding as a means of retrieving the pronunciation of the printed word with reliance on the mechanism of grapheme-phoneme correspondences supplemented with the larger sub-word system of rime units. The next section discusses the main components of phonological decoding in more details.

2.2 The Component Knowledge and Skills of Phonological Decoding

At the centre of phonological decoding skills is the knowledge of spelling-sound correspondences and the skill of employing this knowledge to map sounds onto letters or letter chunks and assemble the sound segments to form the pronunciation of words. In addition, the development of phonological decoding also entails phonological awareness and letter identification (Vandervelden and Siegel 1995; Vellutino 2003).

2.2.1 Phonological Awareness

As Vellutino and Scanlon (1987) indicated, acquiring phonological awareness skills facilitates a conceptual grasp of how the alphabet works (i.e. letters can be associated with sounds) or vice versa. Phonological awareness has been found in numerous studies to be not only positively associated with but also predictive of early phonological decoding ability (Adams 1990; Blachman et al. 2000; Demont and Gombert 1996; Griffith and Gough 1986; Stanovich 1992; Swank and Catts 1994), though it can also be facilitated by learning to read in English (Read et al. 1986; Torgesen et al. 1994). This reciprocal relation has also been documented in L2 studies (Cheung 1999; Hu 2003, 2005; Muter and Diethelm 2001). The operational definition of phonological awareness for the present study is the awareness of and the ability to identify and manipulate the constituent phonological elements in words (Adams 1990; Bentin 1992; Goswami and Bryant 1990; McBride-Chang et al. 1997). It is generally believed that there are at least three levels of phonological awareness, namely (a) awareness of syllables, (b) awareness of sub-syllabic units of onset (the initial consonant or consonant cluster in a syllable) and rime (the vowel and final consonant or consonant cluster), (c) awareness of individual phonemes (the smallest sound units) (Goswami and Bryant 1990; Wagner et al. 1997).

Among the three levels of phonological awareness, phonemic awareness has been generally accepted as the strongest predictor of the acquisition of phonological decoding (Caravolas et al. 2005; Duncan et al. 2000; Harris and Giannouli 1999; Hulme et al. 2002; Muter et al. 1998, 2004; Nation and Hulme 1997; Share 1995; Vandervelden and Siegel 1995). With phonemic awareness, children understand that spoken words consist of a series of discrete sound units (phonemes) and are able to recognise and manipulate these segment sounds. There are different types of phonemic awareness skills: (a) phoneme identification (recognising the common sound in different words, e.g. what is the common sound in words *bike*, *boy*, and *bell*?; recognising the word with the odd sound in three or four words, e.g. which word does not belong? *bus*, *bun*, *rug*); (b) phoneme isolation (recognising individual sounds in a given position in a word, e.g. what sound comes at the end of the word *bed*?); (c) phoneme substitution (replace a phoneme in a word with another phoneme to form a new word, e.g. What word will it be if we change the /r/ in *run* to /s/?);

(d) phoneme blending (combining individual sounds to form a word, e.g. what word is it, /g/, /ɛ/ /t/?); (e) phoneme segmentation (breaking up a word into its individual component sounds, by tapping out or counting the sounds, e.g. how many phonemes are there in *ship*?); (f) phoneme deletion (recognise what word remains when a specified phoneme is removed, e.g. what is *stop* without the /s/?), etc. Different types of phonemic awareness skills may play different roles in the process of acquiring phonological decoding skills. Researchers have examined the relation between different types of phonemic awareness skills and decoding ability (Murray 1998; Vandervelden and Siegel 1995).

Murray (1998) examined the effects of the training in different types of phonemic awareness skills on L1 children's decoding ability. These children were kindergartners aged 5.9 and were highly proficient at recognising letters. It was found that children trained in phoneme identification made significantly greater gains than children trained in phoneme manipulation (phoneme isolation, blending, and segmentation) on a test of phonetic cue reading, a measure of the most rudimentary decoding ability, by which beginning readers use initial or final letters in printed words to cue phonemes, allowing them to select pronunciations among words stored in memory (see details in Sect. 2.4.1). Statistically significant pretest–posttest improvement in phonetic cue reading was only found with the group trained in phoneme identification. Murray thereby suggested that phoneme identification skills seem to be more helpful in developing beginning decoding skills whilst phoneme manipulation skills would be required for a more advanced level decoding skills. According to him, besides the ready access to phoneme identities, fully-developed decoding also implicates at least phoneme blending, because to decode, a reader must unite the phoneme sequence derived from the printed form into a pronunciation.

The stronger association between phoneme recognition and rudimentary phonological decoding skills was also found in Vandervelden and Siegel's (1995) study, which investigated the relationship between different types of phonemic awareness skills and rudimentary phonological decoding ability among L1 children aged 5–8. Initial phoneme recognition and initial consonant segmentation were found to be more strongly related to partial phonological decoding, the rudimentary phase in phonological decoding, i.e. phonetic cue decoding, whereas phoneme deletion and substitution were found to be more strongly related to complete phonological decoding, the more advanced skill in phonological decoding. The researchers suggested this was because the use of rime analogies as an advanced skill in phonological decoding requires the deletion and substitution of initial phonemes. Although phoneme blending skill was not included in their study, it has been suggested in many studies as a requisite for phonological decoding. Ehri et al.'s (2001a, b) meta-analysis of the effect of phonemic awareness instruction on helping L1 children learn to read concluded that decoding words requires phoneme blending skill to transform graphemes into recognizable words. The Rose report on the review of early reading instruction (2006) also demonstrated that pronouncing a word implicates the skill of blending (synthesising) phonemes in order, all through a word.

To recap, phoneme identification/recognition has been generally accepted as the most rudimentary phonemic awareness skill that is most strongly related to initial phonological decoding, i.e. pronouncing a word by associating simply its initial or final letter with the sound (Byrne and Fielding-Barnsley 1990). Phonological decoding also necessitates phoneme blending skill to assemble the sounds mapped onto letters. And the other types of phonemic awareness skills like phoneme deletion and substitution skills may also be implicated in fully-developed phonological decoding.

2.2.2 Letter Identification

Letter identification involves recognising the visual shapes of 26 English lowercase letter symbols and their uppercase counterparts, as well as discriminating the distinguishing features of letters, and knowing the names of letters (Adams 1990). The recognition of letters according to the shapes is essential before children are faced with the task of associating letters with sounds (Rayner et al. 2012; Vellutino 2003). It is common for typically developing readers to initially confuse letters that are mirror images of each other or look alike (e.g. <b> and <d>, <p> and <q>, <m> and <n>). Therefore, in learning to recognise letters, children must be able to identify the features that distinguish one letter from another (Rayner et al. 2012).

There is some uncertainty about whether knowing letter names is necessary for learning to decode words. On one hand, children can decode some words without knowing the letter names (Adams 1990). On the other hand, knowing letter names has also been found to facilitate the learning of letter sounds because many letter names carry information about the letter sounds (Cardoso-Martins et al. 2011; Piasta and Wagner 2010; Share 2004). For instance, the letter <p> is sounded as /p/, and the letter <b> as /b/. Moreover, letter names allow one to talk about letter referents when learning the letter-sound relations, compared to using letter sounds, which usually have different sound representations (Ehri and Roberts 2006). Rayner et al. (2012) thereby suggested learning letter names may constitue a first step toward understanding the alphabetic principle. The UK Primary National Strategy's phonics programme "Letters and Sounds" also includes the teaching of letter names and states the justification for that as follows:

> Letter names are needed when children start to learn two-letter and three letter graphemes (Phase Three) to provide the vocabulary to refer to the letters making up the grapheme. It is misleading to refer to the graphemes "ai" and "th" as /a/-/i/ and /t/-/h/.

(Department for Education and Skills 2007, p. 15)

The evidence and arguments stated above seem to suggest the knowledge of letter names is necessary at least for learning the sounds of letter chunks.

2.2.3   Spelling-Sound Correspondences

It has generally been acknowledged that understanding the correspondences between single letters or letter chunks and their sounds is crucial in learning to decode alphabetic orthographies. Although the English orthography is not entirely regular in grapheme-phoneme correspondences (term used interchangeably with letter-sound correspondences/relations/associations, or abbreviated as GPCs), there is some consistency in the systematic relationship between graphemes and phonemes. Hanna et al. (1971) carried out a study to investigate the spelling regularity of English words. The results showed that among the 17,000 most frequently used English words, about 84% contained regular letter-sound correspondences. Similarly, Crystal (2003) reported that approximately 85% of everyday English words were phonemically regular. And among the 15% of so-called irregular English words, only 3% are highly unpredictable (Blevins 1998). Moreover, Ehri (1998) argued that the decoding of irregular words also draws upon letter-sound associations. According to her, most of the letters in irregular words conform to GPC rules, for example, all but <t> in *listen*. In remembering letters that do not conform to GPC rules, the readers may remember them as extra visual forms, or may remember a special pronunciation of the non-conforming letters. This is supported by Foorman et al.'s (1991) findings that native-speaking children with more letter-sound instruction improved at a faster rate in correct readings of both regular and irregular words. The argument that making use of GPC rules to decode unfamiliar words is the basic mechanism for the learning of sight words (words that are read from memory by sight), whether regularly or irregularly spelled words, has been supported by much research (Gough and Walsh 1991; Ryder et al. 2008; Share 1995). Therefore, teaching the most common grapheme-phoneme correspondences in English is extremely useful for readers in learning to decode English words.

The mechanism of grapheme-phoneme correspondences may be influenced by orthographic context, like the larger sub-word units, i.e. rime units, as suggested by Harley (2008). There are usually one-to-many relationships between letters and sounds in English, especially with vowel letters or letter combinations. However, the uncertainty in the pronunciation of vowels has been found to be much reduced in the orthographic rime units (Cain 2010; Kessler and Treiman 2001; Peereman and Content 1998; Treiman et al. 1995). For example, although the letter <a> has variant pronunciations, the rime units <at>, <ake>, <ast> have relatively more stable spelling-sound correspondences. Although orthographic consonant–vowel units may also help to reduce the uncertainty in decoding vowels, they have been found to be much less consistent compared to orthographic rime units (Treiman et al. 1995). Hence, the use of orthographic rime units are considered as an invaluable tool when trying to resolve the pronunciation or identity of words if there is some uncertainty to its identity (Vousden 2008), and also as the advanced level of phonological decoding (Ehri 1998). Such a relatively more rapid and accurate decoding mechanism that is sensitive to orthographic context evolves progressively from the rudimentary knowledge of correspondences between individual letters and their sounds, along with more and more print experience (Share 1995).

When children learn these relationships well, words that are already in their spoken language become accessible to them when they decode the printed words, and unfamiliar words can be stored in mental lexicon more securely by establishing firm connections between letters and sounds.

We admit that there are other component skills that can be involved in phonological decoding such as working memory and naming speed, which are not included in the present study, because they are beyond the scope of the present study.

2.3   The Importance of Phonological Decoding in Learning to Read English

As Hoover and Gough (1990) stated, decoding is of central importance in L1 reading, for without it, language comprehension (the ability to take semantic information at the word level and derive sentence and discourse interpretations) is of no use (p. 131). With phonological decoding skills, L1 novice readers can derive the phonological representations of the words that are in the oral vocabulary but have not been seen in print before, then the already extant mental lexicon can be accessed for the words, and then the meaning information can be retrieved. After the words in print are read through phonological decoding route four times, the links between the visual forms, sound representations and meanings tend to be consolidated and the words can therefore be retained in the mental lexicon and recognised as sight words via direct lexical access (Reitsma 1983).

Numerous L1 reading studies have indicated that phonological decoding skills are of crucial importance to developing automaticity in word reading (e.g. Ehri 1992; Siegel 1993; Vandervelden and Siegel 1995) and reading comprehension (e.g. Kendeou et al. 2009; Siegel 1993). For example, Vandervelden and Siegel (1995) found that phonological decoding explained more than 80% of the variance on the word reading measures among English speaking children aged from 5 to 8. This adds supporting evidence to Siegel's (1993) study, which showed that phonological decoding as tested by the nonword reading test (a frequently adopted approach to measuring phonological decoding ability, see details in Sect. 3.5.5.1.1) contributed a significant amount of variance in single word reading and reading comprehension among L1 children aged 7–16 years. In addition, Siegel's (1993) study also found the strong correlation between children's performance on phonological decoding tasks and the measures on reading comprehension ($r = 0.82$, $p < 0.0001$). Moreover, there is substantial evidence that L1 children's poor reading performance is strongly associated with weak phonological decoding skills (e.g. Rack et al. 1992; Vellutino et al. 1995). All these evidence suggests that for L1 children, phonological decoding is a critical element in the process of learning to read.

The important role of phonological decoding in learning to read English is also widely accepted in L2/FL contexts (e.g. Haynes and Carr 1990; Koda 2005; Nassaji 2003; Wang et al. 2002). Although L2/FL beginning readers may not have the oral vocabulary size of their L1 counterparts, who already learn to use the language in its spoken form prior to learning it in its printed form and already have a phonologically accessible lexicon when learning to read, the component knowledge and skills of phonological decoding are still of vital importance for L2/FL children to learn to read in English. Woore (2009) suggested four aspects in which phonological decoding is important to L2 learning. Firstly, for the words that are already in the oral vocabulary, learners can get access to the meaning though the phonological decoding route and thereby recognise the words in their printed forms. Secondly, for the new words, complete graphophonic analyses enable the words to be secured in memory and the words are thereby given a unique address that eliminates confusion among similarly spelled words, which is particularly crucial when children's sight vocabulary is expanding. Thirdly, students' proficiency in L2 decoding correlates with their self-confidence and motivation in language learning. Woore (2007) asserted that "the inability to pronounce words fluently or accurately constantly reinforces their own perception of their beginner status" (p. 177). Fourthly, learner autonomy is also affected if learners are unable to pronounce new words and are thereby dependent on the teacher or other means, like electronic dictionary, for their correct sounds.

Some L2/FL studies have indicated the importance of phonological decoding in second language or foreign language learners' reading development (Chiappe and Siegel 1999; Chu 2002b; Nassaji 2003; Wang et al. 2002; Yu and Wang 2001). Chu (2002b) reported the strong correlations between phonological decoding and regular/irregular word reading among Taiwanese EFL children aged from 13 to 14 years old. Phonological decoding measured by nonword reading has also been found as a strong predictor of reading comprehension measures among Chinese EFL children aged 15–16 in Wang and her colleagues' (2002) study. Although in their study, the syntactic awareness and working memory were also found to contribute a significant amount of variance on the reading comprehension measures but the syntactic skills and working memory contributed less than phonological decoding. Yu and Wang's (2001) study also found phonological decoding measured by nonword reading as a strong predictor of single word reading among Chinese EFL children aged around 15 and 16. In addition, the results of their study also showed that measures of nonword reading successfully differentiated among good, average, and poor readers. Poor readers demonstrated the obvious deficits in applying spelling-sound correspondences to decode nonwords. Similarly, the results of Chiappe and Siegel's (1999) examination of 6-year-old L2 children's performance on tasks assessing word reading skill and phonological decoding showed that measures of phonological decoding successfully discriminated between groups of children based on their word reading skill. Similar findings were made in Nassaji's (2003) investigation of the role of higher level syntactic and semantic processes and the lower-level word recognition and phonological decoding in adult L2 learners' (aged 25–35) reading comprehension. Even among the adult L2 learners, phonological decoding, in addition to the other variables, contributed significantly to the distinction between skilled and less skilled

ESL readers, although phonological decoding contributed the least to the variance on reading comprehension, compared with the other variables such as vocabulary and syntactic skills. This is probably because the adult participants were skilled readers and they may therefore not rely much on phonological decoding in their reading. Nassaji (2003) therefore suggested that efficient phonological decoding skills are "not only important factors in beginning reading but also integral components of fluent and skilled reading as well [and their roles hence] must not be neglected even in highly advanced L2 reading" (p. 271).

To summarise, there is a consensus among researchers that phonological decoding plays an important role in the L1/L2/FL reading process, although there are many other variables that may also contribute to the complicated reading process.

2.4 The Acquisition of English Phonological Decoding in L1 and L2/FL Contexts

All recent phase/stage theories of the development of L1 word reading skills propose that children must at some point begin using phonological decoding skills to learn to read in English, which is based on the relationship between spelling and sound (Ehri 1992, 2005a; Frith 1985; Gough et al. 1992; Marsh et al. 1981; Seymour and Duncan 2001). The developmental phases of phonological decoding have been conceptualised as a continuum, e.g. the phase theory by Ehri (1992, 1994, 1999, 2005a, 2020), i.e. from pre-alphabetic, partial-alphabetic, full-alphabetic to consolidated-alphabetic phase, and the phase theory by Marsh et al. (1981), i.e. from rote, linguistic guessing, discrimination net guessing, sequential decoding, to hierarchical decoding stage.

In echo with the phases of L1 children's learning to decode English words, previous research has suggested that children learning English as a second or foreign language acquire reading skills in similar manner to their L1 counterparts, mainly based on their findings that the reading skills of both L1 and L2 children in the process of reading acquisition are correlated with and predicted by the performance on similar tasks such as phonological decoding and phonological awareness tasks (Chiappe et al. 2002; Fitzgerald 1995; Geva et al. 2000; Lesaux et al. 2007; Lipka et al. 2005; McBride-Chang and Treiman 2003; Yin et al. 2007). However, to our knowledge, only Yin et al. (2007) conducted a close and detailed investigation into L2 children's developmental phases of phonological decoding.

This section will firstly discuss L1 children's developmental phases of phonological decoding mainly based on the phase/stage theories by Ehri (1992, 1998, 2002, 2005a) and Marsh et al. (1981), because they described the phonological decoding development in some detail. Then the focus shifts to Yin and her colleagues' findings about Chinese L2 children's developmental sequence of phonological decoding. Finally, factors affecting Chinese L2 children's acquisition of phonological decoding skills will be discussed.

2.4.1 *L1 Children's Developmental Phases in Phonological Decoding*

It has been generally accepted that before drawing on the alphabetic knowledge, L1 children have to "read words by remembering visual or context cues" (Ehri 2005a, p. 140). This phase is labelled as "pre-alphabetic phase" by Ehri (1992, 1999, 2005a), and also as "logographic stage" by Frith (1985), as well as "rote, linguistic guessing stage" by Marsh et al. (1981). Due to the lack of letter knowledge and awareness of constituent sounds in words, learners at this initial phase of learning to read are simply able to capitalize on the non-alphabetic visual cues and rote learn to read words, like reading the logographic script of Chinese (Ehri 1992, 2005a; Frith 1985; Marsh et al. 1981). For instance, they may read words by memorizing specific visual features (e.g. the length or the shape of the word). They may also guess at words based on the cues of linguistic context, e.g. a sentence or a story, or the clues of environmental print, e.g. common labels or logos (Ehri 1992, 1999, 2005a; Marsh et al. 1981). However, the associations between the non-alphabetic features of the words and the sounds in the words are arbitrary and hard to hold in memory, so the words are quickly forgotten and confusion is often caused among words possessing the same or similar visual features. According to Gough and Hillinger (1980), this phase places too much demand on children's visual memory capacity so that it may break down after storing around forty words if the child has not acquired additional reading strategies to distinguish the different visual features of words.

However, when acquiring some knowledge of letters and phonemic awareness skills, children may start to gradually develop their phonological decoding skills through different phases, which will be discussed in the following sections.

2.4.1.1 Partial Alphabetic Phase

The transition from visual cue reading to partial alphabetic decoding is marked by the use of some of the letters in words as symbols for phonemes rather than as arbitrary visual cues to read words by forming partial connections in memory (Ehri 1992). This very initial form of phonological decoding is also labelled by Ehri as phonetic cue decoding phase, and corresponds to Marsh's discrimination net guessing stage, in which the child processes salient graphemic cues to discriminate one printed word from another (Marsh et al. 1981).

As Ehri (1999) described, readers at this point are characterised by the inability to segment the pronunciation of the word into all of its phonemes, and the incomplete knowledge of letter-sound relations, particularly vowels. Ehri (2005a) indicated that this rudimentary phase of decoding requires "not only knowing the names or sounds of letters but also being able to detect some constituent sounds in the pronunciations of words (phonemic awareness)" (p. 143). She gave the example of children remembering how to read *jail* by associating the boundary letters <j> and <l> to their letter names.

It must be admitted that the ability to use partial alphabetic cues to read words does make it easier for readers to store the words in memory, compared with the previous phase. However, because of the limited knowledge of the alphabetic system in this phase, the readers cannot phonologically translate all graphemes of a word into phonemes. They are capable of forming connections between only some of the letters and sounds in words, often preserving the boundary consonant letters, particularly the first letter (Ehri 1999, 2005a; Ehri and McCormick 1998). As a result, words are often misread as other words that share similar letters. To illustrate this, Ehri and McCormick (1998) gave the example of children remembering how to read *block* by linking the letters <b> to sound /b/, and <k> to /k/ in the sound representation of the word, while neglecting other letters and their corresponding sounds, and *block*, therefore, is misread as other words that look similar, such as *book* or *black*. Likewise, as Ehri (1999) indicated, "they have difficulty decoding unfamiliar pseudowords and may give up trying or may substitute a real word sharing some letters with the pseudoword" (p. 91).

In contrast to the previous phase, in which children have no knowledge of letter sounds, children at this partial decoding phase know the sounds of most single consonant letters, but may still lack the full knowledge of the alphabetic system, such as consonant digraphs, consonant clusters, and particularly vowel orthographic units. Vandervelden and Siegel (1995) found in their experimental studies on L1 children's phonological decoding development that "the decoding of initial location consonants is developed first, followed by final consonant decoding and accurate decoding of medial position vowels develops last" (p. 862). Drawing on previous studies, Share (1995) concluded the similar pattern in the development of these rudimentary decoding skills: "consonantal correspondences appear the earliest and easiest to acquire. This advantage is generally attributed to their relatively invariant letter-sound relationships in contrast to vowels" (p. 163).

Treiman et al.'s (1995) findings in their statistical analysis of the properties of the English orthography supported (Share's 1995) conclusion. The results showed that the pronunciation of vowels was very inconsistent across different CVC monosyllabic words (51%), while the pronunciation of initial and final consonants was reasonably consistent (initial consonant = 96%, final consonant = 91%). This indicated very clearly that the spelling-sound consistency of written English is greater for consonants compared to vowels. In English orthography, a vowel grapheme usually has different sound mappings. For example, the vowel letter <a> can be sounded out as /æ/ in *cat*; /ɒ/ in *what*; /ɑ:/ in *glass*; /ɛ/ in *many*; /eɪ/ in *lady*; /ə/ in *about*. Such greater letter-sound variability of English vowels may pose more difficulty for children to decode, compared with consonant letter-sound relations.

Share (1995) also concluded that "final consonant correspondences may be more difficult than initial consonant correspondences" (p. 163). He argued that there are some factors accounting for this. One possibility can be the salience of initial letters in words. It can also be due to the memory limitations, which may restrict phonological decoding to initial letters when the decoding task is slow and effortful. Another possibility can be that final consonants may be "relatively bound within the rime units and hence more difficult to isolate" (p. 163). Similarly, probably because initial consonant blends are also bound in onset units, initial consonant blends require several years to master.

To recapitulate, children at this phase depend mainly on the use of partial phonetic cues (usually initial and final consonant letter name or letter-sound information) to decode words. However, the rudimentary phonological decoding skill does not allow children to decode words completely and may cause words to be misread as other words sharing some letters, usually the first or final consonant letters.

2.4.1.2 Full Alphabetic Phase

Different from the readers in the previous phase, who possess some simple letter-sound knowledge of most single consonant letters, children at the full alphabetic phase of decoding "possess the working knowledge of the major correspondences between letters and sounds, including vowels" (Ehri and McCormick 1998, p. 150). This knowledge enables children to process all the constituent letters in words and blend the generated pronunciations to decode unknown words, in contrast to readers in the previous partial alphabetic phase of decoding, who usually rely on the boundary consonant letter(s) of a word and tend to confuse the word with words sharing the same boundary letters (Ehri 1992, 1999, 2005a). In other words, children at this point are able to use their working knowledge of the major grapheme-phoneme correspondences to decode unknown words completely and more accurately. This phase has also been called as sequential decoding stage by Marsh et al. (1981), in which children are apt to decode words completely, letter-by-letter, most importantly including the vowel letters.

However, the learning of the grapheme-phoneme correspondences is not an easy task. Some GPCs may be more difficult for children to grasp than others. The graphemic complexity seems to affect L1 children's decoding accuracy. Seymour et al. (1992) described L1 children's developmental sequence of acquiring English orthographic structures. Their framework suggests that single consonant letters and common consonant digraphs (e.g. <th>, <sh>, <ch>, <wh>, <ck>) are acquired earlier than less common complex consonants (e.g. <kn>, <wr>, <qu>, <gu>) and consonant clusters (e.g. <pr>, <pl>, <str>, <sn>), single vowel letters earlier than complex vowel orthographic units (e.g. <aw>, <ie>, <i-e>, <a-e>). Laxon et al.'s (2002) study on the effect of graphemic complexity on 6- to 7-year-old L1 children's reading accuracy provided supporting evidence for Seymour et al.'s model of reading development. They found that single vowel letters (e.g. <a>, <e>) were decoded with greater accuracy than complex vowels (i.e. non-split letter combinations representing vowels, e.g. <ay>, <ie>, and split vowel digraphs, e.g. <i-e>, <a-e>) in both familiar words and nonwords. Although Laxon et al. (2002) did not find a significant difference in difficulty between decoding CVC nonwords containing split vowel digraphs and CVC nonwords containing non-split vowel digraphs, the mean error rate of the former structure (51%) is higher than that of the latter (42%). And the acquisition of split vowel digraphs will be discussed in more detail in Sect. 2.4.1.3. Fewer errors were made with three-letter CVC nonwords (e.g. *dob*) than four-letter nonwords that also have a single vowel letter but consonant digraphs (e.g. *dack*). And the CVCC nonwords that also have a single vowel letter but consonant clusters (e.g. *pank*) attracted the highest error rate. The reason can be that complex graphemes (multi-letters) involve more parsing compared with simple graphemes (single letter), or that in the case of consonant clusters, their decoding requires blending more phonemes than in the case of single consonant letters and consonant digraphs.

Although the decoding process at the beginning of this phase is laborious and slow, with more practice of applying the GPC-based decoding skills, children "become familiar with the most frequent sounds symbolised by letters" (Ehri and McCormick 1998). This stage is believed to be the foundation that enables children to attain mature decoding skill in an alphabetic writing system. Although Ehri (1992) proposed a theory of phases rather than of stages to indicate the flexibility of each phase in developing phonological decoding skills, she suggested that mastery of the sequential decoding phase is essential for moving into the next phase.

2.4.1.3 Consolidated Alphabetic Phase

Relying on the simple GPC mechanism that is relatively insensitive to orthographic context acquired in the previous phase, and the accumulation of a sizeable sight word vocabulary bank after more exposure to the printed form of words, children can develop a more complex understanding of the grapheme-phoneme correspondences and transit from the previous phase to this more advanced, consolidated alphabetic phase of decoding (Ehri 1992, 1994, 1999, 2005a, 2020). This phase includes what (Marsh et al. 1981) called as hierarchical decoding phase, in which children can use conditional rules and take account of letter combinations in which one letter signals the phoneme symbolised by another letter (Ehri 1999, 2005a). In other words, letter-sound correspondences become sensitive to orthographic context at this point (Rayner et al. 2012).

Although the acquisition of consonant letter-sound correspondences is relatively easier and earlier than vowel letter-sound correspondences, it is not without its complexities. Drawing on previous research, Share (1995) concluded that variable correspondences for consonants such as the hard/soft <c> present considerable difficulties for beginning readers. Children in this advanced phase of decoding, however, acquire the more sophisticated understanding of the influence of the graphemes occurring in some part of the word on the pronunciation of the other graphemes within the word. They possess the working knowledge of complex letter-sound relations that are sensitive to orthographic context. For instance, the final <e> in *college* or *page* marks the preceding <g> as /dʒ/; <i> in *city* and <e> in *cell* mark the letter <c> as /s/. By the same token, the multiple correspondences of vowels pose greater problem for young readers, but children's sensitivity to orthographic context in this phase increases the accuracy of vowel decoding (Ehri 1999). For instance, they understand that final <e> in *time* and *note* marks long vowels.

Children's sensitivity to the orthographic context in this phase can also be reflected in their sensitivity to the regularities beyond the level of simple grapheme-phoneme correspondences, which is modified in the light of larger spelling patterns recurring within words in their print lexicon (Share 1995). In this phase, building on their possessed knowledge of GPC rules, and exposed to more printed words and sufficient practice of decoding words, children acquire the knowledge of larger spelling patterns such as rime units that recur in words. As described in Sect. 2.2.3, the knowledge of the relatively more consistent orthographic units of rimes is useful in decoding vowel letters or letter combinations relatively more accurately and efficiently (Ehri 1999, 2005a; Ehri and McCormick 1998).

It should be noted here that since reading words by analogy is categorised by Ehri (1992, 1994, 1999, 2005a) as a strategy different and separate from phonological decoding, I think it is necessary to explain how this is handled in the current study. As was pointed out in Ehri's phase theory, reading words by analogy is possible in the previous phase, namely full alphabetic phase, but more common in the consolidated alphabetic phase. Analogies in reading, according to Goswami (1995, p. 108), involve using the spelling-sound correspondence of one word, such as *beak*, as a basis for working out the spelling-sound correspondence of a new word, such as *peak*. Although Ehri categorised the use of analogy as a strategy different and separate from phonological decoding in her phase theory, we hold the same standpoint as Share (1995) and Iversen and Tunmer (1993) that phonological decoding in a broad sense includes not only what Ehri referred to as phonological decoding, namely using the systematic knowledge of the spelling-sound correspondences at the GPC or the rime level, but also the use of the spelling-sound correspondence (at GPC level or at rime level) of a known word as a basis for working out the counterpart of a new word. Different from Goswami (1999), who believed that analogy can be used by children to sound out a printed word at a very early stage of learning to read, Ehri and Robbins (1992) found that using the spelling-sound correspondence of a known word as a basis for working out the counterpart of a new word requires rudimentary knowledge of the initial or final consonant letter-sound correspondences and the skills of segmenting the component sounds in the known words for extracting the letter-sound correspondence of the shared sub-word units and blending the sound of the shared sub-word units and the sound of the remaining letter(s). For instance, in order to read *peak* by analogy to *beak*, children need to possess the knowledge of the letter-sound correspondence of the consonant letter <p>, the skill of segmenting <eak> from <b> within the base word *beak*, and the skill of blending the sound of <eak> and the sound of <p> to form the sound of the new word *peak*. Therefore, it seems logical to argue that the use of analogy is a skill more likely to be developed at a later stage of phonological decoding development (i.e. the full and consolidated alphabetic phases). This argument finds its support from some researchers (Nation et al. 2001; Treiman et al. 1990), who indicated that Goswami's findings about the role of analogy in beginning reading was overestimated, due to the nature of her experiments on one hand that the clue words were presented in view when children were reading test words and therefore not representative of the spontaneous use of analogy, and on the other hand due to the artefact of phonological priming effects (e.g. pronouncing the test word such as *most* by priming it auditorily with its rhyming clue word *toast*, even if the orthographic rime spelling differs). In a word, consistent with the discussion in Sect. 2.1, phonological decoding in the current study is operationalised as sounding out the printed words by using the spelling-sound correspondences (either directly recalled from one's systematic knowledge of the alphabetic codes, or indirectly extracted from the known words that share the same constituent spelling-sound correspondences), at both GPC level and rime level. And it should be noted that phonological decoding is operationalised as a broad term in this study, as the study's focus is not on the differentiation of the two ways of retrieving the spelling-sound correspondences but on whether children showed sensitivity to the orthographic rime patterns.

To sum up, according to the stage/phase theories discussed above, the development of phonological decoding generally follows the route of initially relying on the partial phonetic cue of boundary consonant letters, later to completely decoding constituent graphemes based on the working knowledge of major grapheme-phoneme correspondences that are relatively insensitive to orthographic context, and then to a more complex understanding of the GPCs with sensitivity to the conditional rules and orthographic rime units. It should be noted that as Ehri (2005b) proposed, these phases characterise the predominant types of decoding skills used. Children in the full alphabetic phase use mainly grapheme-phoneme connections to decode words, but they may still show some sensitivity to the orthographic rime units that are very familiar sight words such as <in> and <up>.

2.4.2   L2/FL Children's Developmental Phases in Phonological Decoding

In sharp contrast to the relatively abundant L1 studies on the developmental phases in phonological decoding, there is a scarcity of research on L2/FL children's phonological decoding development (Chiappe and Siegel 1999; McBride-Chang and Treiman 2003; Yin et al. 2007).

Chiappe and Siegel (1999) examined the performance of L1 children and L2 children in the first grade (mean age = 78.4 months) on tasks assessing word reading and phonological decoding. The results showed that the performance profiles of L2 children were very similar to those of the native English speakers. Phonological decoding measures successfully discriminated between average readers and poor readers, but not between L1 readers and L2 readers. Moreover, the analyses of the word recognition error patterns revealed that average readers from both language groups employed grapheme-phoneme correspondences to read unfamiliar words more frequently than poor readers while poor readers from both language groups produced more wild (i.e. guessing) errors than average readers. The findings suggested that second language learners of English may develop their phonological decoding skills in a similar way to native English speakers and become more reliant on grapheme-phoneme correspondences and less reliant on guessing strategies in the process of learning to read.

McBride-Chang and Treiman (2003) added supporting evidence to the finding that L2 children are remarkably similar to their L1 counterparts in their acquisition of the alphabetic principle, i.e. phonological decoding, despite great differences in curricula and language exposure. In their study, 40 Cantonese-speaking children at each of the three kindergarten grade levels in Hong Kong, K1 (mean age $= 3.8$ years), K2 (mean age $= 5.0$ years), and K3 (mean age $= 5.9$ years), were taught to sound out English new words based on letter names, letter sounds, and visual cues. For example, with *BT* as the stimulus, the word *beat* was used in the name condition, *bat* in the sound condition, and *pice* in the visual condition. The training consisted of 3 sessions, each lasting from 10 to 25 min. Each session of the word learning task consisted of a demonstration phase and up to eight test trials. The number of correct responses across trials was recorded for each condition. The mean number and proportion of correct responses across trials were compared among the three different conditions in three grades. The results showed that K2 students made significantly more use of letter name knowledge than letter sounds and visual cues to sound out new words, but no significant difference was found in the use of letter sound knowledge and visual cues. The K3 students also demonstrated a significantly more frequent use of letter name knowledge than the other two strategies while a significant superiority of the use of letter sound knowledge was found among K3 students over the use of visual cues. This suggested a pattern of learning to read English similar to that observed among L1 children learning to read English (see Sect. 2.4.1), namely "the early development of letter name knowledge and early use of this information in learning to read new words, later development of letter sound knowledge and later use of this information in learning to read new words" (p. 142).

Although the studies discussed above suggested the English language learners may develop their phonological decoding skills in a pattern similar to the native English speakers, to my knowledge, the only systematic investigation of the developmental stages of English language learners in reading English words was conducted by Yin and her colleagues' (2007). The researchers administered six language tests and three experimental tasks among 118 Chinese EFL children in primary grade 2 (mean age $= 7.6$ years), grade 4 (mean age $= 10.5$ years) and grade 6 (mean age $= 12.5$ years) from a working-class primary school representative of ordinary urban schools in China. All of the children were native speakers of Mandarin and had been studying English as a foreign language. They studied English in regular classes since grade 1, with 3 English classes per week and each class lasting for 40 min.

A series of tasks were administered to the participants, including an English nonword reading test and an English word reading test. In the English nonword reading task, children were asked to read 80 nonwords in two sessions on two separate days. The 80 nonwords were composed of 60 nonwords and 20 known words as fillers to reduce possible frustration (Yin, personal communication, July 2012). There were four types of nonwords: consonant + vowel + consonant (CVC) (e.g. *hig*, *mux*); consonant + consonant + vowel + consonant (CCVC) (e.g. *bret*, *stib*); consonant + vowel + consonant + consonant (CVCC) (e.g. *nist*, *teld*); and nonwords that are not decodable except by using analogies (e.g. *zight*, *pould*). In each category, there were 15 nonwords plus 5 real word fillers. The maximum score was 60. The English word reading test was a curriculum-based test measuring children's general English word reading ability. Children from each grade were asked to read 40 English words, 20 of which were selected from their current-grade vocabulary, 10 from vocabulary taught in the preceding grades, and 10 from vocabulary taught in the following grades. The maximum score was 40.

The scoring took place into two steps. Firstly, one point was given to each nonword of type 1, 2 and 3 that was correctly decoded using conventional GPC rules, and to the fourth type of nonwords that were read correctly by analogy to known words. The total score of correctly decoded nonwords was calculated for each subject and then the mean percentage of correctly decoded nonwords was calculated for each group, 17% for the second graders, 24% for the fourth graders, and 63% for the sixth graders. A high correlation (0.81) was found between the participants' English nonword reading and English word reading.

In the next step, the number of correct readings of the following six types of graphemic units for each subject was counted: the pronunciations of initial consonant, final consonant, initial consonant clusters, final consonant clusters, middle vowel, and the word parts that were expected to be analogized to known words. On the basis of the six variables, the researchers set three stage markers, i.e. the partial alphabetic marker (the performance on initial consonant and final consonant), the orthographic analogy marker (the performance on reading words that require making an analogy), and the full alphabetic marker (the performance on initial consonant cluster, final consonant cluster, and middle vowel). However, the results did not support the four hypothesized sequence of stages. 39% of children did not fit in the model because some of them were good at the full alphabetic decoding but poor at making analogies, while some were good at making analogies but poor at partial alphabetic reading. Therefore, the initial theory was revised by excluding the orthographic analogy out of the stage sequence. After this, only 8% of the fourth graders did not fit in the revised model of stages: the pre-alphabetic stage, the partial alphabetic stage, and the full alphabetic stage. The proportion of students who fit in the pre-alphabetic and partial alphabetic stages decreased with grades while the proportion of students who fit in the full alphabetic stage increased with grades. These findings revealed that Chinese EFL children experienced similar stages of learning to read English words as native English-speaking children. The researchers admitted varying the cut scores changed the percentage of children falling into each stage while they argued that the developmental pattern remained the same across grades.

In grade 2, namely the initial stage of learning to read, the students made many fewer correct responses in decoding single vowel letters (mean proportion correct = 30%) than initial single consonant letters (mean proportion correct = 79%), and final single consonant letters (mean proportion correct = 67%). Although in grade 4, their performance in decoding single vowel letters (mean proportion correct = 43%) improved, it is still poorer than the decoding of initial single consonant letters (mean proportion correct = 76%), and final single consonant letters (mean proportion correct = 59%). This echoes (Ehri's 1992, 1994, 1999, 2005a) phase theory of learning to read English words, in which L1 children acquire the decoding of vowel graphemes later than the decoding of single consonant letters.

However, it should be noted that Yin and her colleagues only included single consonant letters and consonant clusters in the reading task of CVC, CCVC and CVCC type of nonwords, without involving consonant digraphs. In addition, all of the vowel graphemes in CVC, CCVC and CVCC type of nonwords are single vowel letters (<a>, <e>, <i>, <o> and <u>) and no letter combinations representing vowels (e.g. <ir>, <oi>) are included. Therefore, there is no information concerning Chinese EFL children's acquisition of decoding more complex orthographic units like consonant digraphs and vowel digraphs. Chu's (2002a) evaluation of Taiwanese EFL learners' decoding skills may shed some lights on Chinese EFL learners' decoding performance on the complex orthographic units, because Taiwanese and Chinese children have similar L1 literacy experience (see Sect. 2.5.2.1). In Chu's (2002a) study, the participants were 8th (aged 13–14) and 9th (aged 14–15) graders who had received 1.8 and 2.8 years of formal English teaching respectively. The results of their nonword reading test revealed that they had better knowledge of consonant correspondences than vowel correspondences, and knew single consonant correspondences better than consonant digraph correspondences, based on the comparison of the mean percentage of errors for different types of orthographic units.

Considering that (Yin et al.'s 2007) study did not include the relatively more complex orthographic units such as consonant digraphs and vowel digraphs, it might be somewhat too optimistic for the researchers to suggest that almost all of the sixth graders were classified as being in the full-alphabetic stage. With a closer look at the overall performance of the sixth graders on pronouncing initial consonant clusters (mean proportion correct = 64%) and middle single vowel letter (mean proportion correct = 76%), we find that their overall skills at decoding consonant clusters may not be sufficient to consider them fully fledged readers at the full-alphabetic stage. And based on this assumption, we might argue that among the 39% of all subjects, i.e. the subjects who did not fit in the hypothesized model of four stages, those who were classified as being good at full alphabetic decoding but weak at analogizing might simply be at the very initial stage of full alphabetic stage and not have mastered it yet. As a consequence, this group of subjects had not yet stored enough sight words in sufficient detail to enable them to apply the analogy strategy skillfully.

Furthermore, there are some limitations with the design of the stimuli for the nonword reading test. In the nonword reading task, four categories of nonwords each contain five real words (e.g. *leg, classroom, milk, knee*) randomly mixed with test nonwords (e.g. *neg, clig, tilk, knas*). Chances were therefore that children might have come across the clue words before nonwords sharing the same word parts. In that sense, they might read the nonwords with the aid of the clue words, and this thereby did not really test children's spontaneous ability to decode words. In other words, children's phonological decoding skills may be overestimated.

In conclusion, Yin et al.'s study illustrated that Mandarin-speaking Chinese children progress through similar stages of learning to read English words as L1 children do, i.e. the pre-alphabetic stage, the partial-alphabetic stage and the full-alphabetic stage. But it is a pity that the researchers did not include Ehri's consolidated alphabetic phase in their hypothesized model. In view of the absence of consonant digraphs and vowel combinations, and the limitations of the stimuli design, it is hard to reach the conclusion that most of the sixth graders had really reached the full-alphabetic stage of phonological decoding.

2.5 Factors Influencing Chinese EFL Children's Development of Phonological Decoding

Phonological decoding, as discussed previously, is one of the critical skills for children to master in learning to read in English. Drawing on Cameron's (2001) and Blondin et al.'s (1998) summary of the factors that can influence children's learning to read in English as a foreign language and foreign language learning in general, this section will focus on the factors that are related to Mandarin-speaking children's learning of phonological decoding skills, such as the nature of the written forms of the first language, learner's first language literacy experience, learner's English phonological skills, classroom teaching.

2.5.1 The Difference Between English and Chinese Writing System

When learning to read a foreign language, the child's brain will automatically try to apply the experience and mechanism of reading in their first language (Cameron 2001). The difference in the writing system between the first language and English may hence influence the rate of progress in learning to read in English.

The cipher, i.e. alphabetic decoding skill, is the basis of reading an alphabetic language, although learning to read in English sometimes also needs further information, like orthographic information, to assist in recognising English words (Gough and Walsh 1991). For English language learners speaking another alphabetic language, the orthographic depth of their first language makes a difference. Orthographic depth, according to Rixon (2011), "reflects the symmetry and closeness of relationships between the phonemes of a language and the graphic means that are used to represent them" (p. 49). Chard and his colleagues (2007) reported that an English language learner whose first language is a shallow alphabetic orthography, which has a high proportion of one-to-one grapho-phonemic relationship (e.g. Spanish), might have some difficulties in learning to read English, which has a much less straightforward grapheme-phoneme relationship. They may thereby need to learn some extra decoding skills at the level or beyond the level of grapho-phonemic relationships.

The difference between the Chinese writing system and the alphabetic writing system of English is even sharper. English words contain grapheme-phoneme association, though the relationship is not straightforward. Moreover, English has the distinctive feature of being morphophonemic. A morpheme (e.g. the plural morpheme <s>) can be pronounced differently in different orthographic contexts (/s/ in *cats*, /z/ in *dogs*). However, in the logographic system of Chinese, each character represents a monosyllabic morpheme, giving the language a graph-to-word/morpheme structure instead of a grapheme-to-phoneme structure. And each character is composed of unpronounceable strokes in terms of a set of prespecified sequence rules. For example, in the character 上 (*up*), there is no part that encodes its sound. Siok and Fletcher (2001) indicated that Chinese children's emergent character reading requires elaborated visual orthographic processing to master these rules and assemble the strokes into characters.

Obviously, the two different orthographies demand different optimal processing strategies. The Chinese script demands visual logographic strategies whilst the English script demands alphabetic decoding skills (Liow 1999). Liow found that in learning to read in English, Mandarin-English-speaking children were more likely to adopt "Chinese" word-specific (look-say) strategies that they were encouraged to use for logographs, whereas Malay-English-speaking children were more likely to adopt "Phoenician" rule-based (phonics) strategies because they had been exposed to phonemic awareness training in their shallow alphabetic language of Bahasa Melayu. This is also supported by Chikamatsu (1996), who pointed out that L1 speakers of Chinese exhibited a large reliance on visual information in word decoding strategies. Lin (2008) also reported that Chinese learners tend to adopt their way of reading Chinese characters, i.e. whole-word reading when learning to read English words, which inevitably causes problems with phonological decoding. In a word, due to the nature of Chinese logographic orthography, as Birch (2007) has indicated, Chinese learners tend to transfer their preference for a meaning-based visual processing strategy in reading Chinese to the development of reading skills in English.

2.5.2 Chinese Literacy Experience

Cameron (2001) also indicated that the methodology of teaching L1 literacy skills must be taken into consideration as well. The way the children are taught to read their first language may influence the way early English reading is learned. There are two aspects of L1 literacy experience that will be discussed in this section. One is the experience with the Pinyin alphabetic system that is used as the phonetic transcription for Mandarin Chinese to illustrate the pronunciation of characters. The learning of Pinyin may expose Chinese children to the experience of decoding alphabetic script, and improve their phonological awareness. The other aspect is related to the teaching and learning of character reading, from which children's dominant L1 reading strategy may arise.

2.5.2.1 Experience with the Pinyin System

The traditional way to teach Chinese children to sound out characters is the rote learning approach, by which children are taught to learn characters without any phonological aids. For instance, in Hong Kong, children are taught to read Chinese characters with the look and say method. However, children in mainland China and Taiwan are exposed to the L1 literacy experience of using a transliteration system to mediate their L1 reading. In Taiwan, Zhu-Yin-Fu-Hao is adopted as the phonetic script of characters, which is composed of symbols derived from Chinese characters. In the context of mainland China, which the present study focuses on, the Pinyin system has been used in Chinese language teaching since the 1950s, to provide phonological access to the Chinese characters. The written symbols in Pinyin are composed of letters from the Roman alphabet, e.g. [wo], [jue], [huang], [zhen].

The Pinyin system uses almost all of the 26 letters from the English alphabet except <v> (instead, an additional letter <ü> is used in the Pinyin system) (see Table 2.1). Pinyin breaks down into three parts: tones, initials and finals. Four tone marks (‾ ′ ˇ `) are used along with the letters to denote the pronunciation of characters but as they are not related to the present study, they will not be included in the following discussion. Each Chinese character stands for a meaningful syllable, which is composed of an optional initial (a consonant that begins the syllable, i.e. onset) and a final (a single vowel or vowel compound, i.e. rime). For instance, the Pinyin [ba] of the Chinese character 爸 (father) comprises the initial [b] and the final [a]. Similarly, in the Pinyin [shang] of the character 上 (up), [sh] stands for the initial and [ang] the final. The teaching syllabus of the Pinyin system is at the level of initials and finals. Children are taught to sound out the initials and finals and blend them together to form the pronunciation of characters.

The learning of the Pinyin system undoubtedly familiarise Chinese children with the shapes of the English letters, except <v>. And when learning Pinyin, children are also exposed to the experience of alphabetic decoding using grapheme-phoneme correspondences. However, although Pinyin is also an alphabetic system, it differs from English alphabetic system in terms of spelling-to-sound correspondences.

Firstly, compared with the deep alphabetic orthography of English, Pinyin is a fairly shallow alphabetic system. In English, there are more speech sounds than there are letters of the alphabet. Twenty-six alphabet letters (5 vowel letters and 21 consonant letters) are used to represent 44 phonemes of English (20 vowel phonemes and 24 consonant phonemes, according to British Received Pronunciation, namely RP). This means that an individual sound is connected to more than one letter, e.g. the letters <s> and <h> come together to /ʃ/ in *shop*; <e> and <a> come together to form a vowel digraph for the long vowel /ɛ/ as in *head*. And an individual letter or letter combination can represent different sounds, e.g. <c> represents /s/ in *cinema*, and /k/ in *cat*; <a> can represent /æ/ in *cat*, /ɑ:/ in *class*, and /ɒ/ in *what*. According to Moats (2010), more than 250 graphemes are used to spell the 44 English phonemes. In contrast, as shown in Table 2.1, the Pinyin script simply requires the combination of

Table 2.1 The Pinyin system (Zhao, 1995)

Consonants/ Initials		Vowels/Finals							
		Single vowels		Diphthongs		Nasal vowels		Other vowel compounds	
Pinyin	IPA	Pinyin	IPA	Pinyin	IPA	Pinyin	IPA	Pinyin	IPA
b	p	a	a	ai	ai	an	an	ia	ia
p	pᵃ	o	o	ao	au	en	ən	ie	iɛ
m	m	i	i	ei	ei	ang	aŋ	iao	iau
f	f	u	u	ou	ou	eng	əŋ	iou	iou
d	t	e	ə			ong	uŋ	ian	iɛn
t	tᵃ	ü	y					in	in
n	n	Exceptions:						iang	iaŋ
l	l	i (when preceded by zh, ch, sh, r, z, c, s)	ɨ					ing	iŋ
g	k	e (when preceded by y)	ɛ					iong	iuŋ
k	kᵃ							ua	ua
h	x							uo	uo
j	tɕ							uai	uai
q	tɕᵃ							uei	uei
x	ɕ							uan	uan
zh	tʂ							uen	uən
ch	tʂᵃ							uang	uaŋ
sh	ʂ							ueng	uəŋ
r-	ʐ							üe	yɛ
z	ts							üan	yɛn
c	tsᵃ							ün	yn
s	s								
y	j								
w	w								

Note ᵃrepresents aspiration

the 21[1] initials and 35 finals, and the alphabetic system contains a very high proportion of one-to-one letter-sound correspondences (Bassetti 2007). All individual letters contain the corresponding individual sounds (Lin et al. 2010). More importantly, the spelling-sound correspondences in the Pinyin system are fairly straightforward and consistent (Liow and Poon 1998; Yin et al. 2007). Therefore, the sequential decoding

---

[1] The 21 initials in the Pinyin system consists of all the consonants listed in Table 2.1, except [y] and [w]. They are an orthographic convention for [i], [u] and [ü] when no initial is present.

skill based on simple one-to-one GPCs in learning to read Pinyin may not be sufficient for the decoding of English words. Decoding skills beyond the one-to-one GPC level are required.

Secondly, as Liow and Poon (1998) indicated, in the alphabetic system of Pinyin, the sounds mapped onto the letters are different from those in English. For instance, the letter <x> is consistently sounded out as /ɕ/ in Pinyin but usually as /ks/ or /gz/ in English words such as *box, exam*. Therefore, in order to decode English words, new correspondences between letters and sounds need to be learnt.

Besides the experience of spelling-sound conversion in learning Pinyin, previous studies have also found that children receiving Pinyin instruction performed better in phonological awareness tasks than those who did not and thereby suggested that Pinyin learning may improve children's English phonological awareness (Cheung et al. 2001; Holm and Dodd 1996; Huang and Hanley 1995). But as Liow and Poon (1998) pointed out, it is not clear what level of proficiency can be expected. There has been scant research that has investigated the effect of Pinyin learning on different types of English phonological awareness (Xu and Ren 2004).

Xu and Ren (2004) examined the influence of Pinyin learning on the development of different types of English phonological awareness skills among children in mainland China. They administered Pinyin tests among 87 first graders, 110 third graders and 112 fifth graders. Based on the test results, 20 children scoring the lowest and 20 children scoring the highest were chosen in each grade, namely 120 children in total, 60 children achieving lowest on Pinyin and 60 children achieving highest on Pinyin. Then their English phonological awareness was tested through auditory tasks. The English rhyme awareness, English initial phoneme awareness, English final phoneme awareness were examined using the oddity tasks, in which they would hear three words, and then were required to choose the one whose rhyme, initial phoneme or final phoneme is different from the other two. Another type of phonological awareness task is phoneme counting task, in which children were required to count the number of phonemes contained in the English word they heard. The correlation analysis showed moderate correlation between children's Pinyin literacy skills and English rhyme awareness ($r = 0.42$), English initial phoneme awareness ($r = 0.48$), English final phoneme awareness ($r = 0.45$), but very slight correlation between Pinyin literacy skills and English phoneme counting ability ($r = 0.29$). Compared with the first three tasks involving mainly the skills of identifying and categorising component sounds, the phoneme counting task involves segmenting individual phonemes, which is believed as the essential component skill related to the more advanced level of English phonological decoding (see Sect. 2.4.1.3). However, phoneme segmentation skills are rarely taught in Pinyin learning, which functions mainly at the level of onset and rime. As Chen et al. (2004) and Siok and Fletcher (2001) indicated, Pinyin transcribes the sounds of logographic characters in onset and rime units, rather than phonemes. Children are much exposed to the segmentation at the level of onset and rime, but not any further. This may explain why the performance on Pinyin tests is weakly correlated with the performance on the English phoneme counting task. In addition, although children's performance on Pinyin tests was a better predictor of their Chinese phonological awareness skills, compared to the variable of grade, the opposite trend was found in the regression tests for English phonological awareness skills. The variable of grade turned out to be a better predictor of English phonological awareness than Pinyin skills. This suggests that the development of phoneme segmentation skills may be attributable to the increasing experience of learning English. And the combined results also suggested that Pinyin skills may be facilitative or transferrable to certain types of English phonological awareness, like rhyme identity, initial and final phoneme identity, but is not necessarily beneficial to the type of phonological awareness that may be demanded in learning to read English, such as phoneme segmentation. This is supported by Newman and colleagues (2011), who indicated that "Pinyin training may provide insight into the process of sound segmentation, but not at the level of the phoneme" (p. 255).

2.5.2.2 Experience with Character Reading

In addition to the use of the Pinyin system to teach children the sounds of characters, the analysis of the constituent strokes within a character is also an essential step in teaching and learning of logographic characters. Li et al. (2002) described the common steps for teaching characters. In most cases, a character will be firstly taught to read with Pinyin, e.g. 中 [zhong]. Then, the character will be analysed by the strokes, which have names and writing orders. For instance, 中 has four strokes and the specific sequence of the strokes will be instructed, e.g. firstly the shorter vertical stroke ∣, then ⌐, next the horizontal stroke—to complete the enclosure, and finally with a longer vertical stroke ∣to pass through the enclosure. Finally, the character will be required to be copied several times to memorise the positions of strokes.

It is obvious that Chinese children are instructed with a lot of focus on the visual analysis of how the strokes are assembled into a character. When learning to read in Chinese, a large amount of rote-learning and frequent repetition is obligatory. Ng (2006, p. 149) argued that:

> Pinyin cannot and is not supposed to replace Chinese characters as there are high occurrences of homophones and meaning is still attached to the written form. With the aid of Pinyin, children can sound out new vocabulary, but the characters still need to be remembered as visual codes [....] the nature of the orthography, which is logography with meaning mapped directly onto the written form, requires memorisation of individual characters, each as a separate and holistic entry.

The dominant visual-analysis method of teaching and learning beginning Chinese reading may influence the way beginning English reading is learned. In mainland China, English is taught in primary schools as a foreign language. The number of class hours allocated for English lessons is much fewer than Chinese lessons, and these children do not have as many opportunities to be immersed in an English language environment. Moreover, as mentioned in Sect. 1.2.3.1, the first year of English instruction mainly focuses on developing children's English listening and speaking skills. It is from grade 2 onwards that English literacy skills begin to be introduced to primary students. And Pinyin is usually intensively instructed in the first 4–8 weeks in primary grade 1 before learning to read logographic characters. After that, Pinyin instruction is gradually phased out and only used to teach and learn the pronunciation of new characters. From grade 3 onwards, Pinyin is not printed alongside the characters because the aim of teaching Pinyin is not to achieve Pinyin literacy, but Chinese logography. We can assume that the students in grade 2 have got accustomed to the teaching methodology of Chinese reading and also learned to read in Chinese with reliance on much rote-learning and frequent repetition, as instructed in the classroom. Such rich L1 literacy experience may influence the early learning process of English as a foreign language.

Liu (2010) and Zhu (2005) indicated that many primary school children memorise English words only by rote-learning individual letters mechanically. For example, the children try to remember an English word (e.g. *sound*) mechanically by repeating the names of individual letters within a word (e.g. <s>-<o>-<u>-<n>-<d>, <s>-<o>-<u>-<n>-<d>…), without linking the letters with their sounds. Therefore, they may forget easily the words they have tried very hard to memorise. Such mechanic rote-learning method of English words is similar to the way Chinese children learn to memorise the strokes, namely by rote-learning and frequently repeating the constituent strokes within a character and their writing order.

In conclusion, due to the logographic feature of Chinese language, Chinese beginning readers tend to rely on visual processing strategy when learning to read Chinese characters. The alphabetic system of Pinyin familiarise children with most of the English letters, but new grapheme-phoneme correspondences in English and more advanced decoding skills beyond the one-to-one GPCs need to be acquired.

2.5.3 English Phonology

There are very few studies that investigate the role that knowledge of L2 phonology plays in second language reading (Rixon 2011; Roberts 2005; Wade-Woolley and Geva 2000; Walter 2008). Rixon (2011, p. 89) highlighted the importance of a good operational knowledge of the English phonological system in developing L2 children's phonological decoding skills, which require a mapping of phonology and written mode language:

> English native-speaking children will have a well-established performative grasp of the phonology of their variety of English on which they and their teachers can draw when teaching early reading. In the case of learners for whom English is not a first language, the issue of their still-developing ability to operate with the phonological system of English is particularly urgent to address if phonics is to be the chosen basis for teaching early reading.

She suggested two aspects of English phonological system that are relevant to learning to read in English as a second language, namely phoneme inventory, and phonotactics.

2.5.3.1 English Phoneme Repertoire

Wade-Woolley and Geva (2000) pointed out that for English language learners who learn to decode English words, there is an additional key issue. In most cases, learners do not have full and automatic access to the English phoneme inventory.

Table 2.2 displays (Rixon's 2011) list of the RP phonemes with sample spellings, which she adapted from a table in the "Notes of Guidance" (Department for Education and Skills 2007, p. 23) for the materials pack "Letters and Sounds" developed in support of the UK National Literacy Strategy. As in her study, this English phoneme inventory list is used simply for illustrative purposes in the present study as well. Following Chang's (2001) and Zhao's (1995) description of English phonemes as compared with standard Chinese phonology, the English phonemes that are absent in standard Chinese phonology are listed separately, along with the other English phonemes that are reported to be potentially problematic for Chinese learners.

The phoneme repertoire of Chinese is different from that of English. As shown in Table 2.2, some English phonemes do not have Chinese counterparts and may therefore be difficult to learn, such as /θ/, /ð/, /v/, /æ/, /ɒ/ and /ʌ/. In addition, there are fewer vowel phonemic contrasts in standard Chinese than in RP English (Chang 2001). For instance, the contrast between /ɪ/ and /iː/, /ʊ/ and /uː/ do not exist in Chinese. This means that more effort is required to distinguish them.

The accuracy in discriminating the phonemic contrasts specific to L2 were found highly correlated with children's decoding ability in L2 (Wade-Woolley and Geva 2000). Verhoeven (2000) made a similar statement about the importance of acquiring phonemic contrasts specific to L2 in decoding:

> L2 learners are often less capable of distinguishing sounds in the target language than L1 learners, the acquisition of grapheme-phoneme correspondence rules may be troublesome. Less than full auditory discrimination of phonemes might hamper the assignment of the full range of correct pronunciations to individual letters.

Walter (2008) also emphasised the critical role of reliable L2 phonological inventories in L2 decoding:

> If the learners get to the point where they have a reliable repertoire of L2 phonemes in long-term memory, they will decode written L2 text into well-differentiated words in the phonological loop, and will be able to use these words for comprehension. Therefore, activities that improve recognition of minimal pairs and generally the phonological characteristics of the language may well prepare learners to read better. (p. 470)

In general, it seems that phonological decoding requires not only full access to the English phoneme repertoire but also a reliable repertoire of English phonemes, namely the ability to discriminate different English phonemes.

Table 2.2 Inventory of RP phonemes as compared with standard Chinese phonology (Chang 2001; Rixon 2011; Zhao 1995)

Phoneme		Sample words (Taken from "Letters and Sounds")	RP Phonemes/Phoneme contrasts absent in standard Chinese phonology
Consonants	p	Pen, Happy	
	t	Tap, Butter, Jumped	
	k	Cat, Kit, Duck	
	b	Bat, Rabbit	
	d	Dog, Muddy, Pulled	
	g	Go, Bigger	
	m	Map, Hammer	
	n	Net, Funny	
	ŋ	Ring, Pink	
	f	Fan, Puff, Photo	
	θ	Thin	θ
	ð	Then	ð
	s	Sun, Miss, Cell	
	ʃ	Shop, Sure, Mission, Mention, Partial	
	tʃ	Chip, Catch	
	v	Van	v
	z	Zip, Buzz, Is, Pease, Breeze	
	ʒ	Vision, Measure	
	dʒ	Jet, Giant, Badge	
	w	Wig, Whale	
	r	Rat, Carrot	
	l	Leg, Bell	
	j	Yes	
	h	Hen	
Short vowels	ɪ	In, Gym	ɪ / iː
	e	Egg, Head	
	æ	Ant	æ
	ɒ	On, Was	ɒ
	ʌ	Up, Son, Come	ʌ
	ʊ	Look, Put	ʊ / uː
	ə	Corner, Pillar, Motor, Famous, Favour, Murmur, About, Cotton, Mountain, Possible, Happen, Centre, Thorough, Picture, Cupboard	

(continued)

Table 2.2 (continued)

Phoneme		Sample words (Taken from "Letters and Sounds")	RP Phonemes/Phoneme contrasts absent in standard Chinese phonology
Long vowels	iː	Feet, Sea, He, Chief	ɪ / iː
	uː	Boot, Grew, Blue, Rule	ʊ / uː
	ɜː	Hurt, Her, Girl, Work	
	ɔː	For, Saw, Paul, More, Talk	
	ɑː	Farm, Father	
Diphthongs	eɪ	Rain, Day, Make	
	ɔɪ	Coin, Boy	ɔɪ
	aɪ	Night, Tie, My, Like, Find	
	ɪə	Dear, Deer, Here	
	ʊə		
	eə	Fair, Care, Bear	eə
	əʊ	Boat, Grow, Toe, Go, Home	
	aʊ	Cow, Out	

2.5.3.2   Phonotactics

Rixon (2011) highlighted the immense importance of the command of English phonotactics for L2 learners in learning to decode English words. She defined phonotactics as "the language specific rules for sequential or environmental constraints, concerning numbers of permitted syllable constituents, permitted sequences of consonants in clusters and permitted environments for some vowels and some consonants" (p. 60).

English has a wider range of permissible syllable structures than Chinese does. Chinese contains roughly 400 syllables with four tones (high, rising, low and falling), making up 1,200 distinct tone-syllables (Taylor and Taylor 1995). The syllable structure in Chinese is much simpler than that in English. There are only four types of syllable structures (vowel, consonant + vowel, vowel + consonant, consonant + vowel + consonant). The syllable can be made up of a single vowel or compound vowel, with or without consonant preceding or following it. Only two consonants (nasal consonants, [n] or [ng]) ever follow the vowels in Mandarin (Huang and Hanley 1995). In addition, there are a large number of open syllables (CV) up to 54% of syllable types compared with only 38% of CVC and VC (Wang and Cheng 2008). Moreover, unlike English, consonant clusters such as CC (e.g. <cl->, <-nd>), CCC (e.g. <spl->, <-sps>), and CCCC (e.g. <-lfths>, <-ngsts>) do not exist in Chinese syllables. Therefore, the simplicity of Chinese syllable structure may pose both visual and pronunciation problems to Chinese young learners in learning to decode English words, for example, words containing consonant clusters, which are missing in Chinese phonology.

In addition, as Chang (2001) illustrated, final consonants in general cause a serious problem to Chinese learners. There are only two final consonants ([n], [ng]) in Chinese. What Chinese learners will typically do in reading English words is either drop the final consonant sound altogether or insert an extra vowel or syllable in the cluster. And the absence of consonant clusters in Chinese syllable structure may make the sounding out of initial consonant clusters difficult and final consonant clusters even more difficult.

As Rixon (2011) pointed out, although the reliable operational knowledge of English phoneme repertoire and confident grasp of consonant clusters have been treated as a pronunciation issue, problems in decoding may arise if printed words containing unfamiliar consonant clusters are introduced to young learners of English at an early stage. This is supported by Roberts' (2005) study on the relationships between English articulation, vocabulary, phonemic awareness, and decoding in kindergarteners and first graders learning English as a second language. The results showed that quality of English articulation was significantly related to the L2 children's performance on measures of decoding nonwords and measures of applying phonics knowledge to decoding words, and measures of phonemic awareness. Moreover, these beginning readers' articulation accuracy had a greater influence on their performance in decoding than vocabulary, English oral proficiency, and phonemic awareness.

To recap, the literature generally seems to suggest that in order to grasp the ability to map the phonological representations onto the orthographic units of words, L2 children need to acquire a reliable and full command of English phonemes and be able to articulate them to some extent. This is also why (Rixon 2011) has suggested that teachers and material creators for young learners of English may conflate the instruction of phonological decoding with a framework for teaching or reinforcing pronunciation in English.

2.5.4 Classroom Instruction of Phonological Decoding

As English is instructed as a foreign language in mainland China, the input in English that Chinese children get is mainly from their teachers and English classes. The way the teachers instruct phonological decoding and the range of practice children get in their English lessons is likely to exert some influence on the development of their skills of decoding English words.

Snow and Juel (2005) claimed that the teaching of phonological decoding in early reading instruction is "helpful for all children, harmful to none, and crucial for some" (p. 518). Similarly, Woore (2007) also suggested the necessity of teaching phonological decoding skills to L2 readers, by arguing that for many readers, L2 phonological decoding ability would not automatically develop with experience of their second language, and although some may be able to derive GPC rules from their increasing experience with L2 reading, this process seems to be "lengthy, and uneven in its results" (p. 177).

One major cause of children's insufficient phonological decoding skills may be inadequate instruction that fails to develop knowledge of the spelling system (Ehri 1989). For instance, native-speaking children taught in a whole-word programme demonstrated the lack of phonological decoding skills in word reading tasks, where children produced only words they had been taught and were unable to decode unfamiliar words (Seymour and Elder 1986, cited in Ehri 2005a). Moreover, many studies have showed that both L1 and L2 children taught in the non-phonics programme were found to perform significantly worse in phonological decoding than children taught in the phonics programme (National Reading Panel 2000a; Qiu 2007; Stuart 1999; Torgerson et al. 2006). This research therefore suggests a link between lack of phonics instruction and poor phonological decoding skills.

There is also evidence suggesting that different types of phonics instruction produce differential effects on the development of early phonological decoding strategies. For example, Deavers et al. (2000) assigned 45 L1 children matched on age and reading ability into three groups of phonics instruction, small units instruction emphasising grapheme-phoneme correspondences and phonemic awareness, larger units instruction emphasising onset-rime and rhyme awareness, and combined large and small units instruction as a control group. The three projects ran for two years when children were in Reception and Year 1. The results of nonword reading tests indicated that children receiving small units instruction made significantly more use of GPCs than the other two groups, whereas children receiving larger units instruction demonstrated significantly more reliance on rime-based decoding than children receiving small units instruction, after the familiarity with rime base words was controlled.

The studies discussed above indicate that classroom instruction plays a role in children's acquisition of phonological decoding skills. As L2 children seem to learn to decode English words in a similar manner to their L1 counterparts (see Sect. 2.4.2), it is worthwhile reviewing L1 studies that have investigated the impact of different phonics instructional types on improving children's phonological decoding skills. Therefore, this section will focus on such studies in both L1 and L2 contexts. However, the L2 context will be mainly centered in mainland China and Taiwan, because as discussed in Sect. 2.5.2.1, they both have logographic Chinese as their first language and a set of phonetic scripts for characters, although the phonetic script adopted in Taiwan is composed of symbols derived from Chinese characters while that adopted in mainland China is composed of small Roman alphabetic letters.

2.5.4.1 The Teaching of Phonological Decoding in the L1 Context

This section reviews the L1 studies exploring the impact of different phonics instructional types on children's acquisition of phonological decoding skills, in the following aspects of phonics instruction: the inclusion or exclusion of phonemic awareness training, the synthetic or analytic approach, grapheme-based or rime-based decoding, and the presence or absence of practice in applying phonological decoding skills.

Inclusion or Exclusion of Phonemic Awareness Training

Founded on Rose's (2006) review of the teaching of early reading, the UK Department for Education and Skills (2007) recommended in the notes of guidance for its phonics material pack "Letters and Sounds" that training in phoneme blending and segmenting be included in phonics programmes right from the beginning.

As the first major study on phonemic awareness instruction, Bradley and Bryant's (1983) two-year training study among 65 five-year-old L1 children indicated that phonemic awareness is more effective for word reading only if it is taught in conjunction with alphabetic letters than on its own. But this study did not separate phonological decoding skills from sight word reading ability, and it did not investigate the effect of letter sound instruction in the absence of phonemic awareness training.

Ball and Blachman (1991) designed a careful examination of the effectiveness of phonemic awareness training combined with instruction in letter names and sounds on L1 children's phonological decoding skills, in comparison with the instruction in letter name and sounds with no training in phonemic awareness. The 89 kindergarteners could not read more than three words in the pretest and were therefore regarded as non-readers in the study, although on average, they were able to name around two thirds of the 26 letters, and to sound out around one third of the 26 letters. The participants were randomly assigned to three groups. The first group received training in phoneme segmentation, letter name, and letter-to-sound mapping. The second group only received instruction in letter names and letter-sound correspondences, together with a variety of language activities, such as listening to stories, categorising picture cards according to the same semantic category. And the third group, as a control group, received no intervention. Both intervention programmes were implemented over 7 weeks, during four 20 min sessions per week. The results indicated that both the phoneme awareness group and the language activities group achieved significantly higher letter-sound scores than the control group, but did not differ from each other. However, in the test of decoding phonetically regular words, the phoneme awareness group scored significantly higher than the language activities group and the control group, and the latter two groups did not differ significantly, although the mean number of words read correctly by the language activities group was higher than the control group. It was thereby concluded that letter-name and letter-sound training when provided without phonemic awareness training may not be sufficient to improve native-speaking non-readers phonological decoding ability measured in the test.

Drawing from the findings of the meta-analysis of phonemic awareness instruction studies published by Bus and van Ijzendoorn (1999), Ehri and her colleagues (2001a, b) also draw the same conclusion about the necessity of including phonemic awareness training in teaching pre-schoolers and kindergartners to decode words. The crucial role of phonemic awareness training in beginning reading instruction was also supported by Castles et al. (2018).

To recap, phonemic awareness instruction, with the aid of letters, appears to be more effective in facilitating beginning readers' acquisition of phonological decoding.

Synthetic or Analytic Approach

Although it has been well documented that the explicit approach to teaching phonological awareness appears more effective than the implicit approach, there is lack
of converging evidence with regard to whether it would be more effective to use
the synthetic approach or the analytic approach to teaching phonological decoding
(Johnston and Watson 2005; Rose 2006; Torgerson et al. 2006; Wyse and Goswami
2008).

Torgerson et al. (2006) provided a clear description of the two different approaches
of phonological decoding instruction, namely the analytic phonics approach and
synthetic phonics approach. The analytic phonics approach uses a whole-to-part
approach that avoids having children pronounce sounds in isolation. The letter-sound
relationships are taught in the context of words. For instance, in order to teach the
letter sound of <b> , words such as *bag, boy, book, bank*, are presented to students,
and students are helped to recognise that the example words all begin with the same
sound represented by the letter <b> . Synthetic phonics, however, uses a part-to-
whole approach that teaches letter-sound relationships by articulating the sounds in
isolation. Children learn to translate letters into sounds and then blend the sounds
together. According to Watson (1998), the analytic approach is usually taught after an
initial sight vocabulary has been established and children's attention can be drawn to
certain letters and their sounds in the context of whole words, whereas the synthetic
approach generally starts before students are introduced to word or text reading and
children's attention is drawn to the conversion of letters to sounds and the blending of
the sound segments. Hiskes (1998) pointed out that analytic phonics usually teaches
one letter-sound relationship per week and takes up to three years, while synthetic
phonics can be a very accelerated form of phonics, and can be taught in a few months
as all of the letter-sound relations are taught much more rapidly.

Some studies indicated that the synthetic phonics approach is more effective than
the analytic phonics approach in improving phonological decoding skills (Johnston
and Watson 2005; Rose 2006). Johnston and Watson (2005) conducted a 7 year
longitudinal study to examine the effectiveness of the synthetic and analytic phonics
approaches in teaching decoding. Around 300 children in Primary 1 were divided into
three groups. One group was instructed by the synthetic phonics approach, one by the
standard analytic phonics approach, and one by an analytic phonics programme that
included systematic phonemic awareness instruction without reference to print. It
was concluded from the results that the synthetic phonics approach was more effective than the analytic phonics approach, in improving children's performance on
measures of decoding nonwords, even when analytic phonics approach was supplemented with phonemic awareness training. And the researchers further suggested that
synthetic phonics best be taught at the beginning of Primary 1 as the gains for the
synthetic phonics group were kept till the end of primary years, which was supported
in their recent research (Johnston et al. 2012). The findings from Rose's meta-analysis
of phonics instruction lend supporting evidence to the superiority of the synthetic
phonics approach over the analytic phonics approach in his review of the teaching of
early reading in England. However, his report was challenged by Wyse and Goswami

(2008). They argued that the review did not provide any reliable empirical evidence that synthetic phonics was the best route for most beginning readers to becoming skilled readers. They further analysed the available empirical studies in English and found instead that the data support approaches based on systematic instruction in phonics, no matter whether it is the synthetic or analytic phonics approach. This finding received support from the meta-analyses conducted by the National Reading Panel (2000b) and Torgerson et al. (2006), which suggested that the synthetic and analytic phonics approach are equally effective, as long as they are carried out in a systematic way. And systematic phonics is generally accepted as "the teaching of letter-sound relationships in an explicit, organised and sequenced fashion, as opposed to incidentally or on a when-needed basis" (Torgerson et al. 2006, p. 8). It may refer to systematic synthetic or systematic analytic phonics. Ehri et al. (2001a, b, p. 394) provided a relatively more detailed description of the component elements of the spelling-sound correspondences in systematic phonics programmes:

> In systematic phonics programmes, a planned set of phonics elements is taught sequentially. The set includes not only the major correspondences between consonant letters and sounds but also short and long vowel letters and sounds, and vowel and consonant digraphs (e.g. *oi*, *ea*, *sh*, *th*). It also may include blends of letter–sounds that form larger subunits in words. The larger units taught might include onsets (consonants that precede vowels, such as "j" in *jump* or "st" in *stop*) and rimes (i.e. the vowel and following consonants such as "ump" in *jump* and "op" in *stop*).

In general, there appears to be a general agreement that effective phonics instruction needs to be systematic (Mesmer and Kambach 2022; Piasta and Hudson 2022). However, no conclusions seem to have been reached concerning whether the synthetic approach or the analytic approach represents the optimal method of phonics instruction.

Small Units (Graphemes) or Large Units (Bodies)

In addition to the disputes over the synthetic and analytic approach to teaching phonological decoding, there also seems to be considerable debate over the size of orthographic units (small vs. large, namely GPCs vs. rime patterns) thought to be critical in teaching phonological decoding.

Deavers, Solity and Kerfoot (2000) examined the role of early reading instruction on the nonword reading strategies employed by beginning readers matched on their chronological and reading ages. 45 beginning readers from three schools took part in their study. The phonological decoding instruction in one school emphasised small unit instruction, which covered the direct instruction of phoneme blending and segmentation and letter-sound correspondences. The instruction in the second school emphasised the larger units, namely teaching rhyme, onset-rime and word families alongside letter-sound correspondences. Both projects were run for two years, starting from Reception to Year 1. Children receiving small unit instruction obtained higher accuracy scores than children receiving larger unit in decoding different types of nonwords (regular, e.g. *bish*; irregular, e.g. *boup*) in different conditions (in isolation; with clue words), although the difference between the two instruction types was significant only for the irregular nonwords in isolation. Deavers and her colleagues thereby argued that small units may be particularly helpful for beginning readers, by suggesting that smaller units provide better generalisation to decoding unfamiliar words compared to larger units. Moreover, larger units of rimes may not provide a good basis for generalisation because new words or nonwords are not necessarily likely to contain the rime unit on which the learners have been trained. Another factor that may restrict the use of rime-based decoding strategy is the reading vocabulary size. After controlling for familiarity with rime base words, children receiving larger unit instruction demonstrated significantly greater use of rime-based decoding strategy than children in small unit instructional group. Accordingly, it was suggested that the use of small units (grapheme-phoneme correspondences) is particularly important in phonological decoding in the early stages of reading development; however, there may be a greater role of rime-based decoding strategy with the expansion of reading vocabulary size.

Christensen and Bowey (2005) reported similar findings in their study on the efficacy of three different conditions of instructing phonological decoding. Two instructional conditions were explicit decoding-skills based, one focusing on rime patterns and onset-rime blending, and the other focusing on individual grapheme-phoneme correspondences and the analysis and synthesis of individual phonemes. An implicit phonics programme was used as a control programme, teaching symbol-sound relations as they occurred when reading authentic texts. All three programmes were implemented outside the normal lessons, in which the whole language approach to literacy was adopted. All programmes were conducted for 20 min per day for 14 weeks, among 116 2nd graders with English as their first language. The children were all developing their reading ability normally and knew the majority of the most common sounds of 26 letters. In addition to the pretest, 2 interim tests were conducted first after finishing the modules covering CVC words and second after introducing initial and final consonant clusters. And the posttest was implemented at the end of the intervention. Only the posttest included transfer words, i.e. the words that were not covered in any programmes and thus unfamiliar to the children. Children in both explicit decoding programmes performed consistently better than the implicit phonics group in the accuracy with which they read familiar and unfamiliar transfer words. However, the two explicit decoding programmes did not differ in how successfully the children read the words covered in the programmes, whilst the GPC group decoded significantly more transfer words than the rime group and the control group. Christensen and Bowey suggested that this was probably because the GPC programme required children to attend to all the graphemes in a word thoroughly compared to the rime programme, which focused on the onsets and rimes and did not go further to analyse the component graphemes within the rime patterns. Another of their arguments was that children in their study had not accumulated a sufficient reading vocabulary size yet, which determines the familiarity with the rime patterns embedded in word sets and further critically impacts the use of larger units of rime patterns to decode unfamiliar words or nonwords. Accordingly, consistent with Deavers et al.'s (2000) findings, these results also suggest the small unit instruction may be more effective to the acquisition of phonological decoding skills at the early stage of learning to read, compared to the larger unit instruction. However, the use of rime patterns in decoding may increase with grade level and reading ability (Bowey and Hansen 1994; Treiman et al. 1990) and the rime decoding skills-based programme may be more efficacious for children of higher grade levels and reading ability.

However, some studies found no significant difference in the efficacy between the phoneme-based decoding instruction and the rime-based decoding instruction for 6-year-old poor readers (Savage et al. 2003). The interventions lasted for 9 weeks, with four 20 min sessions per week. Both interventions shared some elements, namely the teaching of letter-sound relations with the use of Jolly Phonics. However, children in the phoneme-based intervention group received additional training at the level of grapheme-phoneme correspondences, mainly in the form of sounding out words by assembling different consonants and a vowel. Children in the rime-based intervention group received additional training at the level of rime units, mainly in the form of sounding out words by assembling different consonants and a rime unit; however, no attention was drawn to the vowel letter within the rime unit. Improvements in the nonword decoding skills were evident between pre- and post-test in both interventional groups. However, no significant difference was found between the two interventions in nonword decoding performance between pre-test and post-test.

The lack of effects based on different sizes of orthographic unit was also shown in Haskell et al.'s (1992) study. They assigned first graders (aged around 7) to three training conditions with different instructional emphasis, one on GPCs, one on onsets and rimes, and one on whole words. The training was run for 6 weeks. The GPC group and the rime group both produced significantly more accurate responses in reading words than the whole word group. But no significant difference was found between the GPC group and the rime group.

Walton and his colleagues (2001) also reported similar findings regarding the effects of teaching rime-based and grapheme-based decoding strategies to first graders with knowledge of letter names but very limited knowledge of letter-sound relations. These children with weak prereading skills (phoneme identity, rhyming, letter sound knowledge) were assigned to the grapheme decoding treatment group, the rime-based decoding treatment group, and the control group with weak prereading skills. Both treatment groups received a 25 min session twice a week, for 11 weeks. They were taught the same prereading skills of phoneme identity (initial, medial, final), oral rhyming, and 15 letter-sound associations (<b>, <f>, <h>, <m>, <r>, <s>, <t>, <d>, <g>, <n>, <a>, <e>, <i>, <o>, <u>), but different decoding strategies, one on smaller units of graphemes and the other on larger units of rimes. The control groups did not receive the teaching in the treatment conditions. Children receiving rime-based decoding training and letter decoding training read equal number of nonwords that can be decoded using either rime-based decoding strategy or GPC decoding strategy, and nonwords that can only be read by GPC decoding strategy. This finding is consistent with what the studies by Christensen and Bowey (2005), Deavers et al. (2000) and Ehri's phase theory suggested about the decoding strategy relying on GPCs as the predominant strategy adopted at the early stage of learning to read in English. However, in decoding unfamiliar words that could only be read by analogy to the rime patterns of clue words (*sight* by rime analogy to *fight*), children in the rime group produced more accurate responses compared to children in the letter decoding training group. Christensen and Bowey (2005) suggested that the words that do not have a direct grapheme-phoneme correspondence, e.g. *sight*, *more* and *walk*, may be decoded more easily using rime patterns, although their study did not reveal any results concerning this. Caution, however, is warranted because clue words with the same rime patterns were read aloud and presented alongside the test nonwords in Walton et al.'s study. The clue-word paradigm in the task of decoding unfamiliar words was believed by some researchers as an artefact of phonological priming (Bowey et al. 1998; Nation et al. 2001). Therefore, although the rime group was superior to the GPC group in decoding those test words with the aid of clue words, no evidence can be found concerning which approach would be more effective when the test words can only be decoded using taught rime patterns in a more natural setting, i.e. without the presence of clue words.

To summarise, there is no conclusive evidence showing whether the decoding instruction at the level of GPCs or the decoding instruction at the rime level is more effective for beginning readers. But it should be noted that both studies that showed the advantage of the GPC-based decoding instruction over the rime-based decoding instruction for beginning children were conducted for longer than the other studies that showed no advantage of either instructional method, with Deavers et al.'s (2000) running for 2 years, and Christensen and Bowey's (2005) running for 14 weeks. In contrast, the intervention duration of the other studies was much shorter, ranging from 6 to 11 weeks, which may lead to the lack of advantage of GPC-based decoding instruction over the rime-based decoding instruction in these studies. Moreover, it appears to be suggested that rime-based decoding strategies may facilitate the decoding of the words that cannot be decoded with the existing GPC knowledge. In addition, the rime-based strategy may become more important and applied more in the decoding task at a later stage, when children's reading vocabulary size is larger. But no studies investigating the efficacy of rime-based decoding instruction at a later stage of learning to read have been found.

The Presence or Absence of Practice and Application

Sufficient practice of decoding skills has been generally accepted as an indicator of a good phonics programme (Chard et al. 2000; Stahl et al. 1998). As Fletcher and Lyon (1998) stated, "a targeted skill cannot be learned without opportunities for practice and application" (p. 49). The National Reading Panel (2000a) also draws an unequivocal conclusion on the role of practice and application of decoding skills: "programmes that focus too much on the teaching of letter-sound relations and not enough on putting them to use are unlikely to be effective in implementing systematic phonics instruction" (p. 10).

Most types of the practice that has been suggested by researchers are decoding words in isolation, or reading texts (e.g. captions, sentences, chants, rhymes, or stories) in which some or most words are regularly spelled and contain the letter-sound correspondences that children have been taught up to that point (Chard et al. 2000; Ehri 2003; Stahl et al. 1998).

Research shows that students who were provided with opportunities for applying their alphabetic knowledge in reading text selections with a high percentage of words that contained taught letter-sound correspondences used more phonologically based word identification strategies than children who read texts consisting predominantly of words that did not match their phonics lessons (Juel and Roper 1985). Although Juel and Roper cautioned against using the results to support one approach to teaching beginning reading over another, their study indicated the impact of practice on the development of phonological decoding skills.

In addition, Ehri (2003) also suggested the optimal phonics programme be deliberately integrated with reading instruction, and gave an example to illustrate the case where letter sound instruction is not integrated with reading instruction:

> [It would be less effective] to teach phonics as a separate subject unrelated to anything else students are taught during the day. For example, children might study letter-sound correspondences for 20 minutes every morning, and then move to reading and writing instruction that bears no connection to the phonics lessons. (p. 14)

In a word, it is generally believed necessary for children to practice their phonological decoding skills and apply their skills in reading activities.

Summary

The studies discussed above reveal disagreements over the choice of effective approaches to teaching phonological decoding in the L1 context. However, they tend to suggest that phonemic awareness training with the aid of letters contributes to the early acquisition of phonological decoding. Systematic phonics instruction is more effective than the implicit and unsystematic phonics instruction. Grapheme-based decoding instruction tends to be more effective than rime-based decoding instruction, at the early stage of learning to decode. And the important role that sufficient practice and application of taught letter-sound relations plays in phonological decoding instruction is stressed. The following section reviews the studies evaluating the effectiveness of phonological decoding instruction in the L2 context, focusing mainly on the context of mainland China and Taiwan.

2.5.4.2   The Teaching of Phonological Decoding in the L2/FL Context

Previous studies on L2 phonological decoding instruction have revealed that phonics instruction is more conducive to developing young English language learners' phonological decoding ability, compared to non-phonics instruction (Chen 2003; Qiu 2007; Stuart 1999).

Stuart (1999) compared the effects of a phonics programme and a whole language programme on L2 children's development of phonological decoding skills. Ninety-six L2 children aged around 5 were assigned to two intervention groups, one using the Jolly Phonics experimental programme (phonemic awareness and phonics) and the other as a control programme taking a whole language approach using Big Books with the introduction of letter names and sounds embedded in the text. The intervention was conducted to whole classes. Children were pretested on phonological decoding, prior to a 12-week intervention, which was implemented for an hour per day. Children were post-tested on it immediately after intervention, and again one year later. The two groups did not differ from each other at the pre-test. However, the Jolly phonics programme performed significantly better relative to the Big Books programme, both at the end of the intervention and a year later, indicating the lasting effects of early, structured and explicit instruction of phonemic awareness and grapheme-phoneme correspondences on accelerating the development of decoding ability in these 5-year-old children with English as their second language, who have initially poor receptive vocabularies for English.

Qiu (2007) compared the effects of the instruction of phonics along with phonemic awareness and the whole language approach on developing the phonological decoding skills of children from mainland China. The 6 week intervention was conducted among children aged roughly 12 years old, with two years of classroom English learning experience in primary schools. The phonics group was trained in phoneme segmentation and blending, and letter-sound relations while the whole language group was involved in activities taken from textbooks, like reading dialogues and words, with rare analysis of letter sounds. The nonword decoding performance of the two intervention groups was matched at the pre-test, but the phonics group significantly outperformed the whole language group in a nonword decoding task at the end of the intervention. This finding is consistent with Stuart's (1999) finding about the advantage of the instruction combining phonics and phonemic awareness over the whole language approach to teaching early reading.

Chen's (2003) study on the effectiveness of the phonics programme combined with phonemic awareness training in developing Taiwanese EFL children's English phonological decoding skills also echoed the findings of the studies discussed above. Twenty-two fifth graders from Taipei were assigned to 2 groups. The intervention ran for 8 weeks, during which the training class was given twice a week, each time for 15–20 min. The experimental group received training in letter sounds, phoneme segmentation and blending, and applying the taught phonics knowledge and phonemic awareness skills in decoding words. During this time, children in the control group only reviewed what they have been taught in the regular English class, including writing the 26 letters of the English alphabets, reading the dialogues taught in the textbook. The results showed that the experimental group significantly outperformed the control group on nonword and unfamiliar word decoding tests.

The studies reviewed above demonstrate how letter sound instruction combined with phonemic awareness training contributes to the development of L2/FL children's phonological decoding. However, to our knowledge, no studies in the Chinese contexts compared the effects of letter sound instruction combined with phonemic awareness training and without. This is probably because those studies usually involve phonics instruction that already included phoneme blending activities (Chu et al. 2007).

In addition, the studies reviewed above did not investigate the effects of different types of phonics instruction on L2/FL phonological decoding skills. This section therefore reviews the L2 studies exploring the impact of different phonics instructional types on children's acquisition of phonological decoding skills, for the same aspects of phonics instruction that the review of L1 studies focused on: the synthetic or analytic approach, grapheme-based or rime-based decoding, and the presence or absence of practice in applying phonological decoding skills.

Synthetic or Analytic Approach

Lee's (2011) study compared the efficacy of the synthetic phonics approach and the analytic phonics approach to teaching phonological decoding among Chinese-speaking children in Taiwan. The children were grade 4 students aged around 10 and started learning English in grade 3. They were assigned to two treatment conditions. One is the synthetic phonics approach, which involved the teaching of letter sounds explicitly along with phonics rules and how these phonemes can be blended to form the words. The other is the analytic phonics approach, which is also concerned with learning letter-sound relations, but adopted the whole-to-part approach to analysing the target component letter-sound relations across words, e.g. the sound of <th> in *thin, think, thick* and *thank*. After the 10-week treatment (80 min per week), both analytic and synthetic groups significantly improved their phonological decoding skills. However, no significant difference was found between the two groups in their effectiveness on developing phonological decoding ability.

Drawing on her own experience, Rixon (2011) argued that the positive effects of synthetic phonics approach might be lessened by the L2/FL children's limited oral/aural vocabulary while the analytic phonics approach seemed to be of more practical use for learners:

> Whatever the merits of the argument for Synthetic Phonics with L1 learners (Johnston and Watson 2005) it would seem to have applicability to EYL learners only in very particular conditions. Most Young Learners of English lack the large oral/aural vocabulary that is needed as a reference point when "building" up and working towards creating words from individual phonemes - words that they themselves would recognize as real English words, that is. Analytical Phonics, which works by encouraging learners to observe and compare the sound and symbol correspondences in words with which they are already familiar aurally and orally, seems to have more prospect of usefulness for EYL. (p. 89)

The synthetic phonics approach serves as a quick "way in" for the beginning L1 readers, involving the instruction of letter sounds in isolation, which are then assembled to form the words. This process requires the working knowledge of the English phonemes as the basis that the synthetic phonics approach can work on. L1 beginning readers possess such knowledge before learning to read while young learners of English are still developing it while learning to read. In that sense, teaching letter sounds within the context of familiar oral/aural words seems to be more practical for L2/FL children, compared to teaching letter sounds in isolation.

To sum up, there is no robust evidence to suggest whether synthetic or analytic phonics approach is more effective in helping Chinese young English language learners develop their phonological decoding skills, although (Rixon 2011) tentatively suggested the advantage of the analytic phonics approach over the synthetic phonics approach for young learners of English.

Small Units (Graphemes) or Large Units (Bodies)

Very few studies have investigated the efficacy of the phonics instruction employing different sizes of orthographic units in the Chinese contexts.

Wu and Chen (2006) compared the effect of small-unit and large-unit phonics training programmes on Taiwanese EFL children's decoding ability. 33 children at primary grade 4 with reading difficulty were selected based on their performance on the screening tests in alphabet knowledge, phonemic awareness and word recognition. Then they were assigned to two phonics programmes. One programme focused on the onset/rime-level of phonological awareness, and rime-based phonics instruction, while the other focused on the phonemic level of phonological awareness, and phoneme-based phonics instruction. The intervention lasted for 10 weeks, two 30 min training sessions per week. Before the intervention, the children had 2 years of English learning at school. Pre- and post-tests on nonword decoding were implemented for both groups. The results showed that both intervention groups enhanced their decoding ability after the training. But children in the phoneme-based phonics programme performed significantly better than children in the rime-based phonics programme on the task of nonword decoding. This converges with the findings by Christensen and Bowey (2005), who found that phoneme-based phonics intervention was superior to rime-based phonics intervention for L1 typically beginning readers in decoding unfamiliar words.

However, no difference between the two types of phonics instruction was found in Lee's (2011) study, which compared the effectiveness of a grapheme-based phonics programme and a rime-based phonics programme on measures of Taiwanese children's decoding skills. The 48 children were fourth graders in a primary school in Taiwan. The English teaching in their school started at grade 3, with 80 min per week. They had knowledge of letter shapes but no experience of phonics. They were given pre-and post-tests on reading nonwords before and after the 10-week intervention. Both the GPC-based and rime-based phonics approach showed positive effect on their decoding performance, but no significant difference was found between the two groups. In terms of the mean score difference, however, the rime group decoded more nonwords containing silent <e>, vowel digraph and diphthongs, and r-controlled vowels, than the GPC group, while the opposite trend was found in decoding monosyllabic nonwords containing short vowels.

Similar to the reviews of L1 studies in Sect. 2.5.4.1.3, there is no converging evidence revealing the advantage of one approach over the other, but they appear to suggest that GPC-based phonics instruction may be more effective for Chinese children with reading difficulties. Rime-based phonics instruction may be more facilitative in teaching decoding the nonwords that contain the relatively more complicated vowel graphemes.

The Presence or Absence of Practice and Application

The importance of applying phonics knowledge in real practice was pointed out in the study by Chu (2011). She investigated the effectiveness of two phonics teaching methods on English word reading and confidence in Taiwanese EFL children. The participants were 117 fifth-grade students in a primary school in Taipei. They started learning English at grade 2 and were matched on word recognition ability. The experimental group received phonics with supplementary decodable text instruction, whereas the control group, consisting of 58 students, received phonics teaching only. The intervention proceeded for five weeks, with three sessions each week, and 20 min per session. Both groups took a pre-test, immediate post-test, and delayed post-test on word reading. The 17 test words were chosen from the five decodable books used in the experimental intervention and were unfamiliar to more than 1/3 of 29 fifth graders in the pilot study. These target words were also included in the word reading practice list in the control group. The findings showed that both methods significantly improved children's performance on reading the 17 words, but that phonics with supplementary decodable text was shown to be more effective than phonics in isolation. But the difference was significant only in the delayed word reading, suggesting a better long-term retention effect produced by the teaching of phonic plus decodable text for practice. In other words, the reading of meaning-involved decodable text may help children to better retain the newly acquired phonics rules. But it should be noted that real words, rather than nonwords, were used in the test, which implied that there might be other factors (rather than phonological decoding skills) interfering in the better performance of the experimental group. For instance, the reading of decodable books may be more conducive to consolidating the memory of the target decodable words than reading them in isolation in the control group.

The results did not provide robust evidence in favour of decodable texts in improving Chinese children's phonological decoding skills. However, as the L1 studies reviewed in Sect. 2.5.4.1.4 suggested, it seems reasonable to assume that any form of practice in applying the phonics knowledge would be beneficial, like reading words, sentences or texts.

Summary

It was not until the beginning of the 21st century that phonics instruction was intro-duced into the primary English curriculum in mainland China and Taiwan. The training studies discussed above demonstrated the positive effect of phonics interven-tion combining phonemic awareness training and instruction in letter-sound relations on developing Chinese-speaking children's phonological decoding skills. However, there is still an outstanding lack of studies investigating the effect of different phonics approaches on children's phonological decoding development. Moreover, none of the phonics training studies in mainland China and Taiwan is a longitudinal one. Neither is there any study evaluating a longitudinal phonics programme embedded in the primary English syllabus.

References

Adams, M. J. (1990). *Beginning to read: Thinking and learning about print*. Urbana-Champaign, IL: Center for the Study of Reading.

Ball, E. W., & Blachman, B. A. (1991). Does phoneme awareness training in kindergarten make a difference in early word recognition and developmental spelling? *Reading Research Quarterly, 26*(1), 49–66.

Bassetti, B. (2007). Effects of hanyu pinyin on pronunciation in learners of Chinese as a foreign language. In A. Guder, X. Jiang, & Y. Wan (Eds.), *The cognition, learning and teaching of Chinese characters*. Beijing, China: Beijing Language and Culture University Press.

Bentin, S. (1992). Phonological awareness, reading, and reading acquisition: A survey and appraisal of current knowledge. In R. Frost & L. Katz (Eds.), *Orthography, phonology, morphology, and meaning* (pp. 193–210). Amsterdam: Elsevier Science Publishers.

Birch, B. M. (2007). *English L2 reading: Getting to the bottom*. Mahwah, N. J.: Lawrence Erlbaum Associates.

Blachman, B. A., Ball, E. W., Black, R., & Tangel, D. M. (2000). *Road to the code: A phonological awareness program for young children*. Baltimore, MD: Paul H. Brookes Publishing Co.

Blevins, W. (1998). *Phonics from A to Z: A practical guide*. New York: Scholastic Professional Books.

Blondin, C., Candelier, M., Edelenbos, P., Johnstone, R., Kubaneck, A., & Taeschner, T. (1998). *Foreign languages in primary and pre-school education: A review of recent research within the European Union*. London: Centre for Information on Language Teaching.

Bowey, J. A., & Hansen, J. (1994). The development of orthographic rimes as units of word recognition. *Journal of Experimental Child Psychology, 58*(3), 465–488.

Bowey, J. A., Vaughan, L., & Hansen, J. (1998). Beginning readers' use of orthographic analogies in word reading. *Journal of Experimental Child Psychology, 68*(2), 108–133.

Bradley, L., & Bryant, P. E. (1983). Categorizing sounds and learning to read: A causal connection. *Nature, 301*(3), 419–421.

Bus, A. G., & van Ijzendoorn, M. H. (1999). Phonological awareness and early reading: A meta-analysis of experimental training studies. *Journal of Educational Psychology, 91*(3), 403–414.

Byrne, B., & Fielding-Barnsley, R. (1990). Acquiring the alphabetic principle: A case for teaching recognition of phoneme identity. *Journal of Educational Psychology, 82*(4), 805–812.

Cain, K. (2010). *Reading development and difficulties* (Vol. 8). Chichester: J. Wiley & Sons.

Cameron, L. (2001). *Teaching languages to young learners*. Cambridge: Cambridge University Press.

Caravolas, M., Volín, J., & Hulme, C. (2005). Phoneme awareness is a key component of alphabetic literacy skills in consistent and inconsistent orthographies: Evidence from Czech and English children. *Journal of Experimental Child Psychology, 92*(2), 107–139.

Cardoso-Martins, C., Mesquita, T. C. L., & Ehri, L. C. (2011). Letter names and phonological awareness help children to learn letter–sound relations. *Journal of Experimental Child Psychology, 109*(1), 25–38.

Castles, A., Rastle, K., & Nation, K. (2018). Ending the reading wars: Reading acquisition from novice to expert. *Psychological science in the public interest, 19*(1), 5–51.

Chang, J. (2001). Chinese speakers. In M. Swan & B. Smith (Eds.), *Learner English: A teacher's guide to interference and other problems* (2nd ed., pp. 224–237). Cambridge: Cambridge University Press.

Chard, D. J., McDonagh, S., Lee, S., & Reece, V. (2007). Assessing word recognition. In J. R. Paratore & R. L. McCormack (Eds.), *Classroom literacy assessment: Making sense of what students know and do* (pp. 85–100). New York: Guilford Publications.

Chard, D. J., Pikulski, J. J., & Templeton, S. (2000). *From phonemic awareness to fluency: Effective decoding instruction in a research-based reading program.* Retrieved September 11, 2011, from https://www.tuninst.net/LANG-ACQUI/ChaPikTem-phoneme-awareness.pdf.

Chen, X., Anderson, R. C., Li, W., Hao, M., Wu, X., & Shu, H. (2004). Phonological awareness of bilingual and monolingual Chinese children. *Journal of Educational Psychology, 96*(1), 142–151.

Chen, Y. (2003). *The effects of phonological decoding training on English word recognition skills in Taiwanese EFL children.* (Unpublished Master dissertaion). National Taipei University of Education.

Cheung, H. (1999). Improving phonological awareness and word reading in a later learned alphabetic script. *Cognition, 70*(1), 1–26.

Cheung, H., Chen, H.-C., Lai, C. Y., Wong, O. C., & Hills, M. (2001). The development of phonological awareness: Effects of spoken language experience and orthography. *Cognition, 81*(3), 227–241.

Chiappe, P., & Siegel, L. S. (1999). Phonological awareness and reading acquisition in English- and Punjabi-speaking Canadian children. *Journal of Educational Psychology, 91*(1), 20–28.

Chiappe, P., Siegel, L. S., & Gottardo, A. (2002). Reading-related skills of kindergartners from diverse linguistic backgrounds. *Applied Psycholinguistics, 23*(1), 95–116.

Chikamatsu, N. (1996). The effects of L1 orthography on L2 word recognition: A study of American and Chinese learners of Japanese. *Studies in Second Language Acquisition,* 18(4), 403–432.

Christensen, C. A., & Bowey, J. A. (2005). The efficacy of orthographic rime, grapheme–phoneme correspondence, and implicit phonics approaches to teaching decoding skills. *Scientific Studies of reading, 9*(4), 327–349.

Chu, H., Yu, Y., Chang, H., Ting, L., Yu, C., & Hu, C. F. (2007). Effectiveness of phonological remediation for children with poor English word reading abilities. *English Teaching & Learning, 31*(4), 85–125.

Chu, H. (2002a). Assessing EFL learners' decoding skills. *English Teaching & Learning, 26*(3), 35–57.

Chu, H. (2002b). Beginning EFL learners' decoding skill and word reading ability. *Taipei Municipal Teachers College Journal, 33,* 471–484.

Chu, M. (2011). *The impact of two phonics teaching methods on English word reading and confidence for Taiwanese EFL children.* (Unpublished Master dissertation). National Yunlin University of Science & Technology, Taiwan.

Crystal, D. (2003). *The Cambridge encyclopedia of the English language.* Cambridge: Cambridge University Press.

Deavers, R., Solity, J., & Kerfoot, S. (2000). The effect of instruction on early nonword reading strategies. *Journal of Research in Reading, 23*(3), 267–286.

Demont, E., & Gombert, J. E. (1996). Phonological awareness as a predictor of recoding skills and syntactic awareness as a predictor of comprehension skills. *British Journal of Educational Psychology, 66*(3), 315–332.

Department for Education and Skills. (2007). *Letters and Sounds: Notes of guidance for practitioners and teachers.* Retrieved September 2, 2011, from http://nationalstrategies.standards. dcsf.gov.uk/node/84969

Duncan, L. G., Seymour, P. H. K., & Hill, S. (2000). A small-to-large unit progression in metaphonological awareness and reading? *The Quarterly Journal of Experimental Psychology: Section A, 53*(4), 1081–1104.

Ehri, L. C. (1989). The development of spelling knowledge and its role in reading acquisition and reading disability. *Journal Of Learning Disabilities, 22*(6), 356–365.

Ehri, L. C. (1992). Reconceptualizing the development of sight word reading and its relationship to recoding. In P. Gough, L. Ehri, & R. Treiman (Eds.), *Reading acquisition* (pp. 107–143). Hillsdale, NJ: Lawrence Erlbaum Associates.

Ehri, L. C. (1999). Phases of development in learning to read words. In J. Oakhill & R. Beard (Eds.), *Reading development and the teaching of reading* (pp. 79–108). Oxford: Blackwell publishers.

Ehri, L. C. (2020). The science of learning to read words: A case for systematic phonics instruction. *Reading Research Quarterly, 55*(S1), S45–S60.

Ehri, L. C., & McCormick, S. (1998). Phases of word learning: Implications for instruction with delayed and disabled readers. *Reading & Writing Quarterly, 14*(2), 135–163.

Ehri, L. C., & Robbins, C. (1992). Beginners need some decoding skill to read words by analogy. *Reading Research Quarterly, 27*(1), 13–26.

Ehri, L. C., & Roberts, T. (2006). The roots of learning to read and write: Acquisition of letters and phonemic awareness. In D. K. Dickinson & S. B. Neuman (Eds.), *Handbook of early literacy research* (Vol. 2, pp. 113–131). New York: The Guilford Press.

Ehri, L. C., Nunes, S., Stahl, S. A., & Willows, D. (2001a). Systematic phonics instruction helps students learn to read: Evidence from the National Reading Panel's meta-analysis. *Review of educational research, 71*(3), 393–447.

Ehri, L. C., Nunes, S. R., Willows, D. M., Schuster, B. V., Yaghoub-Zadeh, Z., & Shanahan, T. (2001b). Phonemic awareness instruction helps children learn to read: Evidence from the National Reading Panel's meta-analysis. *Reading Research Quarterly, 36*(3), 250–287.

Ehri, L. C. (1994). Development of the ability to read words: Update. In R. B. Ruddell, Ruddell, M. R., Singer, H. (Ed.), *Theoretical models and processes of reading* (4th ed., pp. 323–358). Newark, DE: International Reading Association.

Ehri, L. C. (1998). Grapheme-phoneme knowledge is essential for learning to read words in English. In J. Metsala & L. Ehri (Eds.), *Word recognition in beginning literacy* (pp. 3–40). Hillsdale, NJ: Lawrence Erlbaum Assoc.

Ehri, L. C. (2002). Phases of acquisition in learning to read words and implications for teaching In R. Stainthorp & P. Tomlinson (Eds.), *Learning and teaching reading* (pp. 7–28). Leicester, UK: The British Psychological Society.

Ehri, L. C. (2003). *Systematic phonics instruction: Findings of the National Reading Panel.* Retrieved October 2, 2011, from http://www.standards.dfes.gov.uk/pdf/literacy/lehri_phonics. pdf.

Ehri, L. C. (2005a). *Development of sight word reading: Phases and findings.* Oxford: Blackwell Publishing Ltd.

Ehri, L. C. (2005b). Learning to read words: Theory, findings, and issues. *Scientific Studies of Reading, 9*(2), 167–188.

Fitzgerald, J. (1995). English-as-a-second-language learners' cognitive reading processes: A review of research in the United States. *Review of Educational Research, 65*(2), 145–190.

Fletcher, J. M., & Lyon, G. R. (1998). Reading: A research-based approach. In W. M. Evers (Ed.), *What's gone wrong in America's classrooms* (pp. 49–90). Stanford, CA: Hoover Institution Press.

Foorman, B. R., Francis, D. J., Novy, D. M., & Liberman, D. (1991). How letter-sound instruction mediates progress in first-grade reading and spelling. *Journal of Educational Psychology, 83*(4), 456–469.

Frith, U. (1985). Beneath the surface of developmental dyslexia. In K. Patterson, J. C. Marshall, & M. Coltheart (Eds.), *Surface Dyslexia: Cognitive and Neuro-Psychological Studies of Phonological Reading* (pp. 301–330). London: Lawrence Erlbaum Associates.

Geva, E., Yaghoub-Zadeh, Z., & Schuster, B. (2000). Understanding individual differences in word recognition skills of ESL children. *Annals Of Dyslexia, 50*(1), 121–154.

Goswami, U. (1995). Phonological development and reading by analogy: What is analogy, and what is it not? *Journal of Research in Reading, 18*(2), 139–145.

Goswami, U. (1999). Causal connections in beginning reading: The importance of rhyme. *Journal of Research in Reading, 22*(3), 217–240.

Goswami, U., & Bryant, P. (1990). *Phonological skills and learning to read.* Hove: Psychology Press.

Gough, P. B., & Hillinger, M. L. (1980). Learning to read: An unnatural act. *Annals Of Dyslexia, 30*(1), 179–196.

Gough, P. B., Juel, C., & Griffith, P. L. (1992). Reading, spelling, and the orthographic cipher. In P. B. Gough, L. C. Ehri, & R. Treiman (Eds.), *Reading acquisition* (pp. 35–48). Hillsdale, NJ: Lawrence Erlbaum Associates.

Gough, P. B., & Walsh, M. A. (1991). Chinese, phoenicians, and the orthographic cipher of English. In S. A. Brady & D. P. Shankweiler (Eds.), *Phonological processes in literacy: A tribute to Isabelle Y. Liberman* (pp. 199–209). Hillsdale, NJ: Lawrence Erlbaum Associates.

Griffith, P. L., & Gough, P. B. (1986). Acquisition of literacy: A longitudinal study of children in first and second grade. *Journal of Educational Psychology, 78*(4), 243–255.

Hamada, M., & Koda, K. (2011). The role of the phonological loop in English word learning: A comparison of Chinese ESL learners and native speakers. *Journal of Psycholinguistic Research, 40*(2), 75–92.

Hanna, P. R., Hodges, R. E., & Hanna, J. S. (1971). *Spelling: Structure and Strategies.* Boston: Houghton Mifflin.

Harley, T. A. (2008). *The psychology of language: From data to theory* (3rd ed.). Hove and New York: Psychology Press.

Harris, M., & Giannouli, V. (1999). Learning to read and spell in Greek: The importance of letter knowledge and morphological awareness. In M. Harris & G. Hatano (Eds.), *Learning to read and write: A cross-linguistic perspective* (pp. 51–70). Cambridge: Cambridge University Press.

Haskell, D. W., Foorman, B. R., & Swank, P. R. (1992). Effects of three orthographic/phonological units on first-grade reading. *Remedial and Special Education, 13*(2), 40–49.

Haynes, M., & Carr, T. (1990). Writing system background and second language reading: A component skills analysis of English reading by native speakers of Chinese. In T. Carr & B. Levy (Eds.), *Reading and its development: Component skills approaches* (pp. 375–421). San Diego: Academic Press.

Hiskes, D. (1998). Explicit or implicit phonics: Therein lies the rub. *Right to Read Report, 4*(1), 1.

Holm, A., & Dodd, B. (1996). The effect of first written language on the acquisition of English literacy. *Cognition, 59*(2), 119–147.

Hoover, W. A., & Gough, P. B. (1990). The simple view of reading. *Reading and Writing, 2*(2), 127–160.

Hu, C. F. (2003). Phonological memory, phonological awareness, and foreign language word learning. *Language Learning, 53*(3), 429–462.

Hu, C. F. (2005). How much you learn from shared reading may depend on how sensitive you are to the sound structure. *Electronic Journal of Foreign Language Teaching, 2*(2), 14–15.

Huang, H., & Hanley, J. (1995). Phonological awareness and visual skills in learning to read Chinese and English. *Cognition, 54*(1), 73–98.

Hulme, C., Hatcher, P. J., Nation, K., Brown, A., Adams, J., & Stuart, G. (2002). Phoneme awareness is a better predictor of early reading skill than onset-rime awareness. *Journal of Experimental Child Psychology, 82*(1), 2–28.

Iversen, S., & Tunmer, W. E. (1993). Phonological processing skills and the Reading Recovery Program. *Journal of Educational Psychology, 85*(1), 112–126.

Johnston, R. S., McGeown, S., & Watson, J. E. (2012). Long-term effects of synthetic versus analytic phonics teaching on the reading and spelling ability of 10 year old boys and girls. *Reading and Writing, 25*(6), 1365–1384.

Johnston, R. S., & Watson, J. E. (2005). *The effects of synthetic phonics teaching on reading and spelling attainment: A seven year longitudinal study.* Ediburgh, Scotland: Scottish Executive Education Department.

Juel, C., & Roper, D. (1985). The influence of basal readers on first grade reading. *Reading Research Quarterly, 20*(2), 134–152.

Kendeou, P., van den Broek, P., White, M. J., & Lynch, J. S. (2009). Predicting reading comprehension in early elementary school: The independent contributions of oral language and decoding skills. *Journal of Educational Psychology, 101*(4), 765–778.

Kessler, B., & Treiman, R. (2001). Relationships between sounds and letters in English monosyllables. *Journal of Memory and Language, 44*(4), 592–617.

Koda, K. (2005). *Insights into second language reading: A cross-linguistic approach.* New York: Cambridge University Press.

Laxon, V., Gallagher, A., & Masterson, J. (2002). The effects of familiarity, orthographic neighbourhood density, letter-length and graphemic complexity on children's reading accuracy. *British Journal of Psychology, 93*(2), 269–287.

Lee, M. (2011). *The effectiveness of two phonics instructional approaches on Taiwanese EFL young readers' single word reading and spelling.* (Unpublished Master dissertation). National Yunlin University of Science and Technology.

Lesaux, N. K., Rupp, A. A., & Siegel, L. S. (2007). Growth in reading skills of children from diverse linguistic backgrounds: Findings from a 5-year longitudinal study. *Journal of Educational Psychology, 99*(4), 821–834.

Li, W., Gaffney, J. S., & Packard, J. L. (Eds.). (2002). *Chinese children's reading acquisition: Theoretical and pedagogical issues.* Boston: Kluwer Academic Publishers.

Lin, X. (2008). Correlational research on English reading difficulty and phonological skill deficiency. *Journal of Qiqihar University (Philosophy & Social Science Edition), 6*, 94–96.

Lin, D., McBride-Chang, C., Shu, H., Zhang, Y., Li, H., Zhang, J., Aram, D., & Levin, I. (2010). Small wins big: Analytic Pinyin skills promote Chinese word reading. *Psychological Science, 21*, 1117–1122.

Liow, S. R. (1999). Reading skill development in bilingual Singaporean children. In M. H. G. Hatano (Ed.), *Learning to read and write: A cross-linguistic perspective* (pp. 196–213). UK: Cambridge University Press.

Liow, S. R., & Poon, K. K. L. (1998). Phonological awareness in multilingual Chinese children. *Applied Psycholinguistics, 19*(03), 339–362.

Lipka, O., Siegel, L. S., & Vukovic, R. (2005). The literacy skills of English language learners in Canada. *Learning Disabilities Research & Practice, 20*(1), 39–49.

Liu, M. (2010). Problems in the teaching of English phonology in primary schools. *Primary School English Teaching References, 6*, 88–89.

Marsh, G., Friedman, M., Welch, V., & Desberg, P. (1981). A cognitive-developmental theory of reading acquisition. In G. E. McKinnon & T. G. Waller (Eds.), *Reading research: Advances in theory and practice* (Vol. 3, pp. 199–221). New York: Academic Press.

McBride-Chang, C., & Treiman, R. (2003). Hong Kong Chinese kindergartners learn to read English analytically. *Psychological Science, 14*(2), 138–143.

McBride-Chang, C., Wagner, R. K., & Chang, L. (1997). Growth modeling of phonological awareness. *Journal of Educational Psychology, 89*(4), 621–630.

Mesmer, H. A., & Kambach, A. (2022). Beyond labels and agendas: Research teachers need to know about phonics and phonological awareness. *The Reading Teacher, 76*(1), 62–72.

Moats, L. C. (2010). *Speech to print: Language essentials for teachers* (2nd ed.). Baltimore, Maryland: Paul H. Brookes Publishing Co.

Murray, B. A. (1998). Gaining alphabetic insight: Is phoneme manipulation skill or identity knowledge causal? *Journal of Educational Psychology, 90*(3), 461.

Muter, V., & Diethelm, K. (2001). The contribution of phonological skills and letter knowledge to early reading development in a multilingual population. *Language Learning, 51*(2), 187–219.

Muter, V., Hulme, C., Snowling, M., & Taylor, S. (1998). Segmentation, not rhyming, predicts early progress in learning to read. *Journal of Experimental Child Psychology, 71*(1), 3–27.

Muter, V., Hulme, C., Snowling, M. J., & Stevenson, J. (2004). Phonemes, rimes, vocabulary, and grammatical skills as foundations of early reading development: evidence from a longitudinal study. *Developmental Psychology, 40*(5), 665–681.

Nassaji, H. (2003). Higher–level and lower–level text processing skills in advanced ESL reading comprehension. *The Modern Language Journal, 87*(2), 261–276.

Nation, K., & Hulme, C. (1997). Phonemic segmentation, not onset-rime segmentation, predicts early reading and spelling skills. *Reading Research Quarterly, 32*(2), 154–167.

Nation, K., Allen, R., & Hulme, C. (2001). The limitations of orthographic analogy in early reading development: Performance on the clue-word task depends on phonological priming and elementary decoding skill, not the use of orthographic analogy. *Journal of Experimental Child Psychology, 80*(1), 75–94.

National Reading Panel. (2000a). *Teaching children to read: An evidence-based assessment of the scientific research literature on reading and its implications for reading instruction*. Retrieved November 16, 2010, from https://www.nichd.nih.gov/publications/pubs/nrp/Pages/smallbook. aspx.

National Reading Panel. (2000b). *Teaching children to read: An evidence-based assessment of the scientific research literature on reading and its implications for reading instruction (Reports of the subgroups)*. Retrieved November 16, 2010, from http://www.nationalreadingpanel.org/pub lications/subgroups.htm.

Newman, E. H., Tardif, T., Huang, J., & Shu, H. (2011). Phonemes matter: The role of phoneme-level awareness in emergent Chinese readers. *Journal of Experimental Child Psychology, 108*(2), 242–259.

Ng, S. W. C. (2006). *The effects of direct instruction in phonological skills on L2 reading performance of Chinese learners of English*. (Unpublished PhD Thesis). University of London.

Peereman, R., & Content, A. (1998). *Quantitative analyses of orthography to phonology mapping in English and French*. Retrieved May 18, 2012, from http://homepages.vub.ac.be/~acontent/ OPMapping.html.

Piasta, S. B., & Hudson, A. K. (2022). Key knowledge to support phonological awareness and phonics instruction. *The Reading Teacher, 76*(2), 201–210.

Piasta, S. B., & Wagner, R. K. (2010). Learning letter names and sounds: Effects of instruction, letter type, and phonological processing skill. *Journal of Experimental Child Psychology, 105*(4), 324–344.

Qiu, J. (2007). An experimental study on phonics instruction. *Journal of Basic English Education, 9*(1), 29–33.

Rack, J. P., Snowling, M. J., & Olson, R. K. (1992). The nonword reading deficit in developmental dyslexia: A review. *Reading Research Quarterly, 27*(1), 29–53.

Rayner, K., Pollatsek, A., Ashby, J., & Clifton, C. (2012). *Psychology of reading* (2nd ed.). New York: Psychology Press.

Read, C., Zhang, Y., Nie, H., & Ding, B. (1986). The ability to manipulate speech sounds depends on knowing alphabetic writing. *Cognition, 24*(1), 31–44.

Reitsma, P. (1983). Printed word learning in beginning readers. *Journal of Experimental Child Psychology, 36*(2), 321–339.

Rixon, S. (2011). *Beyond ABC: Investigating current rationales and systems for the teaching of early reading to young learners of English.* (Unpublished PhD thesis). University of Warwick.

Roberts, T. A. (2005). Articulation accuracy and vocabulary size contributions to phonemic awareness and word reading in English language learners. *Journal of Educational Psychology, 97*(4), 601–616.

Rose, J. (2006). *Independent review of the teaching of early reading: Final report.* London: Department for Education and Skills Publications.

Ryder, J., Tunmer, W., & Greaney, K. (2008). Explicit instruction in phonemic awareness and phonemically based decoding skills as an intervention strategy for struggling readers in whole language classrooms. *Reading and Writing, 21*(4), 349–369.

Savage, R., Carless, S., & Stuart, M. (2003). The effects of rime- and phoneme-based teaching delivered by learning support assistants. *Journal of Research in Reading, 26*(3), 211–233.

Seymour, P. H. K., & Duncan, L. G. (2001). Learning to read in English. *Psychology: The Journal of the Hellenic Psychological Society, 8*(3), 281–299.

Seymour, P. H. K., Bunce, F., & Evans, H. M. (1992). A framework for orthographic assessment and remediation. In C. M. Sterling & C. Robson (Eds.), *Psychology, spelling and education* (pp. 224–249). Clevedon, England: Multilingual Matters.

Share, D. L. (1995). Phonological recoding and self-teaching: Sine qua non of reading acquisition. *Cognition, 55*(2), 151–218.

Share, D. L. (2004). Knowing letter names and learning letter sounds: A causal connection. *Journal of Experimental Child Psychology, 88*(3), 213–233.

Siegel, L. S. (1993). Phonological processing deficits as the basis of a reading disability. *Developmental Review, 13*(3), 246–257.

Siok, W., & Fletcher, P. (2001). The role of phonological awareness and visual-orthographic skills in Chinese reading acquisition. *Developmental Psychology, 37*(6), 886–899.

Snow, C. E., & Juel, C. (2005). Teaching children to read: What do we know about how to do it? In M. J. Snowling & C. Hulme (Eds.), *The science of reading: A handbook* (pp. 501–520). Malden: Blackwell Publishing.

Stahl, S. A., Duffy-Hester, A. M., & Stahl, K. A. D. (1998). Everything you wanted to know about phonics (but were afraid to ask). *Reading Research Quarterly, 33*(3), 338–355.

Stanovich, K. E. (1992). The psychology of reading: Evolutionary and revolutionary developments. *Annual Review of Applied Linguistics, 12*(1), 3–30.

Stuart, M. (1999). Getting ready for reading: Early phoneme awareness and phonics teaching improves reading and spelling in inner-city second language learners. *British Journal of Educational Psychology, 69*(4), 587–605.

Swank, L. K., & Catts, H. W. (1994). Phonological awareness and written word decoding. *Language, Speech, and Hearing Services in Schools, 25*(1), 9–14.

Taylor, I., & Taylor, M. M. (1995). *Writing and literacy in Chinese, Korean, and Japanese.* Amsterdam: John Benjamins Publishing Co.

Torgerson, C., Brooks, G., & Hall, J. (2006). *A systematic review of the research literature on the use of phonics in the teaching of reading and spelling.* London: Department for Education and Skills.

Torgesen, J. K., Wagner, R. K., & Rashotte, C. A. (1994). Longitudinal studies of phonological processing and reading. *Journal Of Learning Disabilities, 27*(5), 276–286.

Treiman, R., Goswami, U., & Bruck, M. (1990). Not all nonwords are alike: Implications for reading development and theory. *Memory & Cognition, 18*(6), 559–567.

Treiman, R., Mullennix, J., Bijeljac-Babic, R., & Richmond-Welty, E. D. (1995). The special role of rimes in the description, use, and acquisition of English orthography. *Journal of Experimental Psychology: General, 124*(2), 107.

Vandervelden, M. C., & Siegel, L. S. (1995). Phonological recoding and phoneme awareness in early literacy: A developmental approach. *Reading Research Quarterly, 30*(4), 854–875.

Vellutino, F. R., & Scanlon, D. M. (1987). Phonological coding, phonological awareness, and reading ability: Evidence from a longitudinal and experimental study. *Merrill-Palmer Quarterly, 33*(3), 321–363.

Vellutino, F. R., Scanlon, D. M., & Spearing, D. (1995). Semantic and phonological coding in poor and normal readers. *Journal of Experimental Child Psychology, 59*(1), 76–123.

Vellutino, F. R. (2003). Individual differences as sources of variability in reading comprehension in elementary school children. In A. P. Sweet & C. E. Snow (Eds.), *Rethinking reading comprehension* (pp. 51–81). New York & London: The Guilford Press.

Verhoeven, L. (2000). Components in early second language reading and spelling. *Scientific Studies of Reading, 4*(4), 313–330.

Vousden, J. I. (2008). Units of English spelling-to-sound mapping: A rational approach to reading instruction. *Applied Cognitive Psychology, 22*(2), 247–272.

Wade-Woolley, L., & Geva, E. (2000). Processing novel phonemic contrasts in the acquisition of L2 word reading. *Scientific Studies of Reading, 4*(4), 295–311.

Wagner, R. K., Torgesen, J. K., Rashotte, C. A., Hecht, S. A., Barker, T. A., Burgess, S. R., Donahue, J., & Garon, T. (1997). Changing relations between phonological processing abilities and word-level reading as children develop from beginning to skilled readers: A 5-year longitudinal study. *Developmental Psychology, 33*(3), 468–479.

Walter, C. (2008). Phonology in second language reading: Not an optional extra. *TESOL Quarterly, 42*(3), 455–474.

Walton, P. D., Walton, L. M., & Felton, K. (2001). Teaching rime analogy or letter recoding reading strategies to prereaders: Effects on prereading skills and word reading. *Journal of Educational Psychology, 93*(1), 160.

Wang, M., & Cheng, C. (2008). Subsyllabic unit preference in young Chinese children. *Applied Psycholinguistics, 29*(2), 291–314.

Wang, Y., Lin, C., & Yu, G. (2002). Relationship between phonological skill and reading comprehension ability among poor English learners. *Acta Psychologica Sincia, 34*(3), 279–283.

Watson, J. E. (1998). *An investigation of the effects of phonics teaching on children's progress in reading and spelling.* (Unpublished PhD thesis). University of St Andrews.

Woore, R. (2007). 'Weisse Maus in meinem Haus': Using poems and learner strategies to help learners decode the sounds of the L2. *The Language Learning Journal, 35*(2), 175–188.

Woore, R. (2009). Beginners' progress in decoding L2 French: Some longitudinal evidence from English modern foreign languages classrooms. *The Language Learning Journal, 37*(1), 3–18.

Wu, M., & Chen, S. (2006). The effects of two early reading training programs on word recognition in Taiwanese EFL young poor readers: An onset/rime-based approach vs. a phoneme-based approach. *English Teaching & Learning, 30*(4S), 61–80.

Wyse, D., & Goswami, U. (2008). Synthetic phonics and the teaching of reading. *British Educational Research Journal, 34*(6), 691–710.

Xu, F., & Ren, P. (2004). The relation between children's phonological awareness and ability of pinyin in primary school. *Chinese Journal of Applied Psychology*(4), 22–27.

Yin, L., Anderson, R. C., & Zhu, J. (2007). Stages in Chinese children's reading of English words. *Journal of Educational Psychology, 99*(4), 852–866.

Yu, G., & Wang, Y. (2001). A study of the relationship among phonological awareness, pseudoword reading and word recognition ability in poor English learners. *Psychological Science, 24*(6), 683–686.

Zhao, D. (1995). *English phonetics and phonology: As compared with Chinese features.* Qingdao, China: Qingdao Ocean University Press.

Zhu, J. (2005). Reflections on the teaching of English phonology in Chinese primary schools. *Foreign Language Teaching in Schools (Primary Version), 28*(12), 2–5.

Chapter 3
Research Design

This chapter elucidates the research design of this study. It begins by briefly presenting the research purpose and questions in Sect. 3.1, and situating the study within an appropriate research paradigm as displayed in Sect. 3.2. Section 3.3 reports the pilot study, which was set up to test the major research instruments. Section 3.4 gives a description of the sources of data. Then a detailed account and justification of the instruments, the data collection procedures and the data analysis methods used in the main study is presented in Sect. 3.5. The ethical issues are discussed in Sect. 3.6.

3.1 Research Purpose and Questions

The present study describes, interprets and evaluates Chinese EFL children's phonological decoding ability and the teaching of phonological decoding at primary school level, and to a certain extent explores the relationship between children's phonological decoding ability and its teaching, which have rarely been examined together in a single study. Thus, the following research purpose and questions are addressed:

- **The investigation of Chinese children's English phonological decoding ability at the end of their primary schooling**

RQ1: How is children's phonological decoding accuracy affected by different types of orthographic units?

Drawing from the category of orthographic units in terms of different levels of graphemic complexity and letter length adopted in Laxon et al.'s (2002) study (see Sect. 2.4.1.2), the orthographic units investigated in the current study include orthographic units representing consonants (single consonant letter, e.g. <s>; consonant digraph, e.g. <sh>; consonant cluster, e.g. <st>), and orthographic units representing vowels (single vowel letter, e.g. <o>, non-split letter combination representing vowel, e.g. <oi>, split vowel digraph, e.g. <o-e>).

In addition, considering the existence of only two final consonants ([n], [ng]) existing in Chinese and the fact that the morphosyllabic nature of the Chinese language (see Sect. 2.5.3.2) may cause potential problems to Chinese children in learning to read English, the current study also examined the orthographic units in different positions (i.e. initial consonant orthographic unit, medial consonant orthographic unit, final consonant orthographic unit; vowel orthographic unit in monosyllabic word, first vowel orthographic unit in disyllabic word, and second vowel orthographic unit in disyllabic word).

RQ2: What strategies do children at different levels of reading ability employ in sounding out vowel graphemes?

Drawing from the literature review, it was hypothesized that there are three major strategies to sound out the vowel graphemes, GPC decoding strategy with no sensitivity to rime, GPC decoding strategy with sensitivity to rime, and whole word strategy. As suggested in Harley's (2008) model of reading, the phonological decoding route includes two sub-lexical systems (see details in Sect. 2.1), one relying on grapheme-phoneme correspondences, and the other relying on the larger sub-word units, i.e. the orthographic rimes. Children may employ a GPC-based decoding strategy or rime-based decoding strategy to sound out vowel graphemes. Or they may not decode the vowel grapheme at all but read the nonword as a real word which shares the same boundary consonant letter(s), as Ehri (1992, 1999, 2005) suggested the beginning readers at the partial alphabetic phase tend to do in an attempt to sound out a word.

RQ3: How does Chinese children's phonological decoding ability relate to their reading ability?

- **The investigation of the teaching of phonological decoding at primary level from the perspective of textbook design, and actual classroom instruction**

– *Teaching materials*

RQ4: What is the scope and sequence of the component knowledge and skills of phonological decoding as reflected in the textbook?

RQ5: Is practice provided for developing phonological decoding skills in the textbook materials for different grades? If yes, what kind of practice?

RQ6: To what extent are the letter sound relations taught for sounding out the words in each phonics section, and in the textbook vocabulary?

– *Classroom instruction*

RQ7: Is phonics taught in the classroom? If so, how?

RQ8: To what extent is phonological decoding applied in vocabulary teaching?

RQ9: Are text-level reading activities used in the classroom? If so, what activities?

- **The tentative exploration of the impact of the teaching of phonological decoding at primary level on children's phonological decoding ability**

3.2 Research Paradigm

In accordance to the "pragmatism" underpinning the mixed methods research, the research should be "practice-driven", driven by the research questions (Cohen et al. 2011). Drawing upon (Johnson et al.'s 2007) definition of mixed methods research, Cohen et al. (2011, p. 23) provided a detailed description of the pragmatist paradigm:

> [It] draws on, and integrates, both numeric and narrative approaches and data, quantitative and qualitative methods as necessary and relevant, to meet the needs of the research rather than the allegiances or preferences of the researcher, and in order to answer research questions fully.

The underlying principle of the mixed methods approach is believed to fit the overall research stance adopted in this study. As the current study is in its nature descriptive, explanatory and exploratory, a multifaceted approach combining qualitative and quantitative techniques is required. The choice of the research instruments was made following logically from the research questions, which aimed to describe, interpret and evaluate children's phonological decoding ability and the teaching of phonological decoding.

Gathering data on similar target phenomena from different sources and through different methods provides "a more complete picture of the phenomenon under study by combining information from complementary kinds of data or sources" (Denscombe 2008, p. 272). In addition, using multiple methods and sources for collecting data enables the corroboration and triangulation of the data and thereby increases the validity of a study (Lynch 1996). After all, a single source of data may yield biased conclusions. Accordingly, in this study, multiple methods were used wherever possible for each of the following research questions, although some research questions could only be addressed from a single source. It is hoped that the multiple perspectives can cross-validate and complement the findings to capture a more complete and truer picture of the learning and teaching of phonological decoding in the context of mainland China.

Table 3.1 shows which research instrument(s) corresponded to each research question. These instruments will be discussed in detail in Sect. 3.5. Textbook analysis was initially conducted to gain a clear understanding of the materials related to the teaching of phonological decoding. The battery of reading tests was administered at the end of data collection to minimise the possibility of teacher participants altering their behavior in the classroom to align with the researcher's interests.

3.3 The Pilot Study

A pilot study was carried out from December 2011 to February 2012 with the battery of tests for pupils, the classroom observations and the interview questions for teachers, in order to try out those research instruments, and to make necessary

Table 3.1 A cross tabulation of research questions and research instruments

	Textbook analysis	Textbook writer interview	Classroom observation	Teacher interview	Nonword reading test	Real word reading test	Reading comprehension test
RQ1					√		
RQ2					√	√	√
RQ3					√	√	√
RQ4	√	√					
RQ5	√	√		√			
RQ6	√	√					
RQ7			√	√			
RQ8			√	√			
RQ9			√	√			

improvements in the main study. This section describes the administration of the pilot study and the implications for the main study.

3.3.1 Piloting of the Tests

The nonword reading test was piloted among ten Mandarin-speaking grade 5 children from a public primary school in Shanghai. The students were instructed to read aloud 42 nonwords. The students were given the test individually. It was found that they considered it strange to read nonwords and constant encouragement was necessary to reduce their anxiety. Moreover, besides instructions before the test, it was also necessary to give them example nonwords to read first. This was to make sure every subject understood the procedure before they started. In addition, without a microphone, the recording was not clear, especially when there was ambient noise. Two disyllable nonwords (*sopthirm, boakshulf*) were deleted because none of the children sounded them out correctly. Instead, two one-syllable CVC nonwords (*yat, nop*) were added.

The pilot real word test was administered on a one-to-one basis among another group of ten grade 5 pupils in the same school. The time each participant spent on this test varied from 10 to 20 min. As this is a relatively familiar form of test to them, all 10 pupils had no problem with understanding the test procedure.

Another group of ten grade 5 pupils were gathered from the same school to take the pilot reading comprehension test. The original Cambridge YLE reading and writing test, which consists of 6 parts, 40 items in total, takes 30 min. Considering that the adapted[1] reading comprehension test left out the last part and consists of 5 parts, the

---

[1] See details in Sect. 3.5.5.1.3.

time limit was set to 25 min for the piloting test. It took the quickest student 20 min to finish all the questions and all the children managed to finish the test within 25 min. Therefore, the time limit for actual reading comprehension test was set to 25 min.

3.3.2 Piloting of the Teacher Interviews

The teacher interview questions were piloted with two teachers teaching English in the same public primary school, where the pilot tests were administered. They both had over 15 years' experience of teaching primary English. One interview took approximately 50 min and the other an hour.

One of the benefits of piloting the teacher interviews was that it provided invaluable experience of practising the conduct of interviews. For example, it was found necessary to summarise and crystallise issues, which on one hand was a way of showing respect, and on the other hand could avoid misunderstanding and lead to questions. Additionally, the findings revealed that some teachers gave short and general answers to some interview questions, and hence not much data was generated. Thereby, some prompts and probes were prepared for the main study. For instance, the questions like "can you give me an example of…?", "anything else?", or "what are some of your reasons for such preference?".

3.3.3 Piloting of the Classroom Observations

The piloting of classroom observations began in the same week when the real word test and reading comprehension test were piloted. One major benefit of piloting the classroom observations was to get a sense of the English classroom context. And another benefit was the practice of taking field notes based on the observation checklist.

Two grade 2 English classrooms (as representative of the lower grades) and one grade 4 English classroom (as representative of the higher grades) were observed due to the time limit. There were three English lessons per week in grade 2, and five lessons per week in grade 4. Each lesson lasted for 35 min. It took nearly two weeks to finish observing all the lessons covering a whole unit in the three English classrooms. The findings supported what was found in the initial textbook analysis and the piloting teacher interviews—the grade 2 textbook contained much simpler teaching content in "Learn the sounds" section compared with the textbook for grades 3, 4 and 5 (see details in Sect. 5.1) and therefore the time spent on teaching letter sounds in the lower grade (namely the second semester of grade 2) was very short, approximately 3–5 min; very rarely were the component letter-sound relations analysed in teaching the word sound (only two out of 15 words involving phonological decoding in a grade 2 class and one out of 10 words involving phonological decoding in the other grade 2 class). Considering very little data could be generated from the observation of lower grades, the target grade to be observed was decided to be grade 4, which could yield richer data and was best representative of the teaching of phonological decoding in primary English classes.

The findings of the classroom observations also showed that the reading activities at word level and beyond word level were not taught as a separate section but were usually scattered in different lessons for a unit, which shed light on the decision about which lessons to observe (see further details in Sect. 3.4.1).

Another implication of the pilot observations for the main study was that the field notes should include information that could not be traced in the digital audio recordings, such as the grouping of students, teachers' writing on the blackboard, whether the printed form was presented, and teachers' gestures.

3.4 Data Sources

This section presents information about the sources of data collected via the different research methods discussed above.

3.4.1 Profile of Teacher Participants

Primary schools were not easy to reach for conducting classroom observation and the battery of tests. As Eisner (1998) indicated, "access to schools and classrooms is not something that one can take for granted" (p. 171). Eventually, four schools (HL, JZ, SQ and PM) agreed to participate in the study. The four schools are all public (i.e. not private) primary schools in Shanghai, China. None of the schools is a key school[2] or a foreign language primary school.[3] The four schools can be considered representative of ordinary urban public schools in China.

Four teachers who were teaching grade 4 and grade 5 English at the same time in the four different schools when the current study took place (schools HL, JZ, SQ, and PM) agreed to take part in the research. All the four grade 4 teachers who participated in the observation also took part in the interviews. The four teachers all happened to be females. This is a common phenomenon because a large proportion of primary English teachers in China are females. The four teachers were all experienced English teachers. Although two of them had non-English majors, they were confident in

---

[2] In cities in China, there is a distinction between "key schools" and "ordinary schools". Students with the highest academic achievement are admitted into key schools, and those with lower academic achievement are admitted into ordinary schools. In many cities, there are only a few key schools; all the other schools are consequently called ordinary schools, and these represent the majority of urban schools in China.

[3] In foreign language primary schools, more class hours are allocated to English, compared with other schools.

speaking English in class. The general account of each teacher's profile is summarised in Table 3.2.

To understand the teaching of phonological decoding at primary school level, it was decided to observe the English classes in grade 4. There are several reasons for this decision. Firstly, according to the initial textbook analysis and pilot study (see Sects. 5.1.1 and 3.3.3), the grade one textbook contained no teaching content of letter sounds and the grade two textbook contained a very limited amount of relevant content (the sounds of two single consonant letters in each unit, accompanied with two example words for each letter-sound correspondence). Moreover, the teaching focus of the lower grades (grades 1 and 2) was listening and speaking skills. Hence, the fourth grade, where most major letter-sound correspondences of consonant letter or letter chunks are being covered, was considered more likely to reveal the how phonological decoding was taught and at the same time how it was applied in reading words at primary school level. Secondly, as the initial textbook analysis showed, the "Learn the sounds" section in the textbook for grade 4 focuses on the letter-sound correspondences and is therefore more representative of the later stage of teaching of phonological decoding, compared with grade 5, where the major teaching objective is the introduction of the International Phonetic Alphabet (even if the alternative pronunciation of a grapheme is sometimes introduced under the phonetic symbol of a sound (see Table 5.1). Finally, through personal communication with the teachers, I discovered that they all followed the same teaching plan for grade 4. In that sense, we can argue that it is justifiable to observe the grade 4 classes to have a better understanding of how phonological decoding had been taught to the grade 5 students who participated in the nonword reading test.

Drawing from the findings of the pilot classroom observations, the teaching of word reading and text reading was usually scattered in daily teaching. To get a more accurate and more comprehensive picture of how phonological decoding was applied in the reading activities, it was decided to observe all the sessions for a whole unit in each classroom. Table 3.3 presents the number and duration of lessons observed for each grade 4 class.

Table 3.2 Teachers' background information

Teachers	Age	Years of teaching english	Educational level	Major	Grades previously taught	Grades taught during the data collection
HL	36	14	B.A	English	1–5	4 and 5
JZ	40	18	B.A	Non-English	1–5	4 and 5
SQ	33	12	B.A	Non-English	1–5	4 and 5
PM	37	15	B.A	English	1–5	4 and 5

Table 3.3 Grade 4 classes observed

Teachers	Number of lessons observed during the data collection	Total time of observations
HL	7	245 min
JZ	6	210 min
SQ	7	245 min
PM	6	210 min
Total	26	15.2 hrs

3.4.2 Profile of Student Participants

As one of the main purposes of the study is to explore Chinese children's phonological decoding ability at the end of the phonics programme they received in their primary years, it was decided to choose grade 5 children (aged from 10 to 11) as the student participants, who had been taught all the letters and sounds presented in their textbook when the nonword reading test was implemented. Each of the four teachers (HL, JZ, SQ and PM) was asked to nominate from their fifth grade class 5 children of above-average English proficiency, 5 children of average English proficiency, and 5 children of below-average English proficiency. None of them had private lessons on phonics or went to cram schools.

All participants were native speakers of Mandarin and had been studying English as a foreign language on a regular basis for four and a half years since grade 1. Three sessions of 35 min were allocated for English lessons every week in grades 1 and 2; four sessions of 35 min in grade 3; and five sessions of 35 min in grades 4 and 5. Therefore, the participants had received approximately 710 h of English instruction at school. There were no native speakers of English at home.

One student from school JZ, two students from school HL, one student from school SQ, and two students from school PS were excluded because they were not present in all the three tests. Therefore, 54 fifth grade students were retained in the study.

The 54 participants were categorised into three levels of readers, based on their average score of reading comprehension and real word reading tests. As displayed in Table 3.4, the 18 participants whose average scores of reading comprehension and real word reading test rank in the top 18 (average score = 79.65–95.70) are categorised as above average readers, the 18 participants whose average scores of reading comprehension and real word reading test rank the bottom 18 (average score = 25.65–65.15) are categorised as below average readers, and the 18 participants whose average scores of reading comprehension and real word reading test rank the middle 18 (average score = 65.25–78.25) are categorised as average readers. Kruskal–Wallis tests and post-hoc Mann–Whitney tests with Bonferroni adjustment for further pairwise comparison were conducted separately to see if these differences are statistically significant. The results showed significant difference between the three groups of readers ($U = 0.000$, $P < 0.001$).

Table 3.4 The average score of reading comprehension test and real word reading test

Below average readers		Average readers		Above average readers	
Participants	Average score	Participants	Average score	Participants	Average score
JZ12	25.65	SQ3	65.25	PS8	79.65
PS9	37.75	PS11	67.95	SQ9	81.1
JZ6	41.32	HL11	68.45	PS14	82.25
HL5	42.1	HL10	69.9	HL12	82.85
PS13	43.3	SQ4	70.9	JZ9	83.55
JZ7	45.1	HL1	71.15	SQ10	85.2
HL7	51.65	SQ5	72.15	PS15	85.55
JZ11	54.35	JZ15	72.9	HL2	86.77
SQ1	57.25	SQ7	73.55	HL13	87
SQ2	60.05	HL14	73.65	PS1	87.3
JZ1	60.55	JZ3	74.35	SQ11	87.65
PS4	61.05	JZ10	74.45	HL8	88.25
HL3	61.3	PS7	74.55	PS2	88.3
PS12	62.3	SQ8	76.05	JZ4	89.45
HL15	63	PS6	77.15	SQ13	89.6
JZ2	63.15	JZ13	77.65	SQ14	89.65
HL6	64.6	JZ14	78.2	SQ15	91.65
JZ5	65.15	SQ12	78.25	PS5	95.7

It has to be acknowledged that the three levels of readers as each group has a different range of average reading scores. An alternative way of categorising the children could be to fix the scores that counted as high, medium, and low, which would yield different group sizes. But considering that there is no natural grouping of readers around certain scores, the researcher decided to divide them into three groups of equal number.

3.4.3 Textbook Materials

The materials examined in the study include the primary-level English textbook used by the participants, *English (Oxford Shanghai Edition)*[4] (abbreviated as OE), the teacher's book, and the workbook.

Although the focus of the present study is on the analysis of the student's book, the teacher's book is also included in the analysis because it is felt that examining

---

[4] *English (Oxford Shanghai Edition)* is the textbook used in the overwhelming majority of public primary schools in Shanghai. The textbook materials of OE analysed in this study was co-published by Shanghai Educational Publishing House and Oxford University Press in 2011.

the material and the activities suggested in the teacher's book can help to interpret the content related to phonological decoding in the student's book and to examine the role phonological decoding is suggested to play in word and text-level reading activities, even if the teachers do not do all of the suggested activities. In addition, the workbook is also included in the analysis because it may include exercises for practising and consolidating decoding skills.

3.4.4   Textbook Writer

A textbook writer responsible for the textbook materials of OE agreed to be interviewed. She holds a bachelor's degree and has written three textbooks. She used to teach English in primary schools and now works as a researcher of English language teaching, and is responsible for the primary English sector in her own district. She is asked to take multi-functional duties of implementing the curriculum policy, conducting research on English language teaching, providing professional guidance and training to teachers, and monitoring the teaching quality in her district.

3.5   Instruments

This section provides a detailed account and explanation for the instruments used in the study. They are presented according to the sequence in which they were administered. The battery of reading tests was administered at the end of data collection to minimise the possibility of teacher participants altering their behavior in the classroom to align with the researcher's interests.

3.5.1   Textbook Analysis

A textbook analysis was chosen as an instrument in the current study because the textbook plays a crucial role in English language teaching and learning (Hu 2002; Hutchinson and Torres 1994). This is also true in in the context of teaching English to young learners (TEYL). There are four aspects of the influence of the textbook on TEYL that are related to this study (Hutchinson and Torres 1994; Rixon 2011). Firstly, new concepts and approaches to TEYL can be communicated to primary school teachers through concrete examples in textbooks. Secondly, the textbook embodies "a syllabus in terms of linguistic content, and the sequencing, manner, and frequency of presentation and recycling of that content" (Rixon 2011, p. 25). Thirdly, the textbook "provides input into classroom lessons in the form of texts, activities and explanations and so on" (Hutchinson and Torres 1994, p. 317). Fourthly, the textbook provides structured guidance for teachers to follow in the classroom teaching practice.

Garton and her colleagues' (2011) survey of global practices of teaching English to young learners aged 7–11 reported that approximately 61% of primary teachers found the textbook "very useful" in planning lessons and around 28% of the teachers considered it "somewhat useful".

Such influence of textbooks on TEYL may be even more evident in mainland China, where textbooks serve as the primary resource for EFL classroom instruction and good textbooks are therefore integral to the quality of TEYL (Hu 2002). The Chinese National English Curriculum Standards (Ministry of Education 2011) states one reading skill descriptor directly related to phonological decoding skills at the primary level, "able to use phonics rules to read simple English words". Although the curriculum does not clarify what type of words can be categorised as simple, it clearly specifies developing phonological decoding skills as one of the goals for English teaching at primary school level, which is therefore required as one of the guidelines for textbook compilation. The quality of textbooks has the potential to determine the effectiveness of a programme. Considering the function of textbooks as the medium for achieving the "abstract and insufficiently practical" curriculum goals specified in published documents (Wang 2009, p. 285), an examination of the textbook can help to describe and interpret how the textbook is designed to achieve the objective of developing phonological decoding skills, and the potential role of phonological decoding instruction. The textbook analysis aims to provide information for research questions 4, 5, and 6.

Textbook analysis can be carried out through checklists, interviews or observations (McGrath 2002). As McGrath pointed out, the checklist method is systematic, effective and explicit, offering a framework for analysing the elements that are deemed to be important, and allowing for comparison between materials; however, this method may encourage superficial judgements. In-depth analysis by means of interviews or observations is also needed to understand what assumptions and beliefs lie beneath the surface. Therefore, the textbook analysis in this study mainly adopts the framework developed on the basis of UK DfE's criteria for evaluating a phonics programme, whereby the phonological decoding learning and teaching content in the textbook is analysed (see Sect. 3.5.1.2). And the textbook writer and teachers are also interviewed to understand their motives and beliefs in phonological decoding teaching materials (see Sects. 3.5.3 and 3.5.4).

This section gives an account of the procedures for analysing the textbook materials and the rationale for the textbook analysis framework adopted in the study.

3.5.1.1 Procedures

The textbook, teacher's book, and workbook were placed under scrutiny according to the research questions. Relevant information and data were stored in Excel spreadsheets for further numerical manipulation where necessary.

3.5.1.2   Framework for Textbook Analysis

In order to collect relevant data to address research questions 4, 5 and 6, a framework for textbook analysis was employed. As there is no official guideline on how to deliver phonics instruction to EFL children, the framework mainly drew on the relevant core criteria for evaluating a phonics programme developed by the UK Department for Education (2010). The notes of guidance for the UK Primary National Strategy's phonics programme "Letters and Sounds" (Department for Education and Skills 2007) are also referred to, because the UK programme is developed in line with the DfE core criteria for phonics programmes, and hence provides detailed information on the features of high quality phonics work, which can be included in the framework for textbook analysis. In other words, such documents do not exist in the context of teaching EFL in China, hence my recourse to them to theoretically frame the textbook analysis. The explanations and justifications for the framework of textbook analysis for each research question are presented as below.

RQ4 What is the scope and sequence of the component knowledge and skills of phonological decoding as reflected in the textbook?

- 4-a The scope of component knowledge and skills of phonological decoding that are covered in the textbook (i.e. phonological awareness, letter names and shapes, letter-sound relations, rime patterns)
- 4-b The sequence in which the component knowledge and skills of phonological decoding are arranged

It has been generally agreed that the salient feature of an effective phonics programme for reading is the quality of being systematic, namely teaching a planned set of phonics elements (see details in Sect. 2.5.4.1.2). Sufficient scope and an incremental sequence of phonics elements is also at the top of the UK DfE core criteria list for evaluating a phonics teaching programme. We can therefore argue that the scope and sequence are two important elements that need to be included in the textbook analysis framework.

As discussed in Sect. 2.2, phonological awareness skills, knowledge of letter names and shapes and knowledge of spelling-sound relations are the essential component knowledge and skills required for developing phonological decoding and to be taught in regular classroom context. As shown in Table 3.5, the UK Primary National Strategy's phonics programme "Letters and Sounds" includes these three elements.

The development of phonological awareness skills along with speaking and listening skills is placed at the initial phase of the phonics programme, because this is recognised by DfES as crucial for paving the way to making a good start to learning to read. Then the shapes and names of the 24 letters of the alphabet, and one sound for each letter are taught, followed by more complex letter-sound relations, such as letter combinations. It should be noted that although rime patterns are not included in the "Letters and Sounds" programme, Ehri et al. (2001) indicated that a systematic phonics programme may also include the larger sub-word units of

Table 3.5 Phases of phonics instruction suggested in the UK Primary National Strategy's phonics programme "Letters and Sounds"

Phases	Teaching objectives	Letter-sound relations progression
Phase 1 (the beginning of the EYFS[a])	Developing children's speaking and listening skills, phonological awareness (awareness of rhymes and alliteration) and oral blending and segmenting	/
Phase 2 (up to 6 weeks at the EYFS)	Knowing 19 letters of the alphabet and one sound for each; Blending and segmenting VC and CVC words; Introducing the reading of two-syllable words and simple captions	Week 1: s a t p Week 2: i n m d Week 3: g o c k Week 4: ck e u r Week 5: h b f /ff l / ll ss
Phase 3 (up to 12 weeks at the EYFS)	Knowing the remaining 7 letters of the alphabet and one sound for each; Knowing another 18 letter combinations so that children know one way of representing each of 44 phonemes; Blending and segmenting CVC words including graphemes of more than one letter and two syllable words	Week 1: j v w x Week 2: y z (zz) qu Week 3: ch (*chip*) sh (*shop*) th (*thin/then*) ng (*ring*) Week 4: ai (*rain*) ee (*feet*) igh (*night*) oa (*boat*) Week 5: oo (*boot, look*) ar (*farm*) or (*for*) Week 6: ur (*hurt*) ow (*cow*) oi (*coin*) ear (*dear*) Week 7: air (*fair*) ure (*sure*) er (*corner*)
Phase 4 (4 to 6 weeks at the EYFS)	Blending adjacent consonants in words and apply when reading unfamiliar texts; Practising reading monosyllabic and polysyllabic words containing adjacent consonants	Week 1: adjacent consonants at the final position (nt, ts, lp, st, lt, mp, nd, nk, ft, pt, sk, xt, lk, lf, ct, nth, lsh, nch) Week 2: adjacent consonants at the initial position (fr, st, sp, pl, tr, gr, fl, gl, tw, sn, sw, cl, dr, br, sm, thr, cr, pr, bl, sc, sk, shr, spr, str, str, scr)

(continued)

Table 3.5 (continued)

Phases	Teaching objectives	Letter-sound relations progression
Phase 5 (Year 1)	Knowing new graphemes for reading; Knowing alternative pronunciations for graphemes; Reading phonically decodable polysyllabic words	Weeks 1–4: Teach new graphemes for reading (about four per week) ay (*day*), ou (*out*), ie (*pie*), ea (*seat*), oy (*boy*), ir (*girl*), ue (*blue, due*), aw (*lawn*), wh (*when, who*), ph (*phone*), ew (*blew, few*), oe (*Joe*), au (*August*), ey (*money*), a-e (*make*), e-e (*these*), i-e (*like*), o-e (*home*), u-e (*June, use*) Weeks 5–7: Teach alternative pronunciations of graphemes for reading (about four per week) a (*lady, fast, what, wasp*), e (*he, frequent*), i (*find*), o (*old*), u (*music, put, playful*), ow (*snow*), ie (*thief*), ea (*head*), er (*her*), ou (*soup, could, shoulder*), y (*by, gym, happy*), ch (*school, chef*), c (*cell*), g (*gym*), ey (*they*)
Phase 6	Applying phonic skills and knowledge with increasing fluency when reading unfamiliar words in texts	

[a]The EYFS: the Early Years Foundation Stage

rimes. Moreover, it is also of critical importance in the development of phonological decoding skills (see details in Sect. 2.4.1.3). Therefore, it was decided to check whether rime patterns are incorporated in the teaching scope as an element in the textbook analysis framework.

The decision on the sequence of introducing sets of letter sounds is based on incremental development, from simple to more complex, namely from single consonant letters to consonant digraphs and clusters, and from single vowel letters to letter combinations representing vowels. The more complex letter-sound relations that are sensitive to orthographic context (e.g. <a-e>, <i-e>, <i> in *city* and <e> in *cell* mark the letter <c> as /s/) are not introduced until the final stage.

In addition, the decision on the sequence of introducing sets of letter sounds also involves the attempt to enable children to get a quick way into applying phonics knowledge and skills to decode words. The most frequently used letter sounds (e.g. <s>, <t>, <p>, <n>, <m>, <d>) are introduced before the less frequently used ones (e.g. <j>, <v>, <w>, <x>, <y>, <z>). Moreover, the short vowel sounds of the five single vowel letters, which are most frequently used (e.g. the sound of <a> as /æ/), are introduced at the very early phase, along with single consonant letters. This is a typical characteristic of the synthetic phonics approach, which according to Rose (2006) enables children to start decoding words right from the beginning. For instance, after learning the first set of letter sounds of <s>, <a>, <t>, and <p>, children can map the sounds to the letters in words such as *at, as, sat, tap, pat*, and *sap*, and blend the letter sounds to form the pronunciation of the words. However, there is still no agreement on whether the synthetic approach would be as effective for EFL children as it is suggested for L1 children. Rixon (2011) has suggested that the analytic phonics approach may be more suitable to EFL children (see Sect. 2.5. 4.2.1).

The possibility that some alternative pronunciations of graphemes (the sounds of <a> as /eɪ/ in *lady*, /ɑː/ in *fast*, /ɒ/ in *what* and *wasp*) might interfere with the learning of the major and frequent letter sounds (<a> as /æ/ in *cat*) is also taken into account in deciding the teaching sequence of letter sounds. As Nation (2009) has suggested about the sequence of teaching spelling-to-sound correspondences to ESL/EFL students, although some alternative pronunciations of graphemes are also important features, they should be postponed, if possible, or not emphasised until the corresponding major and frequent letter sounds are well known (p. 151).

To answer research question 4, all these aspects of the textbook were systematically examined. The analysis also remained open to new elements emerging from the textbook.

RQ5 Is practice provided for developing phonological decoding skills in the textbook materials for different grades? If yes, what kind of practice?

- 5-a Whether there are any activities for practising phonological awareness skills in different grades (such as nursery rhymes, songs, and games to develop awareness of rhymes and alliteration, phoneme blending and segmenting)
- 5-b Whether there are any activities for practising phoneme articulation and discrimination in different grades
- 5-c Whether there are any activities for consolidating the knowledge of letter names and shapes in different grades (e.g. singing the alphabetic song, and multisensory activities, like drawing, painting and making models)
- 5-d Whether there are any activities for practising spelling-sound correspondences and applying them to decode words in different grades (e.g. sounding out letter sounds, word building, and reading captions, sentences, and texts such as stories and poems)

The core criteria developed by the UK Department for Education (2010) list the practice of applying phonic knowledge and skills to decode words and read decodable texts, as one of the essential elements for ensuring a high quality phonics programme. Previous research also suggests the importance of practice in consolidating the taught knowledge and skills of phonological decoding (see Sect. 2.5.4.1.4).

The UK Primary National Strategy's phonics programme "Letters and Sounds" sheds some light on the activities that can be used to help children develop phonological decoding skills progressively. As EFL children seem to learn to decode words in similar ways as their L1 counterparts (see Sect. 2.4.2), we can argue that the activities that are effective for L1 children may also have similar effects for EFL children.

At the very initial phase of the "Letters and Sounds" programme, special emphasis is given to the rich experience of songs and nursery rhymes to help both L1 children and children learning English as an additional language to "tune into the rhythm and sound of English" as a means to pave the way for developing phonological decoding skills (Department for Education and Skills 2007, p. 24). In addition, children's attention is also drawn to the alliteration, i.e. the identity of the initial sound in words, through nursery rhymes, captions and different types of games. Besides the identification of phonemes and rhymes, phoneme blending is practised throughout the six phases of phonics instruction suggested in the "Letters and Sounds" programme for the purpose of sounding out words (see Table 3.5).

Activities of articulating speech sounds and discriminating phonemes are also suggested for children at this initial phase of learning to read. It should be noted that the programme guides point out the challenge for children in the early stages of learning English as an additional language: "[they] may need time to observe others [speak the language] and rehearse the spoken challenge; as in any turn-taking activities they should not be asked to take the first turn (Department for Education and Skills 2007, p. 40). This note suggests that for EFL children, the learning of English speech sounds may be challenging and it may take more time to prepare them for learning to decode English words than their L1 counterparts. Because of the difference between L1 and L2 children in their grasp of English spoken language, the UK Primary National Strategy's phonics programme guidance appears vague in suggesting when children should move on from the foundation work in phase one to the following phase of systematic phonics instruction. As the guidance pointed out, this is because some children may be ready more quickly for phonics instruction while some children may still need more time to acquire the speaking and listening skills. The decision regarding when children should move on to the systematic phonic work is important as it may impact whether children are able to learn to decode words successfully and effectively. The guidance also recognises that some activities in the foundation phase (e.g. phoneme blending, phoneme identification) can be valuable to run alongside and complement the systematic phonic work in the following phases. Therefore, it would be interesting to find out how the balance between oral skills (e.g. phonological awareness skills, phoneme articulation and discrimination) and systematic phonic work is handled in the phonics programme for Chinese EFL children.

In the UK "Letters and Sounds" programme, letter names and shapes are taught alongside letter sounds, through multisensory activities, e.g. drawing, painting and making models of letters, and singing the alphabetic song. The activities used for practising letter-sound relations include sounding out the letter or letter combinations, blending all the sounds throughout the word, and reading captions, sentences, and texts such as stories and poems.

The OE textbook, teacher's book, and workbook were scrutinised for the relevant activities and practice, with reference to the guidelines in the "Letters and Sounds" phonics programme developed with the support of the UK Primary National Strategy. There can be ambiguity in deciding whether the language activities are relevant to phonological decoding or not, because the practice of phonological decoding can be implicitly embedded in some general language activities such as reading aloud texts. It was decided to focus the textbook analysis on the activities that are explicitly designated for training phonological decoding skills, by reference to the detailed description and guidance provided in the teacher's book.

RQ6 To what extent are the letter-sound relations taught for sounding out the words in each phonics section, and the textbook vocabulary?

- 6-a To what extent are (high-frequency) letter-sound relations embedded in the textbook vocabulary (particularly in monosyllabic words) explicitly covered in the textbook?
- 6-b To what extent are letter-sound relations taught for sounding out words (particularly in monosyllabic words) in "Learn the sounds" section of each unit?
- 6-c To what extent are letter-sound relations taught for sounding out words (particularly in monosyllabic words) in the vocabulary list for each unit?

Using phonics rules to read simple words is specified in China's national English curriculum standards as one of the objectives that are required to be achieved at the end of primary schooling (Ministry of Education 2011). Although the national curriculum does not clarify which types of words are simple words, we would assume that the words that are referred to as simple words are probably monosyllabic words, although we have to admit that some monosyllabic words are not phonically regular, like *have*. Accordingly, after the analysis of the whole pool of OE vocabulary, the monosyllabic words were analysed to generate a separate list of letter-sound relations embedded in monosyllabic words, in order to find out whether the design of the phonics syllabus covered most of the letter-sound relations required for the decoding of monosyllabic words. Although the ultimate aim is to teach all the letter-sound correspondences, it is impossible to cover all correspondences, because class hours are limited on one hand and on the other hand it may be more practical to include the correspondences which have higher frequency of occurrence within textbook vocabulary. Hence, it was decided as a next step to examine whether the high-frequency letter-sound correspondences embedded in the whole pool of textbook vocabulary and in the pool of monosyllabic words are explicitly covered in the textbook. The present study draws upon Kuo's (2011) analysis of the coverage of phonics rules governing the basic words in the English textbooks in Taiwan, and her operationalisation of high-frequency letter-sound correspondences as the ones that have more than 20 occurrences in the word pool, for comparisons to be made between the two contexts, which both have Chinese as L1.

The UK DfE core criteria that define the best features of an effective phonics teaching programme (Department for Education 2010) specifies one of the features as involving children in practising reading decodable words with reliance on their learnt phonics knowledge and skills so that they can experience success and learn to rely on phonological decoding strategies. This suggests that the words used to practise phonics knowledge and skills need to be words that are decodable via taught letter-sound relations. Therefore, question 6-b aims to examine whether the design of the OE phonics programme takes into account of the decodability of the words that are used to practise the component knowledge and skills of phonological decoding.

Another core criterion that the UK Department for Education (2010) suggested for an effective phonics teaching programme is that phonological decoding is applied as the first and prime approach to reading words. However, considering the teaching of letter sounds spans years, from the second term of grade 2 till the end of grade 5, some simple decodable words at lower grades may not be fully decodable because certain component letter-sound relations are taught to the children at a later stage and therefore probably not for their use when those words are taught. We can argue that if a large proportion of words in each unit are not fully decodable, this may discourage learners from applying phonological decoding as the first and prime approach to reading words. Therefore, it is practical to address RQ 6-c, by examining in more detail the extent to which the vocabulary (particularly monosyllabic words) in each unit can be fully decoded by applying taught letter-sound relations.

For the purposes of this study, the tools of Excel 2010 were deemed sufficient. The data was stored and manipulated mainly in Excel spreadsheets, namely "Letter-sound relations in the textbook phonics syllabus" (see example in Table 3.6), "Vocabulary in each unit" (see example in Table 3.7), and "Letter-sound relations in textbook vocabulary" (see example in Table 3.8), for answering RQs 6-a, 6-b, and 6-c.

The letter-sound relations and the practice words in the textbook phonics syllabus were entered into the Excel spreadsheet "Letter-sound relations in the textbook phonics syllabus" (see Table 3.6). Then, by reference to the information in the first four columns, the numbers and percentages of decodable monosyllabic words in all monosyllabic words, and decodable polysyllabic words in all polysyllabic words were counted.

The OE textbook only provides a word list in the textbook for each semester, thereby 10 word lists in total. Some words appear in several word lists because the textbook design takes into account the recycling of vocabulary. For instance, *run* is introduced in the first semester of grade 2, and repeated in the second semester of grade 2, grade 4 and grade 5. In order to retrieve the letter-sound relations embedded in the textbook vocabulary, the first step was to type all the wordlists into the Excel spreadsheet "Vocabulary in each unit", alongside the source of the words, such as the grade, module and unit (see Table 3.7). That is to say, in the general vocabulary list, the word *run* appears 5 times. In other words, *run* has five entries in the general vocabulary list. By adopting this way of entering words, the general vocabulary list composes 2053 word entries, some of which are the same.

It was decided to treat compound words, such as football, as one word, but to divide phrases (e.g. *dog food*), hyphenated words (e.g. *lost-property*) into separate words. Phrases such as ice cream were also treated as two individual words. This is because the hyphen serves as a blank space o separate two words. Words such as *build* were treated as different from their inflected forms such as *built*. The acronyms such as PE were excluded. The "remove duplicates" function in Excel 2010 was used in the "vocabulary" column to generate the list of textbook vocabulary, which contained no repeated words. In this list, there are 1068 different words, which include 586 monosyllabic words and 482 polysyllabic words.

The list was then stored in the Excel spreadsheet "Letter-sound relations in the textbook vocabulary", for extracting the letter-sound relations embedded in the vocabulary. After that, each word was separated into its component letters within individual syllables. Consonant clusters were treated as a unit to keep in accordance with the textbook syllabus of letter-sound relations. For instance, *around* was separated into

Table 3.6 Layout of the Excel spreadsheet for "Letter-sound relations in the textbook phonics syllabus"[a]

Columns

A	B	C	D	E	F	G	H	I	J	K	L
Grade	Module-unit[a]	Letters	Sounds	Monosyllabic words	Monosyllabic words (N)	Decodable monosyllabic words (N)	Decodable monosyllabic words (%)	Polysyllabic words	Polysyllabic words (N)	Decodable polysyllabic words (N)	Decodable polysyllabic words (%)
3A[b]	M4U1	u	/ʌ/	Duck[c], Sun, Russ, Run, Up	5	3	60%	Summer	1	0	0%
4A	M4U3	th	/θ/	Thin, Think	2	2	100%	/	/	/	/
5A	M1U1	y	/i/	/	/	/	/	Easy, Very, Happy, Early	4	1	25%

[a] Each textbook has 4 modules (general topics) and each module has three units

[b] 3A represents the first semester of grade 3. 3B represents the second semester of grade 3 etc

[c] Underlined words are the ones that cannot be fully decoded using taught letter-sound relations

Table 3.7 Layout of the Excel spreadsheet for "Vocabulary in each unit"

Grade	Module-unit	Vocabulary	Monosyllabic (M)/Polysyllabic (P) words
4A	M1U1	Classmate	P
4A	M1U1	Desk	M

Table 3.8 Layout of the Excel spreadsheet for "Letter-sound relations in the textbook vocabulary"

Words	Letters	Sounds	Monosyllabic (M)/Polysyllabic (P) words
Bus	b	/b/	M
Bus	u	/ʌ/	M
Bus	s	/s/	M
Sixteen	s	/s/	P
Sixteen	i	/ɪ/	P
Sixteen	x	/ks/	P
Sixteen	t	/t/	P
Sixteen	ee	/iː/	P
Sixteen	n	/n/	P

four component units, <a>, <r>, <ou>, and <nd>. Table 3.8 displays the layout of the Excel spreadsheet for letter-sound relations embedded in the textbook vocabulary.

It has to be admitted that the division of words into component letter units was not always a straightforward process. Careful consideration was given to the decision. For example, in deciding whether *rough* should be divided into <r>, <ou>, <gh> or <r>, <ough>, the other words containing <gh>, like *light*, *right*, *eight*, were also taken into account. Considering <igh> was counted as a grapheme consisting of three letters but representing a single phoneme /aɪ/ in the textbook syllabus, in order to keep in accordance with the syllabus and keep consistency in analysis, it was decided to choose the latter way to separate *rough*, namely into <r> and <ough>.

Based on the spreadsheet "Letter-sound relations in the textbook vocabulary" (see Table 3.8), pivot tables were used to summarise and count the occurrence of letter-sound relations embedded in the whole pool of textbook vocabulary (see Table 3.9), and in the pool of monosyllabic words (see Table 3.10). A sort to bring the letter-sound relations that occur most frequently within vocabulary to the top of the table was carried out, thus yielding the list of high-frequency letter-sound relations with more than 20 occurrences within the complete vocabulary pool and the monosyllabic word pool. Then the lists of letter-sound relations embedded in the whole pool of textbook vocabulary (see Table 3.9) and in the pool of monosyllabic words (see Table 3.10) were compared with the list of letter-sound relations in the textbook phonics syllabus (see Table 3.6) to examine which letter-sound relations are covered in the textbook phonics syllabus and which are not. The outcome of comparison for each letter-sound correspondence was recorded in the column for "Covered in OE phonics or not".

Table 3.9 The occurrence of letter-sound relations in OE vocabulary

Letters	Sounds	Frequency of occurrence in OE vocabulary	Covered in OE phonics or not
t	/t/	224	√
i	/ɪ/	175	√
m	/m/	134	√
n	/n/	222	√
…			
tch	/ʧ/	5	/
…			
squ	/skw/	1	/

Table 3.10 The occurrence of letter-sound relations in OE monosyllabic words

Letters	Sounds	Frequency of occurrence in OE monosyllabic vocabulary	Covered in OE phonics or not
t	/t/	93	√
n	/n/	79	√
…			
tch	/ʧ/	3	/
…			
squ	/skw/	1	/

To address RQ 6-c, based on the previously created Excel spreadsheet "Vocabulary in each unit", and by reference to the list of letter-sound relations in the textbook phonics syllabus, the words were categorised as decodable (√) and not decodable (/) by using taught letter-sound relations (see Table 3.11). Pivot tables were used to count and summarise the decodable words (particularly decodable monosyllabic words) in each unit of the textbook.

Table 3.11 Vocabulary in each unit plus the decodability

Grade	Module-unit	Vocabulary	Monosyllabic/Polysyllabic words	Decodable or not
4A	M1U1	Classmate	P	/
4A	M1U1	Desk	M	√
4A	M1U1	Eleven	P	/
4A	M1U1	Every	P	/
4A	M1U1	Fifteen	P	/

3.5.2 Classroom Observation

The main reason for choosing classroom observation to collect data is to gain a clearer and more comprehensive picture of the classroom teaching of phonological decoding and thereby address research questions 7, 8 and 9. The research method of classroom observation, in Dörnyei's (2007) words, "is a highly developed data collection approach typical of examining learning environments" (p. 176). The observation of the teaching and learning activities in naturalistic classrooms enables a situated understanding of learning, the impact of certain teaching approaches on learning outcomes, and the factors that facilitate or inhibit learning (Lightbown 2000). While the classroom observation is invaluable for gathering descriptive contextual information about the phenomenon under study, only observable phenomena can be observed, and this does not necessarily lead to the understanding of the reason behind the actions and events within the research setting (Dörnyei 2007).

Similar to interviews, observations can range in degree of structure, from structured, semi-structured, to open observations (Lynch 2003). Considering the highly complex nature of the classroom research setting, and the descriptive and exploratory nature of the study, the semi-structured observation approach was adopted. Instead of using a highly structured observation scheme, an observation checklist was used for keeping a running record of the teaching process related to phonological decoding.

This section describes the observation checklist, illustrates the procedures for collecting the data from classroom observations, and outlines the methods of analysing the data.

3.5.2.1 Observation Checklist

A semi-structured observation checklist (see Table 3.12) was used in the study so that what happened about phonological decoding in English classes could be recorded comprehensively.

3.5.2.2 Procedures

On the first day of observation, the researcher was introduced to each class by the English teacher. In order to minimise the possibility of being observed altering their behaviour to align with the researcher's interests, it was decided not to fully disclose the goals of the research by telling the teachers and students that my research was about exploring a range of issues in primary English teaching and hope that the end product could contribute to improving children's English proficiency. In addition, in order not to interfere with the natural classroom teaching, I chose to play the role of the non-participant observer, seating myself at the back of the classroom and taking notes. To reduce the possibility that the presence of the observer in the classroom setting might be distracting to children, the observation started in one lesson before

Table 3.12 Observation checklist

Categories	Subcategories
Background information	– Class size – Length and frequency of lessons
Content of observed lessons	Tasks or activities used in the following aspects: – Phonological awareness – Phonics (Presentation, practice, review) – Sounding out words in vocabulary instruction – Reading at text level
Teaching aids and materials	– Use of teaching aids (Flashcards, kits, toys, etc.) – Use of textbook materials – Use of supplementary materials
Teacher's role	What the teacher does and what he/she expects children to do
Students' role	What the students do
Classroom grouping	– Individual work – Group work

the teacher began a new unit so that children would not be too curious about the presence of the observer and get distracted when the actual observation of a whole unit started.

The whole class was recorded for all observations. The researcher observed classes using two means: firstly by audio-recording of all the lessons and secondly by taking notes to record all the aspects listed in the observation checklist, especially specific incidents that cannot be detected via audio-recording, e.g. teachers' writing on the blackboard.

The classroom observation in each school usually lasted for nearly two weeks, though the observation of some classes took more than two weeks to finish, due to holidays and term exams.

3.5.2.3   Data Analysis

The digital recording of the classroom observations was firstly transcribed and saved on Microsoft Word. The software SoundScriber was used to aid in the transcription of digitised sound files. The approximate time spent on phonics instruction, and reading at text level was noted down in the transcription, while the time spent on sounding out words was not because it was usually very short and difficult to separate from the other activities of vocabulary learning. The transcript files were later exported to QSR NVivo where the files were organised according to each participant teacher. The second stage was data reduction and organisation, which will be described in more detail below. Two distinct approaches to data analysis and presentation were used. First, as there was no relevant coding scheme to refer to, the grounded theory approach was used to analyse the data. The other approach is the quantitative analysis.

The amount of time spent on certain relevant activities were counted and presented in graphs or tables.

Coding of Observation Data Transcripts

The coding process is generally referred to as the data reduction and organisation by highlighting extracts of the transcribed data and labelling the data for generating themes/categories and concepts that can be easily identified, retrieved, or grouped for analysis through description and explanation (Cohen et al. 2011; Dörnyei 2007). An exploratory open strategy was employed to code the classroom observation data in the sense that the observation data was examined for emerging categories, by looking for anything pertinent to research questions 7, 8 and 9, namely in the three aspects of phonics instruction, reading at word level, and reading at text level. During the coding process, it was also borne in mind that new insights from the data that are not derived from the research questions or literature review may also be important and therefore coded as well.

The first round of data reduction aimed at identifying and extracting the teaching and learning activities aimed specifically at phonological decoding skills for reading. Such relevant activities included phonics instruction, the teaching of word sound in vocabulary instruction, and other activities of reading beyond word level, like sentences or texts. The phonics instruction was found to mainly occur in teaching the section "Learn the sounds". In examining the transcript data relevant to the application of phonological decoding in sounding out words, the target words chosen for coding included the words extracted from the textbook wordlist for the observed unit, and the new words that were not in the textbook wordlist but appeared in the unit or were supplemented by the teacher. However, it should be noted that the above-mentioned activities without the presence of printed form provided to pupils were not coded, e.g. watching the video of a story without script, or sounding out a word without the presence of its printed form, because those activities were more like listening and speaking activities, which did not involve the actual process of mapping printed forms onto speech sounds. However, listening to teacher reading aloud text with the text in sight was counted as a reading activity because that offers children opportunities to link the printed word with the sound they hear.

The second round of coding the data for phonics instruction involved reading and rereading the observation data for any emerging categories of activities and assigning codes to them. Take the following coding of an extract of practising the letter-sound correspondence (<ir> - /ɜː/) in phonics instruction as an example.

T   Follow me. /IR/. *(Teacher tells letter sound)*
SSS /ɜː/. *(Class repeats letter sound)*

...

T   I-R, *(Teacher tells letter name)* /ɜː/. *(Teacher tells letter sound)*
SSS I-R, *(Class repeats letter name)* /ɜː/. *(Class repeats letter sound)*

T   ##, you try
S   I-R, (Teacher directs individual student to repeat the letter name) /ɜ:/. (Teacher directs individual student to repeat the letter sound)
T |inviting the next student| you try
S   I-R, (Teacher directs individual student to repeat the letter name) /ɜ:/. (Teacher directs individual student to repeat the letter sound).

After multiple iterations of reading through the data, the crude categories were refined and restructured. For example, the first two codes in the excerpt above were combined together to one label "T models and class repeat-LS" (teacher models and class repeats letter sound), and the last two codes combined to one label as "IS asked to repeat-LSC" (individual student asked to repeat letter-sound correspondences), because those are basically the same activities. The codes generated for the activities used in the phonics instruction are listed in Appendix D.

The analysis of the data relevant to the teaching of word sound in vocabulary instruction involved two steps of coding. Firstly, if the word sound was taught to students as a whole without any decoding of its sub-word components, the label "whole word reading" was assigned to the word. If a word involved decoding, the component letter or letter combinations that were explicitly decoded as a separate unit were asterisked (see Appendix L). Then, the proportion of words involving phonological decoding or whole word reading, and the proportion of different types of focal sub-word units were calculated.

The analysis of the data for the reading activities beyond the word level went through similar stages as the analysis of the data for phonics instruction activities. The emerging codes focused on two primary areas: (a) reading activities (e.g. individual reading; listening to teacher reading aloud; choral reading); (b) reading materials (e.g. textbook materials; supplementary materials) (see Appendix D). Then the crude codes of reading activities were refined and grouped into two summary codes: reading activities at the first encounter with the materials and rereading the materials. It was decided to combine the different types of reading activities used in the rereading stage but keep the subcategories of reading activities at the first encounter with the materials. This is because the types of the reading activities children were engaged in when they firstly encountered the reading materials can reveal whether children were given the opportunities to decode words independently or linking the component sub-word units to their phonological representations. We concede that it is not known whether children truly apply their phonological decoding skills when engaged in these reading activities.

Inter-Rater Reliability Checks

To ensure the coding of the observation data was reliable, a sample transcript along with the list of codes was sent to a second coder, who had three years' experience of teaching English to young learners in China before doing the MA Course in TEFL at Essex University. After the second coder had finished coding, the reliability was calculated by adding the total number of instances which we both coded in the same way, divided by the total number of instances in the sample transcript multiplied by 100%. The percentage of our agreement on the classroom observation of phonics instruction was 92.2%, on the classroom observation of the use of phonological decoding in teaching word sound 98.5%, and on the classroom observation of the reading activities beyond the word level 97.1%. Any disagreements were discussed and resolved through a discussion between the researcher and the second coder.

3.5.3 Teacher Interview

To complement the findings from the textbook analysis and classroom observation, and to achieve a better understanding of the complex phenomenon, teacher interviews were carried out to yield supplementary and in-depth data for research questions 5, 7, 8 and 9. Similar to the interview with textbook writer (see Sect. 3.5.4), semi-structured interviews were adopted with teacher interviewees, with a set of open-ended questions prepared in advance.

This section describes and explains the design of the teacher interview questions, the procedures of interview, and the approach to analysing the interview data.

3.5.3.1 Semi-structured Interview Questions

Questions in the teacher interview (see Appendix E) were designed to provide complementary information and explanations for some research questions (see Table 3.1). Most specifically, the questions aimed to find out whether teachers used any methods and activities different from what were observed in class and to explore the explanations for their choice of these teaching techniques as well as the challenges they encountered in teaching phonological decoding and applying it in reading tasks. It should be noted that the interviews were administered after the classroom observations in order that the teachers were not aware of the exact focus of this study during the classroom observations and thereby would not change their normal practice to give more focus to phonological decoding.

There were four sections in the teacher interview. The first section was about the teacher's experience of teaching primary English. The second section concerned the methods teachers employed to teach the sounding out of words and whether they had a preference for any certain type(s) of methods to teach their students to sound out English words. The questions in the third section related to the teaching of phonological decoding, most specifically letters and sounds. And teachers were also invited to discuss the challenges they encountered in helping children develop the ability to decode English words using phonics rules. Throughout the interview, the teachers were encouraged to use the words or texts from the observed unit as an example to illustrate their description of the methods and activities. It is noteworthy that although the interview was semi-structured, the questions in section two were designed to be asked before the questions in section three. This is due to the concern that the exposure to the questions concerning phonological decoding might bias interviewees when answering questions in section two.

3.5.3.2 Procedures

A total of four teacher interviews were conducted after series of observations in order not to affect the teachers' behaviour in class. Each interview was carried out individually in Mandarin and was digitally audio-recorded. Each interview lasted between 35 and 50 min. The interview took place either in the conference room or an empty classroom, to avoid interruptions. And all the interviews were conducted in an informal and conversational atmosphere.

3.5.3.3 Data Analysis

Full transcripts of four interviews were transcribed in Chinese. Teachers' responses to the questions varied greatly in the sense that some teachers gave thorough explanations for questions with examples to illustrate their ideas while some teachers gave short and general answers. The results showed that the number of words in the longest interview was about 9000 Chinese characters while the shortest contained about 5000 Chinese characters.

For coding the data, all transcribed interviews were imported into a QSR NVivo file. The answers related to the interview questions were then extracted for further coding. The coding categories were formulated according to purpose of the investigation as well as the themes and patterns emerging from the interview data.

3.5.4 Textbook Writer Interview

The interview with the textbook writer aimed to corroborate and triangulate the findings from the textbook analysis. It was also thought to be interesting to probe into the intentions behind the design of the materials related to phonological decoding. Therefore, the textbook writer interview is designed to provide complementary information for research questions 4, 5, and 6.

There are different types of interviews, such as structured interviews, unstructured interviews, and semi-structured interviews (Dörnyei 2007). As Dörnyei (2007, p. 135) noted, they vary in terms of the degree of structure in them, with structured interviews at one extreme involving prepared, elaborate, and tightly controlled interview scheme, and unstructured interviews at the other extreme with no detailed interview guide prepared in advance. The structured interviews have the strength of allowing comparability across interviewees, but there is little spontaneity and flexibility in the interview process and limited richness of the data. In contrast, the unstructured interview allows much more flexibility and establishes a more relaxed atmosphere for interviewees to talk about the targeted phenomenon. In between the two types of interviews lies semi-structured interviews, which according to Dörnyei (2007) is the most frequently used research method in applied linguistics. In this format, a set of interview questions are prepared in advance to be used as a guide. The questions are open-ended and not necessarily asked in the same order. In this way, interviewees are encouraged to elaborate on certain issues. In the present study, the aim of an interview was to elicit as much information as possible about the writer's thinking behind the phonological decoding content (see research questions 4, 5, and 6). Therefore, the suitable interview type for this study was semi-structured, because it allowed the interviewer to be clear about the information that needs to be obtained, and also ensured that anything relevant that came up spontaneously was encouraged.

This section describes and explains the design of the textbook writer interview questions, the procedures adopted for the interview, and the approach to analysing the interview data.

3.5.4.1 Semi-structured Interview Questions

Questions in the textbook writer interview (see Appendix F) were designed to provide complementary information and explanations for some research questions (see Table 3.1). Most specifically, the questions aimed to find out how the textbook was designed to develop children's phonological decoding ability, and whether the textbook design took into consideration the integration of the teaching of phonological decoding into the teaching of reading at word level and beyond word level.

The first question was a warming up question, which invited the textbook writer to give a brief description of the textbook materials. The second section aimed to find out how the textbook was designed to help children develop the ability to sound out words using phonics rules. Questions 3–9 focused on the textbook design of teaching letters and sounds, including the teaching objective of the relevant sections in the textbook, the logic behind the design of the content, the sequence of introducing different content, and the principle behind the design of relevant activities for practice. Question 10 investigated whether the textbook design took into account the integration between the teaching of phonological decoding and the teaching of reading at word level or beyond word level. The last question investigated whether there is any training for teachers on how to teach phonological decoding.

3.5.4.2 Procedures

A textbook writer interview was conducted. The interview was carried out in Mandarin and was digitally audio-recorded. It lasted for 40 min. The interview took place in the interviewee's office. And the interview was conducted in an informal and conversational atmosphere.

3.5.4.3 Data Analysis

The analysis of the textbook writer interview data followed the same procedure as the analysis of the teacher interview data. The analysis began with the transcription of the full scripts of the interview in Chinese, followed by the coding of the data in QSR NVivo.

The answers relevant to the interview questions were extracted and coded according to the purpose of the investigation, namely to provide complementary and supporting evidence to the findings of the textbook analysis on phonological decoding, and to explore the principle and logic behind the design of relevant content in the textbook and accompanying materials.

3.5.5 Battery of Tests

A battery of tests was used in the current study to address research questions 1, 2 and 3. A real word reading test and reading comprehension test were employed to assess children's reading ability at word and text level. A nonword reading test was used to assess children's phonological decoding proficiency. Nonword reading tests are a commonly used technique to assess phonological decoding proficiency (Ehri 1991; Emery 2005; Gough and Juel 1991; Harris and Giannouli 1999; Koda 2005; Rack et al. 1992; Share 1995; Siegel 1993), and "one of the purest tests of phonological decoding skill" (Snowling 1995, p. 134). Unlike a list of real words, which can be read by phonological decoding, or by sight, namely by retrieving the sound information as a whole through the stored entries in mental lexicon, nonwords do not have stored lexical entries or support from context, and thereby can only be pronounced by using phonological decoding (Chard et al. 2007; Chu, 2002a, 2002b; Harris and Giannouli 1999; Wentink et al. 1997). Therefore, nonword reading tests can be regarded as a more accurate measurement of phonological decoding ability.

However, there has been some criticism of nonword reading. Rack and his colleagues (1992) indicated that reading nonwords would be considered as an unnatural activity so that young children might misunderstand the task. For example, they might believe that they have to guess what real words could be represented by the unfamiliar letter strings that were presented to them.

Despite the unnatural characteristics of nonword reading, given what has been discussed above, a nonword reading test is still believed to be an effective way to measure phonological decoding ability. We think that providing trial nonword items for practice before the test may be helpful to familiarise the participants with the task, together with an explanation before the test that nonwords are not real words but meaningless words that do not exist in English vocabulary, which may also help the young participants to understand the task more clearly.

This section gives a detailed presentation of the construction of the nonword reading test, real word reading test and reading comprehension test, the procedures for

Table 3.13 The 42 nonword test items

1	lun	15	knud	29	wect
2	fod	16	wret	30	selt
3	lik	17	vock	31	lext
4	tep	18	muth	32	zelp
5	rel	19	zess	33	cleals
6	juf	20	toch	34	stount
7	yat	21	haif	35	twesk
8	nop	22	soin	36	snump
9	fote	23	galk	37	floket
10	kile	24	cight	38	zaycred
11	bage	25	grop	39	malras
12	hime	26	plaf	40	fraklenk
13	whik	27	snet	41	chensert
14	shos	28	prug	42	shemslip

administering the tests, and the quantitative and qualitative approaches to analysing the data.

3.5.5.1 Test Construction

The Nonword Reading Test

The items in the nonword reading test included 42 nonwords, 36 of which were monosyllabic, and 6 disyllabic (see Table 3.13).

The 36 monosyllabic nonwords ranged in terms of difficulty, including 20 CVC (consonant + vowel + consonant) nonwords (e.g. *tep, whik, zess, soin*), 4 CVCe items (e.g. *fote, hime*), 4 CVCC (consonant + vowel + consonant cluster) nonwords (e.g. *wect, selt*), 4 CCVC (consonant cluster + vowel + consonant) nonwords (e.g. *grop, plaf*), and 4 CCVCC (consonant cluster + vowel + consonant cluster) nonwords (e.g. *twesk, snump*). The 20 CVC nonwords were composed of 8 CVC items containing a single consonant letter, a single vowel letter and a single consonant letter (e.g., *lun, tep, yat*), 4 CVC items containing initial consonant digraph letters, a single vowel letter and a single consonant letter (e.g. *whik, knud*), 4 CVC items containing a single consonant letter, a single vowel letter and final consonant digraph letters (e.g. *vock, toch*), and 4 CVC items containing a single consonant letter, a single vowel digraph/trigraph and a single consonant letter (e.g. *soin, haif*). As the present study focuses on decoding the printed orthographic units, no distinction was made between monophthong and diphthong sounds. Neither the fact that English is stress-timed rather than syllable-timed was taken into account.

Table 3.14 Pivot table for summarising the rime-level sub-word units in OE monosyllabic words

Row labels	Count of rime-level sub-word units
op	5
Drop	1
Hop	1
Pop	1
Shop	1
Stop	1

In order to find out whether Chinese children are able to decode vowel graphemes with sensitivity to the rime patterns (i.e. vowel + coda, e.g. <un>, <ump>), 22 monosyllabic nonwords that contain the same rime-level graphemic patterns as some monosyllabic word(s) in the textbook vocabulary list were designed. For example, the nonword *lun* contains the rime <un> shared by a set of monosyllabic words in the textbook vocabulary, i.e. *run*, *sun*, and *fun*.

Before designing the 22 monosyllabic nonwords, a pivot table was used to summarise the occurrence of the rime patterns contained in the monosyllabic words in the OE vocabulary list (see Table 3.14).

Based on the summary table of all the rime patterns contained in the textbook vocabulary, 11 nonword test items that share the rime-level sub-word units with one monosyllabic word in the text vocabulary list and 11 that share the rime-level sub-word units with at least two monosyllabic words in the text vocabulary list were designed (2 out of the 11 nonwords have 2 base words[5]; 2 have 3 base words; 4 have 4 base words; 2 have 5 base words; 1 has 10 base words, as shown in Table 3.15).

Each nonword was checked in the Oxford English Dictionary Online to make sure that none of them exists in English and hence there was no likelihood for the subjects to have encountered them before testing. Reading accuracy was recorded but reading speed was not taken in account because reading speed was considered not related to the purpose of this test, i.e. to investigate the subjects' proficiency in phonological decoding skills, to examine the relationship between scores on phonological decoding test and scores on reading comprehension test, and to discover possible strategies Chinese children might use in decoding nonwords. The resulting 42-item measure has a Cronbach's alpha of 0.84, which indicates that it has a high level of internal consistency and is therefore reliable.

The Real Word Reading Test

A list of 150 real words was designed to test children's ability to read English words that were taught before and were phonically decodable (namely decodable with reliance on GPC rules) (see Appendix C). Fifteen words were chosen from each of

---

[5] Base words refer to the monosyllabic words in the textbook vocabulary list that share the same rime-level sub-word units as the test nonwords. For example, *run* is one of the base words for *lun*.

Table 3.15 List of all monosyllabic words in the textbook vocabulary list that share with the nonwords the same rime-level sub-word units

	Monosyllabic nonword test items	Monosyllabic words containing the same rime-level graphemic patterns
1	lun	Run, Sun, Fun
2	fod	Nod
7	yat	At, Cat, Chat, Fat, Hat, Sat, Rat, Tat, That*, What*
8	nop	Drop, Hop, Pop, Shop, Stop
10	kile	While, Smile
11	bage	Age
12	hime	Time
15	knud	Bud
16	wret	Get, Let, Net, Wet
17	vock	Clock, Rock, Sock
19	zess	Chess, Dress, Guess, Mess
22	soin	Join
23	galk	Talk, Walk
24	cight	Bright, Night, Light, Right
25	grop	Drop, Hop, Pop, Shop, Stop
27	snet	Get, Let, Net, Wet
28	prug	Hug
31	lext	Next
32	zelp	Help
34	stount	Count
35	twesk	Desk
36	snump	Jump

Notes The underlined words are basic words, which are highlighted in the textbook vocabulary list and attract much more attention in the teaching and learning process, compared to extended words, which are not underlined. Although *what* and *that* are words that frequently appear across the textbook, they are not listed as basic vocabulary in OE, probably because they are not content words

the 10 textbooks (one book for each semester). Among the 150 real word items, there are 115 monosyllabic words (77%) and 35 disyllabic words (23%). In addition, there were 87 nouns (58%), 28 verbs (19%), 17 adjectives (11%), and 18 other types of parts of speech (12%). This proportion of test words in different parts of speech is consistent with that of the textbook vocabulary in different parts of speech. It should be noted that this test was not meant to examine the participants' vocabulary size but to test their competence in reading the textbook vocabulary that they had been taught before and that was phonically decodable.

Considering that participants' sensitivity to the rime patterns depends on the familiarity with particular rime patterns (see details in Sect. 2.4.1.3), among the 150 real words are 35 monosyllabic words, which were tested to find out whether the participants were able to sound out the base words whose rimes children may rely on when decoding nonwords (see Appendix B). These base words share with their nonword counterparts the same rime-level sub-word units (vowel + final consonant / coda). For example, *hop*, *shop* and *stop* share the same rime-level graphemes, i.e. <op>, with the nonword *nop*. When decoding the nonword *nop*, children may rely on their knowledge of the rime of <op> as /ɒp/. It is believed that if a child is not able to sound out the graphemic pattern representing the rime, e.g. <op>, in any of the base words, e.g. *hop*, *shop*, *stop*, he/she will not be able to deduce the rime and further apply this knowledge in decoding *nop*. In other words, to use the knowledge of rime to decode nonwords requires knowledge of base words. If a child does not know any words of the component rime, we cannot expect the child to deduce the rime. For example, one should be able to read the words containing the rime <un>, e.g. *run* or *sun*, in order to deduce the component rime <un> in *lun*. The more children encounter the rime pattern repeated in words, the more likely the rime pattern will be consolidated. This is because the OE textbook does not involve the teaching of rime. Most of the time, the pupils might need to deduce the rime units from words that they already know, though it was found in class observations that on very few occasions certain rimes were taught in class on the basis of a group of textbook words.

In addition, it is believed that the base words from which children deduce or summarise their knowledge of the shared rime must come from the vocabulary list of the participants' primary English textbook, which is the major source of their English input. It has to be admitted that children might pick up additional English words from other sources such as English cartoons and storybooks; however, the number of such words is likely to be limited according to personal communication with primary school teachers, who indicated that the pupils rarely read other English materials except the textbook after school. Moreover, each individual child might have access to different out-of-class materials, which made it difficult to test. Accordingly, it was decided to base this test on the participants' textbook vocabulary list, i.e. the words that share the rime-level graphemic patterns with the nonwords as shown in Table 3.14, as we could be confident that they had learnt them.

For the 11 nonwords with more than one base word that share the same rime-level graphemic patterns, we decided to choose the base words that that are basic vocabulary (see explanation in Sect. 3.5.5.1.1), except for *kile*, which has two base words and both of them are extended vocabulary. The other exception is *yat*, whose base words that are extended vocabulary, i.e. *what* and *that*, were also included in the test, in case children might rely on the phonological rime /ɒt/ or /ət/ of the rime-level sub-word unit <at>. By choosing the basic vocabulary, on which more teaching and learning attention had been focused and therefore were more likely to be part of the children's mental lexicon, compared with the extended vocabulary, we can confidently say that a child does not know the spelling-sound correspondence of the component rime or is not sensitive to the rime pattern, if he/she cannot sound out any of the rime pattern in the base words that received most teaching and learning attention. Meanwhile, we can also minimise the possibility of categorising the children who fail to decode an extended word, i.e. a possibly unfamiliar word, as not knowing the rime. For example, in the case of *nop*, there is more than one textbook word of the same component rime, e.g. *drop*, *hop*, *pop*, *shop*, *stop*, *hop*, *shop* and *stop* were chosen as test items because they are basic words. The list of the base word test items can be found in Appendix B. The resulting 150-item measure has a Cronbach's alpha of 0.90, which indicates that it has a high level of internal consistency and is therefore reliable.

Reading Comprehension Test

Phonological reading skills are regarded as "the single most important determiner of reading proficiency in English" (Emery 2005, p. 126). A reading comprehension test was therefore designed to test reading proficiency and further compare Chinese learners' English reading proficiency with their phonological decoding skills.

The reading comprehension test was taken from one of the most widely used standardised English test for young learners, i.e. Cambridge Young Learners English tests (Cambridge ESOL Examinations 2007), which is aimed at children in primary and lower secondary education. The Movers level was chosen after consulting the primary teachers, who suggested this level was more suitable for the grade 5 children, considering their vocabulary size and grammar knowledge. The original test was composed of six parts, but the sixth part was left out, because the grammatical points in this part were mostly not taught before (e.g. relative clauses).

Moreover, care was taken not to "contaminate" the reading test by high levels of writing requirements, as McKay (2006) suggested for assessing young language learners. Firstly, neither copying nor writing words was required in the adapted reading test. Children were only asked to choose the answers.

In addition, the vocabulary list of the YLE test did not correspond with that of the participants' primary English textbooks. Therefore, considering that this test was not meant to measure children's English vocabulary size or knowledge of grammar, all the words in the test were taken from the vocabulary list of the participants' textbooks. Accordingly, although we tried to retain the questions as in the whole test, some questions that contained untaught vocabulary had to be taken out and substituted with other questions from other tests at the same Movers level. Or some untaught words were substituted with taught ones, e.g. substituting *stomachache* with *toothache*, or annotated with Chinese meaning in brackets, e.g. *clown* (小丑). Moreover, in light of the fact that the participants had just begun the first lessons on the past tense at the time of this test and they might still be confused with the unfamiliar past tense, all the sentences in the past tense were rewritten in the present tense in this test. These adjustments were not thought to alter the validity of the test for the purposes of this study, given its focus on phonological decoding skills.

The test is composed of five parts. Each part begins with 1–2 examples. In the first part, the participants were asked to match words and definitions. There were 8 pictures, each with the words that they illustrate written under them, and 6 definitions.

The pupils must find the word which matched each definition and write it beside its definition. In the second part, the pupils were required to look at a big picture and read six sentences about it. Then they had to judge whether the sentences described the picture correctly or not. In the third part, participants read a short written dialogue, for which three different responses were given for what the second speaker said in her turn. The participants chose the correct response by circling letters. In the fourth part, participants read a text with five gaps and looked at the words and pictures in a box next to the text. They then chose the correct words to fill in the gaps. The missing words are nouns, adjectives or verbs. There are two extra inappropriate words. They were also asked to choose the best title for the story from a choice of three. The fifth part was a story in the past tense in the original version, which was rewritten in the present tense. The story was divided into three sections each with an illustration. The pictures did not provide answers to the questions. Children were required to read the story and choose the right words to complete 10 sentences. The resulting 34-item measure has a Cronbach's alpha of 0.82, which indicates that it has a high level of internal consistency and is therefore reliable.

To recapitulate, this test was designed to examine specifically the participants' English reading proficiency, excluding words that were not in the vocabulary list of the participants' taught textbooks, or unfamiliar grammar such as the past tense. The scoring procedure is detailed in Sect. 3.5.5.3.1.

3.5.5.2   Testing Procedure

The nonword reading test was administered at the end of data collection during the month of April 2012. It took about 5–20 min to administer. Children were tested individually in a quiet room. All the instructions were in Chinese. Before the test, each individual child was told that the strings of letters they were going to read aloud were nonwords, which did not exist, and that the results would only be used for the purpose of research. The microphone of a digital voice recorder was attached to their collars to record their pronunciation of these nonwords. Considering the possibility that some children may not be accustomed to using a computer, all words were printed in Times New Roman 72-point font size on A4 pages, in lowercase letters, with the number of each nonword in the top left corner. If any nonwords were skipped, the children would be instructed to go back to the missed nonword with reference to its number. Five example nonwords (*fev*, *phin*, *drish*, *creet*, *somed*) were given to subjects to make sure they got the general idea of the procedure before they started. There was no time limit for a subject to respond to each item. No feedback on the accuracy of a response was given but encouragement was generous throughout the test. If any child got stuck with a nonword, he or she would be given time to think it over and meanwhile be encouraged to make an attempt to read it aloud. During the test, the sound that participants mapped onto each nonword was recorded in IPA symbols as the basis for further transcription. In addition, if a child made several attempts to sound out a nonword, only the last attempt would be transcribed. At the end of the test, each child was asked individually whether he or she had taken any courses outside of class and whether those courses offered any phonics instruction or instruction on letter-sound relations.

After the nonword reading test was administered to one participant after another, the same group of children were given the real word test individually. As the only time available for administering these two tests was the lunch break, it took approximately 7–8 days to finish administering the two tests in each school. Finally, they were gathered in a quiet classroom during the lunch break to take the reading comprehension test, which lasted for 25 min. To recap, the three tests were administered to the same group of participants in three different sessions.

3.5.5.3 Data Analysis

Before the data was analysed, the 42 nonwords were presented to four native speakers of English (two British, two American). They assigned the same pronunciations to those nonwords, except 7 items, *muth*, *haif*, *plaf*, *floket*, *zaycred*, *malras*, *fraklenk*. All the pronunciations that the four native speakers of English assigned to the 7 items were accepted as correct. For instance, two pronounced *muth* as /mʌθ/, two as /muːθ/. Both pronunciations of *muth* were counted as correct. The accepted pronunciations of these 42 nonwords are listed in Appendix A.

Scoring Procedure

The scoring procedure was divided into the following steps:

Firstly, one point was given to each nonword that was decoded correctly, based on the list of accepted pronunciations. There could be a maximum score of 42. The scores revealed the proficiency of the subjects' decoding skills.

Secondly, one point was given to a correct answer in the reading comprehension test. There could be the maximum score of 34 points. The correlation between nonword reading test scores and reading comprehension test scores was investigated to examine whether the phonological decoding ability, as indicated in the nonword reading test, was an accurate indication of reading comprehension ability.

Thirdly, one point was given to a word that was read aloud correctly in the real word test. There could be a maximum score of 150 points. Any partial error would be given a score 0. For example, if *light* was pronounced as *right*, it would be counted as a wrong response and no point would be given.

Coding Procedure of Nonword Decoding

The errors of nonword decoding were firstly categorised into two general types, i.e. vowel decoding errors and consonant decoding errors. Then according to the position of consonant orthographic units, consonant decoding errors were further classified as errors of decoding initial consonant orthographic units (e.g. <pl> in *plaf*), medial consonant orthographic units (e.g. <m> and <sl> in *shemslip*), and final consonant orthographic units (e.g. <f> in *plaf*). Similarly, vowel decoding errors were further classified as errors of decoding vowel graphemes in monosyllables (e.g. <a> in *plaf*), the first vowel in disyllables (e.g. <e> in *shemslip*), and the second vowel in disyllables (e.g. <i> in *shemslip*). And according to the complexity of consonant orthographic units, consonant decoding errors were categorised into errors of decoding single consonant graphemes (e.g. <t> in *wret*), consonant digraphs (e.g. <wr> in *wret*), and consonant clusters (e.g. <pr> in *prug*). Similarly, vowel decoding errors were broken up into errors of single vowel letters (e.g. <e> in *wret*) and non-split letter combinations representing vowels (e.g. <oi> in *soin*), split vowel digraphs (e.g. <o-e> in *fote*). For instance, if *plaf* was read as /pju:f/, there would be one consonant error (/p/ for <pl>) and one vowel error (/ju:/ for <a>). And then the consonant error could be further categorised as an initial consonant cluster error, and the vowel error further classified as a single vowel error.

The first round of analysis showed that the mean success rate of decoding vowel graphemes (43%) was significantly lower than the mean success rate of decoding consonant graphemes (77%) (see details in Sect. 4.1.1). Thereby, further qualitative and quantitative analyses were conducted on the participants' performance on decoding vowel graphemes in order to find out the possible strategies they might use in the decoding process. As one third of the 6 disyllabic nonwords involved omission of a vowel, it was decided to focus this further analysis on the 36 monosyllabic nonwords, whose vowels were all sounded out by the participants.

The coding procedure is driven by the data, i.e. item-based and below is the coding scheme for the possible strategies used to sound out the vowel graphemes in nonwords. There are two main categories of strategies, whole word strategy and decoding strategy. And the decoding strategy is then analysed in further sub-categories.

(1) Whole word strategy is characterised by assigning the nonword with a sound of the real word in the OE vocabulary list that shares some letter component(s) of its nonword counterpart. For example, *cleals* was sounded out as *clean*, *whik* as *walk*, *grop* as *group* or *drop*, *soin* as *soon*, *shemslip* as *shopping*. In this case, the participants did not pay close attention to the internal structure of the nonword but read the item as a whole word, which resembles the nonword to some extent.

(2) The decoding strategy is categorised into major grapheme-phoneme correspondence (major GPC) strategy and minor grapheme-phoneme correspondence (minor GPC) strategy.

The difference between the two types of strategies lies in whether the sound a child mapped onto the vowel letter is a major GPC or a minor GPC. Major GPCs are operationalised in this study as the letter-sound correspondences covered in the textbook phonics syllabus (see Appendix J). For example, in the participants' primary phonics syllabus, the sounds of the letter <o> is introduced as /ɒ/ in *dog, shop, photo*, as /əʊ/ in *go, old*, and as /ʌ/ in *other* and *son*. Moreover, these major GPCs usually include the correspondences that occur most frequently among primary textbook vocabulary. For instance, <o> is translated to /ɒ/ in 77 word types, /əʊ/ in 58 word types and /ʌ/ in 24 word types.

Minor GPCs are operationalised as the letter-sound relations that are not covered in the textbook phonics syllabus but occur in some textbook vocabulary. These correspondences usually occur less frequently, i.e. in much fewer words in the participants' textbook vocabulary list (see Appendix J). For instance, compared with the above-mentioned major sounds of <o>, the other sounds of <o> occur less frequently in the primary textbook vocabulary (/ʊ/ in 2 words, e.g. *into*; /u:/ in 8 words, e.g. *do*), except /ə/, the schwa sound, found in 34 primary words, e.g. *lesson*. These untaught and less frequent letter-sound relations are classified as minor grapheme-phoneme correspondences in this study.

The major GPC strategy is further classified into the following three types of strategies, as detailed in category a-1, a-2, and a-3 in Table 3.16.

(3) All other responses of vowel decoding that cannot fall into any of the strategy types listed above were classified as "others". These responses can be the outcome of children's wild guessing or other unknown factors.

The reliability of the coding scheme was checked by asking a Ph.D. graduate who did her research on second language reading at University of Essex, to code the possible strategies used by 8 randomly selected participants to sound out the vowel graphemes in the 36 monosyllabic nonwords. The results yielded an average of 90.63% agreement. Any discrepancies in coding were resolved through discussion between the researcher and the second coder.

Quantitative and Qualitative Approach to Data Analysis

Both qualitative and quantitative approaches are adopted to analyse the data from the tests. To answer the first research question (repeated below), binary logistic regression analyses in SPSS were used.

RQ1: How is Chinese children's phonological decoding accuracy affected by the orthographic units at different levels of complexity (single consonant letter, consonant digraph, consonant cluster; single vowel letter, non-split letter combination representing vowel, split vowel digraph) and at different positions (initial/medial/final consonant orthographic unit; vowel orthographic unit in monosyllabic words, first vowel orthographic unit in disyllabic word, second vowel orthographic unit in disyllabic word)?

This is because the dependent variable (success of decoding graphemes) is categorical and dichotomous (either $0 =$ failure or $1 =$ success). And the independent variables, both complexity and position, are also categorical. Moreover, the binary logistic regression model does not require the assumption of normality in the distribution of scores (Field 2009). Figure 3.1 displays the non-parametric distribution of participants' nonword reading test percentage scores. And the Kolmogorov–Smirnov test was used to see if the distribution of the three test percentage scores is significantly different from a normal distribution. The results of the Kolmogorov–Smirnov

Table 3.16 Codes for decoding strategies

Codes for decoding strategies		Description	Examples
a. Decoding-MAGPC (Decoding-major GPC)	a-1 Decoding-MAGPC-NR (Decoding-major GPC-no rime-level base words)	When dealing with the 14 monosyllabic nonwords that do not have base words of the same rime-level graphemic patterns, children have no rime pattern to resort to, only their knowledge of major GPCs	For example, in the case of decoding *rel*, which has no base words of the same rime-level graphemic patterns in primary textbook vocabulary, if a child sounded it out as /ri:l/ or /rel/, the response would be coded as Decoding-MAGPC-NR, because the participant had no rime pattern to resort to, but his/her knowledge of the major GPCs (<e> can be mapped onto /ɛ/ or /i:/)
	a-2 Decoding-MAGPC-SR (Decoding-major GPC-sensitive to rime pattern)	When dealing with the 22 monosyllabic nonwords that have base words of the same rime-level graphemic patterns (e.g. *lun*), children decode the vowel grapheme of a nonword based on its major GPC, with sensitivity to the rime-level letter pattern (e.g. <un>) Whether a child knows the rime pattern is tested with the rime-level base word(s) listed in Appendix B	For example, with sensitivity to the rime pattern of <ock>, a child was more able to decode the vowel letter <o> in *vock* as /ɒ/ instead of other major phonemes such as /əʊ/ or /ʌ/. Hence, if a participant was able to sound out <ock> in both base words, *clock* and *sock*, we can assume that he might know how to sound out the rime <ock>. And if he decoded the vowel grapheme in the nonword *vock* correctly as that in the rime-level base words, we can further assume that he might decode the vowel letter <o> with sensitivity to the rime pattern <ock> and thereby code this response as "Decoding-MAGPC-SR"

(continued)

Table 3.16 (continued)

Codes for decoding strategies		Description	Examples
	a-3 Decoding-MAGPC-IR (Decoding-major GPC-insensitive to rime pattern)	This strategy is characterised by using the major grapheme-phoneme correspondences covered in the textbook phonics syllabus (see Appendix J) to decode the vowel graphemes in the 22 monosyllabic nonwords that have base words of the same rime-level graphemic pattern, without showing sensitivity to the rime patterns	For example, in the case of decoding *lun* as /lju:/, the child might use one of the major GPCs, <u> -/ju:/, without sensitivity to the rime pattern of <un> . Or in the case of decoding *fod* as /fɒd/, as the participant was not able to decode <od> in *nod*, we assume that he/ she did not possess the knowledge of the rime pattern of <od> , and therefore could not use the rime strategy (as explained in a-3) but used knowledge of major GPC to decode the vowel letter
b. Decoding-MIGPC (Decoding-minor GPC)		This strategy is characterised by using minor grapheme-phoneme correspondences, as explained above (see Appendix J)	If a child decoded the letter <o> in *nop* as /ə/, / ʊ/ or /u:/, the response would be coded as using minor GPC strategy (Decoding-MIGPC). Another example, when *cleals* was decoded as / keɪs/, the response would also be coded as "Decoding-MIGPC", because except the major sounds of the grapheme <ea> (/i:/, /ɛ/) introduced in the primary phonics syllabus, <ea> can be sounded out as /eɪ/ in another two primary grade textbook words, i.e. *break, great*

Notes There is a possibility that children might stick to major GPC strategy in decoding vowel graphemes, without resorting to rime patterns, although they might know the rimes. For example, PS5 is found to decode the letter *u* always as /ʌ/, so his code for *lun* and *prug* can be either Decoding-MAGPC-SR or Decoding-MAGPC-IR. JZ13 decoded the letter <o> always as /ɒ/, and therefore the responses for *fod, nop* and *vock* can be either coded as Decoding-MAGPC-SR or Decoding-MAGPC-IR. Similarly, as JZ1, JZ11 and HL2 decoded <a> always as /æ/, their codes for *yat* can be either Decoding-MAGPC-SR or Decoding-MAGPC-IR

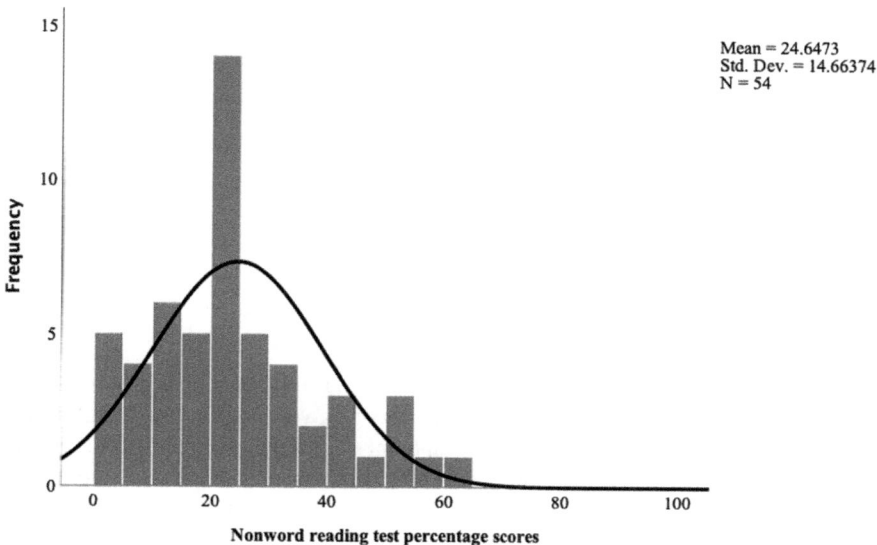

Fig. 3.1 The distribution of nonword reading test percentage scores

Table 3.17 The number of consonant graphemes of different levels of complexity and position

Complexity	Position			
	Initial	Medial	Final	Total
Single consonant	26	8	29	63
Consonant cluster	10	2	9	21
Consonant diagraph	6	/	4	10
Total	42	10	42	94

test showed that the percentage score on the nonword reading test, D (54) $= 0.14$, p < 0.05, is significantly non-normal.

There are a total of 94 consonant graphemes and 48 vowel graphemes in both monosyllabic and disyllabic nonwords. Each grapheme has 54 responses (54 participants). Table 3.17 displays the number of consonant graphemes of different levels of complexity and position. And the number of vowel graphemes of different levels of complexity and position is outlined in Table 3.18.

A binary logistic regression analysis was firstly conducted to investigate how Chinese children's phonological decoding performance is affected by graphemic unit types, i.e. whether vowel graphemes or consonant graphemes are more or less difficult for the children.

Further binary logistic regression analyses were conducted to explore how Chinese children's phonological decoding performance is affected by the complexity

Table 3.18 The number of vowel graphemes of different levels of complexity and position

Complexity	Position			
	Vowel in monosyllable	1st vowel in disyllable	2nd vowel in disyllable	Total
SV	26	5	5	36
VC	6	1	1	8
Split VD	4	/	/	4
Total	36	6	6	48

Note SV single vowel letter (e.g. *a*), *VC* non-split letter combination representing vowel (e.g. *oi*), *Split VD* split vowel digraph (e.g. *a-e*)

of graphemes (single consonant letter/consonant digraph/consonant cluster; single vowel letter/non-split letter combination representing vowel/split vowel digraph).

Finally, the effect of the position of graphemes (initial consonant/medial consonant/final consonant; vowel in monosyllables/the first vowel in disyllables/the second vowel in disyllables) on decoding performance was also investigated through binary logistic regression analyses.

To answer the second research question (What strategies do children at different levels of reading ability employ in sounding out vowel graphemes?), each response for vowels in monosyllabic nonwords was assigned a code according to the code category detailed in Sect. 3.5.5.3.2 Then the occurrences of each type of vowel decoding strategies were counted and input into SPSS for quantitative analysis. Kruskal–Wallis tests and post-hoc Mann–Whitney tests with Bonferroni adjustment for further pairwise comparison were performed separately for different types of vowel decoding strategies. The independent variable consists of three categorical and independent groups of participants according to their reading performance (above average, average, and below average). And the dependent variables are the different types of strategies (decoding-MAGPC-NR; decoding-MAGPC-IR; decoding-MAGPC-SR; decoding-MIGPC; whole word strategy; other), measured in frequency of occurrence.

To explore the third research question (How does Chinese children's phonological decoding ability relate to their reading ability?), both quantitative and qualitative methods were used. Given the results of the tests of normality, Spearman's correlation coefficient (for non-parametric data) instead of the Pearson correlation test was used to reveal the correlation between nonword reading test scores and reading comprehension test scores, and between nonword reading test scores and real word reading test scores. After the quantitative analysis, 6 children who were ranked top 3 and bottom 3 in terms of reading ability were picked out for further qualitative analysis, with a view to revealing how their phonological decoding skills relate to their reading ability and to looking in detail at their phonological decoding skills.

3.6 Ethical Considerations

An official in charge of primary education from Shanghai Education Bureau was firstly approached through personal contact. She then kindly gave me a list of public primary school principals that I could contact. In order to ask for the permission for the study to be carried out in the schools, the participant information sheet and the consent form were given to the principals in face-to-face meetings. After receiving permission from the principals, the teachers who were teaching both grade 4 and grade 5 when the current study took place, were contacted and sent the participant information sheet and the consent form. Their grade 5 students who participated in the battery of tests were also sent the participant information sheet and the consent form for their parents to sign. The English teachers helped to collect them from the student participants before the administration of the tests. The textbook writer was contacted through personal contact. Before the interview, she was also sent the participant information sheet and the consent form to sign.

All the participants were informed at the very beginning that they could withdraw at any time. Only one pupil withdrew before the tests and a new pupil replaced him. No participants quit during the course of the study.

References

Cambridge ESOL Examinations. (2007). *Cambridge young learners English tests (Movers)*. Cambridge: University of Cambridge, ESOL Examinations.

Chard, D. J., McDonagh, S., Lee, S., & Reece, V. (2007). Assessing word recognition. In J. R. Paratore & R. L. McCormack (Eds.), *Classroom literacy assessment: Making sense of what students know and do* (pp. 85–100). New York: Guilford Publications.

Chu, H. (2002a). Assessing EFL learners' decoding skills. *English Teaching & Learning, 26*(3), 35–57.

Chu, H. (2002b). Beginning EFL learners' decoding skill and word reading ability. *Taipei Municipal Teachers College Journal, 33*, 471–484.

Cohen, L., Manion, L., & Morrison, K. (2011). *Research methods in education* (7th ed.). London: Routledge Falmer.

Denscombe, M. (2008). Communities of practice: A research paradigm for the mixed methods approach. *Journal of Mixed Methods Research, 2*(3), 270–283.

Department for Education and Skills. (2007). *Letters and Sounds: Principles and practice of high quality phonics*. Retrieved September 2, 2011, from http://nationalstrategies.standards.dcsf.gov.uk/node/84969.

Department for Education. (2010). *Phonics teaching materials: Core criteria and self-assessment*. Retrieved September 2, 2011, from https://www.gov.uk/government/publications/phonics-teaching-materials-core-criteria-and-self-assessment.

Dörnyei, Z. (2007). *Research methods in applied linguistics*. Oxford: Oxford University Press.

Ehri, L. C. (1991). Development of the ability to read words. In R. Barr, M. L. Kamil, P. B. Mosenthal, & P. D. Pearson (Eds.), *Handbook of reading research* (Vol. 2, pp. 383–417). Hillsdale, NJ: Erlbaum.

Ehri, L. C. (1992). Reconceptualizing the development of sight word reading and its relationship to recoding. In P. Gough, L. Ehri, & R. Treiman (Eds.), *Reading acquisition* (pp. 107–143). Hillsdale, NJ: Lawrence Erlbaum Associates.

Ehri, L. C. (1999). Phases of development in learning to read words. In J. Oakhill & R. Beard (Eds.), *Reading development and the teaching of reading* (pp. 79–108). Oxford: Blackwell publishers.

Ehri, L. C. (2005). *Development of sight word reading: Phases and findings.* Oxford: Blackwell Publishing Ltd.

Ehri, L. C., Nunes, S., Stahl, S. A., & Willows, D. (2001). Systematic phonics instruction helps students learn to read: Evidence from the National Reading Panel's meta-analysis. *Review of educational research, 71*(3), 393–447.

Eisner, E. W. (1998). *The enlightened eye: Qualitative inquiry and the enhancement of educational practice.* Upper Saddle River, NJ: Prentice Hall.

Emery, H. (2005). *An investigation into the nature and causes of reading and spelling errors made by Arab ESL learners.* (Unpublished PhD thesis). Cardiff University.

Field, A. (2009). *Discovering statistics using SPSS.* London: Sage.

Garton, S., Copland, F., & Burns, A. (2011). *Investigating global praticies in teaching english to young learners.* Retrieved 15 December, 2011, from http://www.teachingenglish.org.uk/public ations/global-practices-teachingenglish-young-learners.

Gough, P. B., & Juel, C. (1991). The first stages of word recognition. In L. Rieben & C. Perfetti (Eds.), *Learning to read: Basic research and its implications* (pp. 47–56). Hillsdale, NJ: Erlbaum.

Harley, T. A. (2008). *The psychology of language: From data to theory* (3rd ed.). Hove and New York: Psychology Press.

Harris, M., & Giannouli, V. (1999). Learning to read and spell in Greek: The importance of letter knowledge and morphological awareness. In M. Harris & G. Hatano (Eds.), *Learning to read and write: A cross-linguistic perspective* (pp. 51–70). Cambridge: Cambridge University Press.

Hu, G. (2002). Recent important developments in secondary English-language teaching in the People's Republic of China. *Language Culture and Curriculum, 15*(1), 30–49.

Hutchinson, T., & Torres, E. (1994). The textbook as agent of change. *ELT journal, 48*(4), 315–328.

Johnson, R. B., Onwuegbuzie, A. J., & Turner, L. A. (2007). Toward a definition of mixed methods research. *Journal of Mixed Methods Research, 1*(2), 112–133.

Koda, K. (2005). *Insights into second language reading: A cross-linguistic approach.* New York: Cambridge University Press.

Kuo, L. (2011). *The role and efficacy of phonics instruction in the early literacy development of young Taiwanese EFL learners.* (Unpublished PhD thesis). University of Warwick.

Laxon, V., Gallagher, A., & Masterson, J. (2002). The effects of familiarity, orthographic neighbour-hood density, letter-length and graphemic complexity on children's reading accuracy. *British Journal of Psychology, 93*(2), 269–287.

Lightbown, P. M. (2000). Classroom SLA research and second language teaching. *Applied linguistics, 21*(4), 431–462.

Lynch, B. K. (1996). *Language program evaluation: Theory and practice.* Cambridge: Cambridge University Press.

Lynch, B. K. (2003). *Language assessment and programme evaluation.* Edinburgh: Edinburgh University Press

McGrath, I. (2002). *Materials evaluation and design for language teaching.* Edinburgh: Edinburgh University Press.

McKay, P. (2006). *Assessing young language learners.* Cambridge: Cambridge University Press.

Ministry of Education, China. (2011). *English curriculum standards for compulsory education.* Beijing: Beijing Normal University Press.

Nation, I. S. P. (2009). *Teaching ESL/EFL reading and writing.* New York: Routledge.

Rack, J. P., Snowling, M. J., & Olson, R. K. (1992). The nonword reading deficit in developmental dyslexia: A review. *Reading Research Quarterly, 27*(1), 29–53.

Rixon, S. (2011). *Beyond ABC: Investigating current rationales and systems for the teaching of early reading to young learners of English.* (Unpublished PhD thesis). University of Warwick.

Rose, J. (2006). *Independent review of the teaching of early reading: Final report.* London: Department for Education and Skills Publications.

Share, D. L. (1995). Phonological recoding and self-teaching: Sine qua non of reading acquisition. *Cognition, 55*(2), 151–218.

Siegel, L. S. (1993). Phonological processing deficits as the basis of a reading disability. *Developmental Review, 13*(3), 246–257.

Snowling, M. J. (1995). Phonological processing and developmental dyslexia. *Journal of Research in Reading, 18*(2), 132–138.

Wang, Q. (2009). Primary English in China: Policy, curriculum and implementation. In M. Nikolov (Ed.), *The age factor and early language learning* (pp. 277–309). Berlin & New York: Mouton de Gruyter.

Wentink, H. W. M. J., Van Bon, W. H. J., & Schreuder, R. (1997). Training of poor readers' phonological decoding skills: Evidence for syllable-bound processing. *Reading and Writing, 9*(3), 163–192.

Chapter 4
Chinese Children's Phonological Decoding Ability

This chapter reports findings and provides discussion of both quantitative and qualitative analyses of the collected data concerning Chinese EFL children's phonological decoding ability in accordance with the research questions as stated in Chap. 3. Firstly, results of quantitative analyses of participants' performance in decoding orthographic units of different types are presented and discussed to address research question 1. Secondly, results showing the differences between above average readers, average readers, and below average readers in using a range of strategies to sound out vowel graphemes are presented and discussed to address research question 2. Finally, answers to research question 3 are concerned with participants' phonological decoding ability in relation to their reading ability.

4.1 Performance in Decoding Different Orthographic Units

4.1.1 Vowel Graphemes Versus Consonant Graphemes

As shown in Fig. 4.1, the mean accuracy rate in decoding consonant graphemes (77%) is higher than the mean accuracy rate in decoding vowel graphemes (43%). The results from the binary logistic model indicate that consonant graphemes lead to a significantly higher degree of success compared with vowel graphemes (B = 1.466, Std. Error = 0.0517, Wald Chi-Square = 802.686, df = 1, p < 0.001).

The greater number of errors with decoding vowel graphemes compared to consonant graphemes found in this study is in keeping with previous studies showing that vowel misreadings are much more common than consonant errors (Bryson and Werker 1989; Tal and Siegel 1996). This is also in line with Vandervelden and Siegel's (1995) and Share's (1995) conclusion on L1 children's phonological decoding development that consonantal decoding appears earlier and is easier to acquire than vowel decoding (see details in Sect. 2.4.1.1).

K. Hua, *The Learning and Teaching of Phonological Decoding in Chinese EFL Children*, https://doi.org/10.1007/978-981-97-6891-2_4

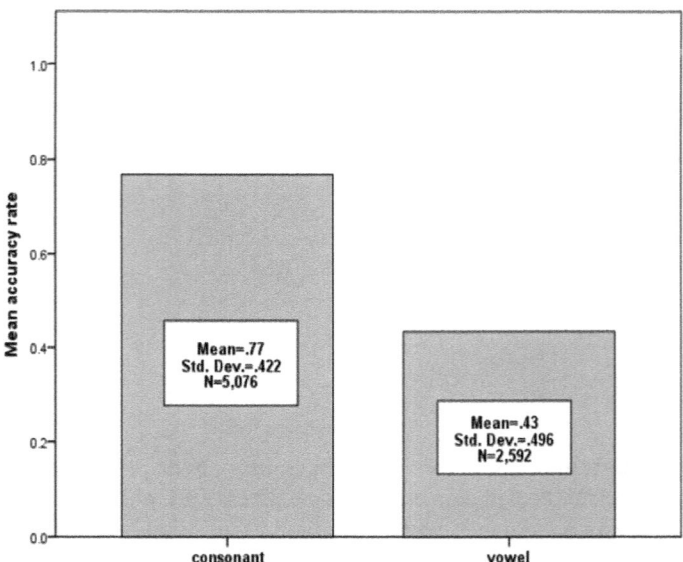

Fig. 4.1   The mean accuracy rate in decoding vowel graphemes and consonant graphemes

4.1.2   The Effect of Graphemic Complexity

As shown in Fig. 4.2, the mean accuracy rate in decoding single consonant graphemes (86%) is the highest, consonant digraphs (71%) the second, and consonant clusters (53%) the lowest. The results from the binary logistic model further indicate that single consonant graphemes lead to a significantly higher degree of accuracy than consonant digraphs (B = 1.083, Std. Error = 0.1101, Wald Chi-Square = 96.908, df = 1, p < 0.001), and consonant digraphs lead to a significantly higher degree of accuracy than consonant clusters (B = 0.681, Std. Error = 0.1131, Wald Chi-Square = 36.237, df = 1, p < 0.001).

The mean accuracy rate in decoding single vowel graphemes (49%) is the highest, non-split letter combinations representing vowels (31%) the second, and split letter combinations representing vowels (16%) the lowest (See Fig. 4.3). The results from the binary logistic model further indicate that single vowel graphemes lead to a significantly higher degree of accuracy than letter combinations representing vowels (B = 0.756, Std. Error = 0.1148, Wald Chi-Square = 43.421, df = 1, p < 0.001), and letter combinations representing vowels lead to a significantly higher degree of accuracy than split letter combinations representing vowels (B = 0.770, Std. Error = 0.2159, Wald Chi-Square = 12.710, df = 1, p < 0.001).

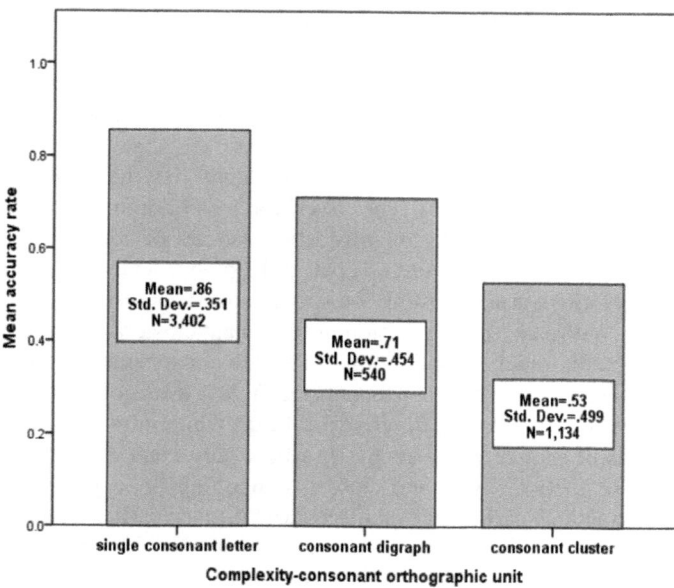

Fig. 4.2 The mean accuracy rate in decoding consonant graphemes of different levels of complexity

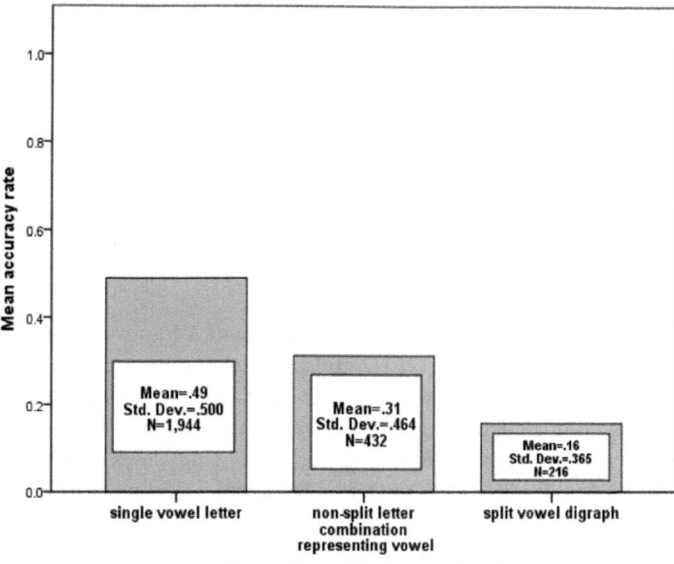

Fig. 4.3 The mean accuracy rate in decoding vowel orthographic units of different levels of complexity. *Note* A split vowel digraph refers to a digraph consisting of two vowel letters that are split by a consonant, for example, <a-e> in *make*

4.1.2.1 The Effect of Complexity on Consonant Decoding

Among the three types of consonant graphemic structures, consonant clusters are found to be the most problematic segment type for the participants, compared to single consonant graphemes and consonant digraphs.

The problem with consonant clusters, on one hand, may be attributable to the inherent difficulty of this segment type. Even for L1 children, the acquisition of consonant clusters is "one of the longest-lasting aspects of speech acquisition in normally developing children" (McLeod et al. 2001, p. 99). As indicated in Smit and her colleagues' (1990) normative study on speech sound acquisition of L1 children in the age range 3–9 years, the acquisition of consonant clusters not only starts later but is also completed much later than that of single consonants. According to the results of their study, most single consonants reach 90% levels of acquisition before age 7, except /ŋ/, /θ/, /ð/, /s/, /z/, /ʃ/, /ʧ/, /ʤ/, /-l/, /r/, while most consonant clusters reach 90% levels of acquisition after age 7, except consonant cluster consisting of a stop and /w/ (e.g. /tw/, /kw/), and clusters containing /l/ (e.g. /pl/, /fl/), which reach 90% criteria much earlier, between age 4;0–5;6, even earlier than some above-mentioned difficult single consonants. Some 8- to 9-year-olds are still mastering consonant clusters. Therefore, all the evidence with L1 children may also suggest that for Chinese young learners of English, consonant clusters would also be a more problematic phonological segment type to produce and it is primarily a developmental problem.

Chinese children's problem with consonant clusters may be exacerbated by the fact that this type of graphemic units does not exist in Chinese Pinyin, which is used to transcribe Mandarin speech using letters from the Roman alphabet (Huang and Hanley 1995; Zhao 1995). On the contrary, according to Locke (1983), one third of English monosyllables have a consonant cluster as onset, and because of the phonemes /s/, /z/, /t/ and /d/ that can indicate grammatical morphemes, consonant clusters predominate at the coda position. Therefore, in the process of acquiring English phonology, consonant clusters may be more challenging for Chinese learners, whose native language only has single consonant letters and consonant digraphs (<zh>, <ch>, <sh>) as onset and coda.

As discussed in Sect. 2.5.3, articulation accuracy was found to bear a significant relation to and a strong influence on L2 children's decoding performance (Roberts 2005). Although the articulation of consonant clusters has been treated as a pronunciation issue, problems in decoding may arise if printed words containing unfamiliar consonant clusters are introduced to young learners of English (Rixon 2011). In other words, the development of L2 children's phonological decoding skills necessitates a good operational knowledge of the English phonological system.

With a closer look at the errors that the participants made, cluster reduction (omission of one element in a consonant cluster) predominates among their responses. For example, *prug* was sounded out as /pjuːg/, and *twesk* as /twiːs/. Such error pattern is also the most common type that younger L1 children make with consonant clusters in their normal phonological acquisition (Ohala 2008). As error patterns are not the focus of this study, they are not discussed in detail here. But it is evident that some Chinese children aged 10–11, who had received 710 h of English instruction at school, were still on the road to mastering consonant clusters.

As to the errors with consonant digraphs, the biggest problem is with the <wr> in *wret* and <kn> in *knud*. 36 out of 54 children (66.7%) decoded <wr> wrongly, 30 children (55.6%) decoding it as /w/ and 5 children (5.6%) as /wʌr/. 46 out of 54 children (85.2%) children decoded <kn> wrongly, 13 children (24.1%) decoding it as /k/, and 30 children (48.2%) decoding both /k/ and /n/ and inverting /n/ after the vowel, producing the sound of *knud* as /kɪnd/ or /kʊnd/, etc. The mean error rate of the other 8 consonant digraphs (<wh> in *whik*, <sh> in *shos*, <ck> in *vock*, <th> in *muth*, <ss> in *zess*, <ch> in *toch*, <ch> in *chensert*, <sh> in *shemslip*) is 16.2%. The poor performance for these two digraphs may be related to the low input of words containing them. In their textbook vocabulary, there are only three words containing <wr> , *write, writer* and *wrong*, and three words containing <kn> , *knee, knife*, and *know*. In contrast, there are 7 words containing <wh> pronounced as /w/, 37 containing <sh> as /ʃ/, 27 containing <ck> as /k/, 38 containing <th> as /θ/, 19 containing <ss> as /s/, 23 containing <ch> as /tʃ/. In that sense, children are more likely to be familiar with the grapheme-phoneme correspondences of the consonant digraphs that occur more frequently in their textbooks, compared with those that occur much less frequently. Therefore, <wr> and <kn> , the two digraphs described as "less common complex consonants" by Seymour et al. (1992) caused more problem for children to decode. If the two less common complex consonants were left out of the category of consonant digraphs, the mean accuracy rate for consonant digraphs would be 83.8%, which is near the mean accuracy rate of single consonant letters (86%). In addition, those two digraphs (<kn> and <wr>) were not included in their phonics syllabus and children may therefore not have been able to discover the correspondences between the two digraphs and their sounds and apply the correspondence in the decoding task. A pedagogical implication of this finding could be that it is necessary to teach directly the letter-sound relations, at least for some children who are not analytic decoders, as Adams (1990) suggested.

In a word, the data supports the claim made by Seymour et al. (1992) which suggests that single consonant letters and common complex consonants (e.g. <th>, <sh>, <ch>) are acquired before less common complex consonants (e.g. <kn>, <wr>) and consonant clusters.

4.1.2.2 The Effect of Complexity on Vowel Decoding

Graphemic complexity also has an effect on the performance in decoding vowel orthographic units. Chinese children in the present study tend to make most errors with split vowel digraphs, less with non-split vowel digraphs, and least with single vowel letters. This echoes (Seymour et al.'s 1992) model of L1 children's developmental sequence of acquiring English orthographic structures and Laxon et al.'s (2002) study on the effect of graphemic complexity on L1 children's reading accuracy (see details in Sect. 2.4.1.2). Both L1 studies suggest that single vowel letters are acquired earlier than complex vowel graphemes, namely vowel digraphs (e.g. <ay>) and split vowel digraphs (e.g. <a-e>).

Participants' performance on decoding different types of vowel orthographic units is also in accordance with L1 children's developmental phases of acquiring phonological decoding skills (Ehri 1992, 2005a). As discussed in Sect. 2.4.1, the decoding of split vowel digraph requires "more complex understanding about the influence of graphemes occurring in one part of the word on the sounds of graphemes in other parts of the word" (Ehri and McCormick 1998, p. 155) and is therefore usually acquired at a later stage than single vowel letters and non-split vowel digraphs.

Further evidence can be found in Davis and Bryant's (2006) 2-year longitudinal study on the acquisition of split vowel digraphs among two age groups of L1 children (aged 7 and 8). In their study, both groups of children reached ceiling levels of scores for the correct reading of single vowel letters (above 90%) while many more mistakes were found with split vowel digraphs. Among 7-year-olds, the mean success rate of decoding split vowel digraphs was approximately 25% and rose up to 64% two years later. And among 8-year-olds, the mean success rate of decoding split vowel digraphs was approximately 38% and rose up to 81% two years later.

To recap, the complexity of orthographic units does matter in children's decoding performance. The orthographic units of greater complexity may need more attention in the teaching and learning process. Or they may just need more time to develop, because we could not expect Chinese EFL children at that stage to be able to deal with the complex graphemic units, given that they might not have yet acquired English phonological representation, nor English articulation, and that they have had limited input. Attention in terms of teaching may do very little until these foundations are in place.

4.1.3   The Effect of Graphemic Position

Figure 4.4 displays that the mean accuracy rate of decoding consonant orthographic units in different positions. Initial consonant graphemes (80%) are the highest, followed by final consonant graphemes (76%), and medial consonant graphemes (65%). The results from the binary logistic model indicate that initial consonant graphemes lead to a significantly higher degree of accuracy than final consonant graphemes (B = 0.332, Std. Error = 0.0769, Wald Chi-Square = 18.598, df = 1, p < 0.001), and final consonant graphemes lead to a significantly higher degree of accuracy than medial consonant graphemes (B = 0.764, Std. Error = 0.1116, Wald Chi-Square = 46.897, df = 1, p < 0.001).

As shown in Fig. 4.5, the mean success of decoding the first vowel graphemes in disyllables (0.65) is the highest, the second vowel graphemes in disyllables (0.41) the second, and the vowel graphemes in monosyllables (0.40) the lowest. The results from the binary logistic model indicate that the first vowel graphemes in disyllables lead to a significantly higher degree of success than the second vowel graphemes in disyllables (B = 1.006, Std. Error = 0.1640, Wald Chi-Square = 37.657, df = 1,

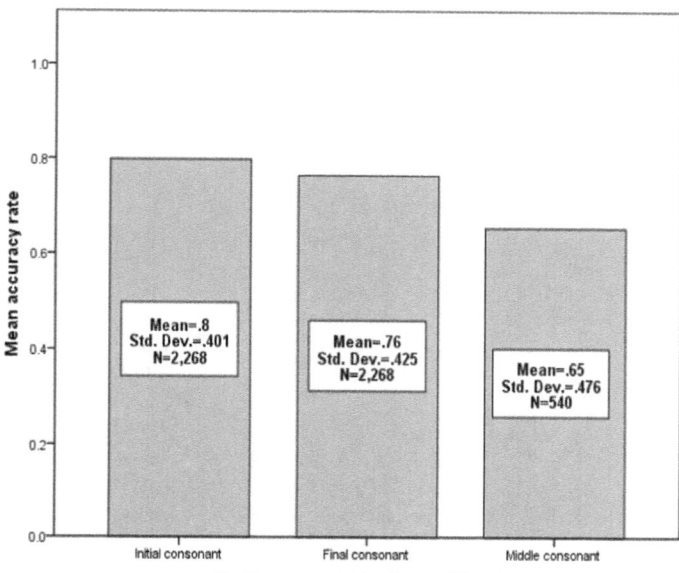

Fig. 4.4 The mean accuracy rate of decoding consonant graphemes of different levels of position

p < 0.001), also higher than the vowels in monosyllables (B = 0.925, Std. Error = 0.1278, Wald Chi-Square = 52.398, df = 1, p < 0.001).

As consonant clusters were found to be the most problematic consonant ortho-graphic unit, a further binary logistic regression test was conducted to investigate whether there is any difference between consonant clusters at different positions, by adding the interaction of position and complexity in the regression model. The results showed that initial consonant clusters lead to a significantly higher degree of accuracy than final consonant clusters (B = 0.500, Std. Error = 0.1262, Wald Chi-Square = 15.673, df = 1, p < 0.001) while there is no significant difference between medial consonant clusters and final consonant clusters (B = 0.177, Std. Error = 0.2129, Wald Chi-Square = 0.693, df = 1, p = 0.405).

It is obvious from the results that the second vowel and the medial consonant in disyllables posed the biggest problem to the participants, compared with initial/final consonant graphemes and the first vowel in disyllables. Around 31% of the responses for the 6 disyllabic nonwords were found to be in the form of monosyllables. That is to say, on a third of the occasions, children in this study only produced the sound of one of the two syllables, most of the time the initial consonant followed by the first vowel and the final consonant. This is probably because decoding disyllables is a more demanding cognitive task compared with monosyllables. It requires larger working memory and syllabification skills. The children in this study were still young and their working memory is still developing; therefore, decoding nonwords of greater length might overload it. Another explanation could be that some children

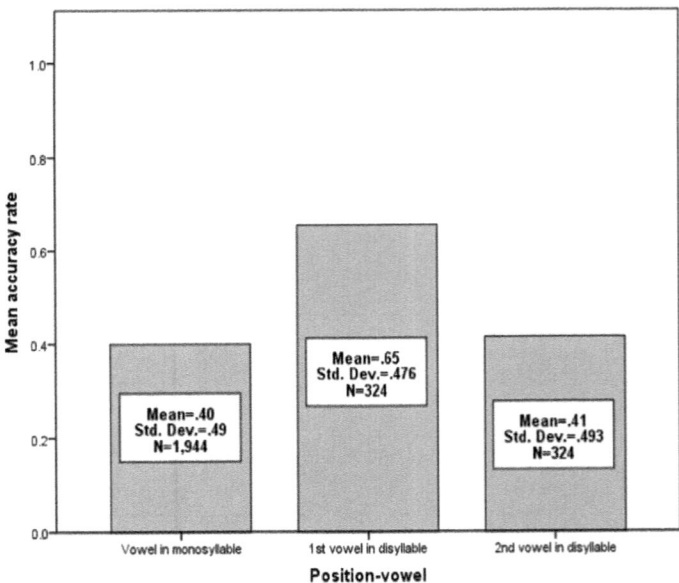

Fig. 4.5 The mean accuracy rate of decoding vowel orthographic units of different levels of position

did not decode the letters sequentially with careful attention and the graphemes in the middle, such as medial consonant graphemes and the second vowel graphemes were thereby ignored.

The greater error rate with final consonant graphemes than that involving initial consonant graphemes resonates with L1 studies (Share 1995; Vandervelden and Siegel 1995) that suggest final consonant decoding poses more difficulty than initial consonant decoding. Chinese children's greater difficulty in decoding final consonants may also be related to the sharp contrast between English and Chinese syllable structure. The former is much more complex than the latter. A typical syllable in Chinese consists of an optional initial (always a consonant) and a final (a vowel or a vowel followed by a nasal consonant). For example, a Chinese syllable can be like [en], [len], [ao], [liang], etc. There is a predominance of CV syllables and only two nasal consonants are available at the coda position, i.e. <n> and <ng>. In contrast, an English syllable can contain a vowel preceded by up to 3 consonants and followed by up to four, which may be represented as CCCVCCCC (e.g. *strengths*/streŋkθs/). Accordingly, Chinese children have not had as much experience with decoding the final consonant graphemes in their L1 as English children do. Therefore, for Chinese EFL children, besides acquiring the GPC correspondences, they also need to acquire the English phonological system, in order to develop phonological decoding skills. In addition, each Chinese character represents a syllable; therefore, Chinese children may not have experience with syllabifying multisyllabic words in their native language.

The greater accuracy of the first vowel in disyllables than that of the vowel in monosyllables may be due to the item construction. There is only 1 out of 6 first vowel graphemes in disyllables that is a vowel digraph, i.e. <ay>. However, 10 out of 36 vowel graphemes in monosyllables are vowel digraphs, 4 of which are split vowel digraphs. This may explain this difference in difficulty between the vowel graphemes in these two positions. The difference is not the outcome of position but of complexity.

To sum up, the development of phonological decoding skills for L2 children does not only require the knowledge of grapheme-phoneme correspondences but also the acquisition of English phonology. Graphemic type, complexity and position all play a role in Chinese children's phonological decoding performance. Generally speaking, vowel graphemes pose more difficulty than consonant graphemes; less common and complex graphemes more difficulty than single and common graphemes; medial graphemes more difficulty than graphemes at other positions. With the awareness that certain types of graphemes may cause more difficulties than others, teachers can possibly make more efforts on those aspects and help their students to develop phonological decoding skills, although we have to admit that sometimes children might find it difficult because they are not yet developmentally ready to acquire it, and no amount of teaching will change it.

4.2 Strategies of Sounding Out Vowel Graphemes

This section aims to investigate the qualitative differences between readers of different abilities in how they sound out vowel graphemes. A quantitative analysis was also performed to explore whether there is any difference between each group of readers as a function of the type of vowel decoding strategy.

Table 4.1 reports the frequency, means, and standard deviations for the three main strategies used by each reading group in sounding out the vowel orthographic units in the 36 monosyllabic nonwords, i.e. decoding strategy (e.g. sounding out *rel* as /rel/), whole word strategy (e.g. sounding out *rel* as *ruler*), and other strategies (e.g. sounding out *rel* as /ru:/). Then statistical analysis of the subcategories of decoding strategy and other strategies is also reported.

Kruskal–Wallis tests were firstly performed separately for the three general types of strategies among the three reading groups. The results of these tests (see Table 4.2) indicate that the use of decoding strategy, whole word strategy, and other strategies to decode vowel graphemes differed significantly at least between two reader groups. Under the category of decoding strategy, significant differences were found in using major GPC based decoding strategy with sensitivity to rime, and major GPC based decoding strategy in nonwords with no rime-level base words.

Then post-hoc Mann–Whitney tests were conducted to evaluate pairwise differences between the three reader groups in using the sub-categorised strategies whose p values were found less than 0.05, as mentioned above (i.e. Decoding-MAGPC-SR; Decoding-MAGPC-NR; Whole word; Others). A Bonferroni correction was applied

Table 4.1 Mean frequency of vowel decoding strategy type for each monosyllabic nonword

	Above average (N = 18)			Average (N = 18)			Below average (N = 18)		
	F (%)	M	SD	F (%)	M	SD	F (%)	M	SD
1. Decoding	450 (69.4%)	25.00	3.71	344 (53.1%)	19.11	4.86	275 (42.4%)	15.28	3.30
(1) Decoding-MAGPC-SR	139 (21.5%)	7.72	3.21	79 (12.2%)	4.39	1.33	46 (7.1%)	2.56	2.04
(2) Decoding-MAGPC-IR	97 (15.0%)	5.39	1.85	97 (15.0%)	5.39	2.12	99 (15.3%)	5.50	1.54
(3) Decoding-MAGPC-NR	177 (27.3%)	9.83	2.04	134 (20.7%)	7.44	2.28	105 (16.2%)	5.83	2.01
(4) Decoding-MIGPC	37 (5.7%)	2.06	1.16	34 (5.2%)	1.89	1.41	25 (3.9%)	1.39	0.78
2. Whole word	87 (13.4%)	4.83	1.92	145 (22.4%)	8.06	3.02	193 (29.8%)	10.72	3.66
3. Others	111 (17.1%)	6.17	3.35	159 (24.5%)	8.83	3.94	180 (27.8%)	10.00	2.54
Total	648			648			648		

Note F total frequency of using a certain type of strategy to sound out the vowel grapheme, *M* mean frequency of using a certain type of strategy to sound out the vowel grapheme, *SD* standard deviation

Table 4.2 Kruskal Wallis test for different types of vowel decoding strategies among the three reading groups

	Chi-Square	df	Asymp. Sig
1. Decoding	28.521	2	0.000***
(1) Decoding-MAGPC-SR	27.52	2	0.000***
(2) Decoding-MAGPC-IR	0.152	2	0.927
(3) Decoding-MAGPC-NR	22.755	2	0.000***
(4) Decoding-MIGPC	3.951	2	0.139
2. Whole word	23.365	2	0.000***
3. Others	10.757	2	0.005**

Note ** $p < .01$; *** $p < .001$

and thereby all effects are reported at a 0.0167 (0.05/3) level of significance. Table 4.3 reports the results of these tests.

A significant difference was found in decoding vowel graphemes (e.g. <u> in *lun*) based on major GPCs and with sensitivity to rimes (e.g. the major sound of <u> as /ʌ/ as in the rime pattern <un>) (i.e. Decoding-MAGPC-SR) between each pair of reader groups. Above average readers used this strategy significantly more frequently than average readers (U = 52.500, p < 0.001), and significantly more frequently than below average readers as well (U = 19.500, p < 0.001). The average readers also used this strategy significantly more than below average readers (U = 19.500, p < 0.001).

When dealing with nonwords for which the children have no rime patterns to resort to (e.g. *muth*), above average young readers used major GPC based decoding strategy (e.g., sounding out *muth* as /mʌθ/ or /muːθ/ by using the major grapheme-phoneme correspondences of <u>, namely /ʌ/ and /uː/) significantly more than average readers (U = 68.5000, p = 0.003) and also significantly more than below average readers (U = 23.000, p < 0.001). But there was no significant difference between average readers and below average readers in using major GPC strategy to decode nonwords with no rime-level base words (U = 90.500, p = 0.021), although the mean frequency of using major GPC strategy to sound out the vowel grapheme in nonwords with no rime-level base words was greater for average readers (M = 7.44) than for below average readers (M = 5.83).

Above average readers were found to use whole word strategy (e.g. sounding out *muth* as *month* or *mouth*) significantly less than average readers (U = 59.000, p = 0.001) and also significantly less than below average readers (U = 20.000, p < 0.001). But no significant difference was found between average readers and below average readers in using this strategy (U = 100.000, p = 0.049).

Although the mean frequency of using other strategies (e.g. sounding out *plaf* as /pjuːf/, neither by using the major or minor GPCs of <a> or reading it as a real word) was the highest with below average readers (10.00), less with average readers (8.83) and the least with above average readers (6.17), significant difference was only found between above average readers and below average readers (U = 59.500, p = 0.001).

Table 4.3 Mann–Whitney test for pairwise differences of vowel decoding strategy use among the three groups

Vowel decoding strategies	Above average—average readers		Average—below average readers		Above average—below average readers	
	Mann–Whitney U	Asymp. Sig.	Mann–Whitney U	Asymp. Sig.	Mann–Whitney U	Asymp. Sig.
Decoding-MAGPC-SR	52.500	0.000***	65.500	0.002**	19.500	0.000***
Decoding-MAGPC-NR	68.500	0.003**	90.500	0.021	23.000	0.000***
Whole word	59.000	0.001**	100.000	0.049	20.000	0.000***
Others	107.500	0.083	113.500	0.123	59.500	0.001**

Note ** $p < .01$; *** $p < .001$

As no participants read aloud every nonword as a real word, it can be concluded that all of them had passed beyond the pre-partial alphabetic phase of word learning, in which L1 children do not show any knowledge of letter-sound relations at all but rely on nonalphabetic visual cues and rote learning, for instance, reading look because it has two eyes in the middle. The three groups of readers showed great disparity in their knowledge of major grapheme-phoneme relations. But the extent to which they used the decoding strategy is significantly different among readers of different abilities. It is obvious from the results that above average readers tended to use decoding strategies significantly more but the whole word strategy significantly less, compared to average and below average readers. The decoding strategy requires knowledge of major grapheme-phoneme correspondences to map sounds onto segment graphemic units. The whole word strategy, however, is a logographic recognition process, in which nonwords are substituted with similar real words. This suggests that good readers tend to be more analytic, relying upon major grapheme-phoneme correspondence knowledge to decode nonwords, while poor readers tend to be more holistic in learning to read English words, relying upon word-specific knowledge, e.g. specific knowledge about the sound of a word as a whole visual form, which cannot by itself be used to read nonwords (Baron 1979; Bowey 2008; Gough and Walsh 1991). At the outset of learning to read, a holistic approach can enable children to accumulate a small number of sight words. However, with inadequate grapheme-phoneme correspondence knowledge, holistic children will find it increasingly difficult to form word-specific orthographic representations because there are simply too many orthographic representations to remember; their word reading development may therefore be hindered (Bowey 2008; Byrne et al. 1992). In contrast, with adequate alphabetic knowledge, analytic readers, like the Phoenician readers in Byrne et al.'s (1992) longitudinal study, will probably achieve higher levels in word reading.

Above average readers also tend to rely more on rime patterns when decoding vowel graphemes, compared to average and below average readers. In other words, good readers usually have a better knowledge of rime units, especially common rime patterns such as <at>, <un>, <ump>, etc. This supports (Ehri's 1992, 1999, 2005a) phase theory of learning to read English words. L1 children at the partial or full alphabetic phase operate primarily with grapheme-phoneme correspondences to decode vowels, while L1 children at a more advanced level, i.e. the consolidated alphabetic phase, operate with more sensitivity to the rime spelling patterns, i.e. the larger chunks that are consolidated out of grapheme-phoneme relations after recurring experience with the grapheme-phoneme correspondences embedded in rime units. The rime units are important because a vowel grapheme, which usually has several sound mappings, is more stable and consistent in rimes and therefore facilitates word decoding accuracy (Cain 2010; Treiman et al. 1995). Larger chunks of rime units can also reduce the total number of units processed in words and thereby speed up decoding speed (Ehri and McCormick 1998).

In accordance with Yin et al.'s (2007) study on stages in Chinese children's reading of English words, the discussion above may also suggest that Chinese young learners of English follow a developmental sequence of learning to read English words similar to their L1 counterparts as suggested by Ehri (1992, 1999, 2005a). Chinese learners start with a holistic approach to reading a word and become more analytic with the increasing proficiency in English. With the enlarging sight vocabulary and working knowledge of major grapheme-phoneme correspondences, they achieve a more complex understanding of the effect of orthographic context on GPC decoding and acquire the rime-based decoding skill.

To sum up, in decoding vowel graphemes, good readers tend to be analytic, associating major sound representations to segment graphemic units, relying on rime units if applicable, and with whole word visual strategy or guessing strategy less involved.

4.3 Phonological Decoding Ability in Relation to Reading Ability

This section firstly reports the results of quantitative comparisons of children's nonword reading test scores in the four different schools. Then the results of quantitative correlational analyses of participants' nonword reading test scores with their reading comprehension test scores and real word reading test scores are presented, followed by a discussion of the results. Next the three most advanced and three least advanced readers' performance on the nonword reading test is discussed in detail in connection with their reading ability.

Table 4.4 displays the descriptive statistics of correct scores and percentages of correct scores on the nonword reading test, reading comprehension test and real word reading test. Descriptive statistics of children's scores in the nonword reading test are grouped according to different schools in Table 4.5. In general, the nonword reading performance of children in the four schools was relatively low (mean percentage of correct answers = 16 in school JZ, 21 in school HL, 29 in school PS, and 32 in school SQ).

Table 4.4 Descriptive statistics of the scores and percentage scores on nonword reading test, reading comprehension test and real word test

	Nonword reading test (Total = 42)		Real word reading test (Total = 34)		Reading comprehension test (Total = 150)	
	Number of correct responses	Percentage score	Number of correct responses	Percentage score	Number of correct responses	Percentage score
Mean	10.4	24.7	23.6	69.4	109.1	72.7
SD	6.2	14.7	5.2	15.2	26.8	17.8
Max.	27	64.3	32	94.1	147	98.0
Min.	1	2.4	7	20.6	46	30.7

Note SD standard deviation

Table 4.5 Descriptive statistics of the nonword reading test scores in four schools

Schools	No. of participants	Mean	SD	Min.	Max.	Mean % correct
JZ	14	6.9	4.737	1	18	16
HL	13	8.9	4.734	2	18	21
PS	13	12.2	5.890	5	24	29
SQ	14	13.4	7.111	3	27	32

Note SD standard deviation

In order to find out whether the nonword reading test scores differed significantly between the four schools, a Kruskal–Wallis test was firstly performed. The results indicate that children's performance in the nonword reading test differed significantly at least between two schools (Chi-Square = 9.897, p < 0.05). Then post-hoc Mann–Whitney tests were conducted to evaluate pairwise differences between the four schools in their nonword decoding performance. A Bonferroni correction was applied and thereby all effects are reported at a 0.0083 (0.05 divided by 6 for 6 comparisons) level of significance. The only significant statistical difference was found between school JZ and school SQ. Children in school SQ performed significantly better than school JZ in decoding nonwords (U = 40.500, p < 0.0083). The striking advantage of school SQ over school JZ in the nonword reading performance will be explained in Sect. 6.2, which explores the link between children's phonological decoding ability and the relevant instruction they received.

In order to investigate the relationship between children's performance in the nonword reading test, the reading comprehension test and the real word reading test, correlation tests were computed. The output for Spearman correlations on the three scores are displayed in Table 4.6 below. The significance value for the correlation coefficient between nonword reading test scores and reading comprehension test scores (0.723) is less than 0.01; therefore, it can be concluded that there is a strong and positive relationship between the two scores. Similarly, the significance value for the correlation coefficient between nonword reading test scores and real word reading test scores (0.831) is also less than 0.01, which suggests a strong and positive correlation between these two scores. In other words, the participants who usually get higher scores in the nonword reading test also score higher in both the reading comprehension test and the real word reading test.

This study, along with studies of L1 children (Hamada and Koda 2010; Vellutino et al. 1995) and EFL beginning readers (Chu 2002; Peng and Tao 2009; Wang et al. 2002; Yin et al. 2007) demonstrates that phonological decoding ability has a strong positive relationship with both reading comprehension ability and real word reading ability. It also further supports the importance of phonological decoding skills in learning to read English words and developing English reading comprehension ability (see Sect. 2.3).

When learning to read English words, if a word is unfamiliar to a child in its written form, phonological decoding helps the child to translate the printed form of the word into its sound representation and then locate the word in the mental

Table 4.6 Spearman correlation test of the percentage scores on nonword reading test, reading comprehension test, and real word reading test

			Reading comprehension test	Real word reading test
Spearman's rho	Nonword reading test	Correlation coefficient	0.723	0.831
		Sig. (1-tailed)	0.000	0.000
		N	54	54

lexicon. But this requires the word to be already extant in the child's oral vocabulary. However, even if the word is not in one's oral vocabulary, phonological decoding can also serve as "a powerful mnemonic system" to form the connection between its spelling and pronunciation out of one's knowledge of the English alphabetic system, allowing the word to be secured in the mental lexicon and later to be accessed directly as a sight word (Ehri 2005b, p. 172). Therefore, no matter whether the word is in the child's oral vocabulary, phonological decoding is a prerequisite for efficient word recognition.

In addition, this study also underscores phonological decoding ability as a good predictor and necessary component of Chinese learners' English reading comprehension ability. This resonates with the simple view of reading (Chen and Vellutino 1997; Hoover and Gough 1990; Protopapas et al. 2012), which holds decoding together with oral language comprehension as two necessary components for skilled reading. Hoover and Gough (1990) specifically noted that for beginning readers, decoding skills involve the derivation of "appropriate phonological representations for novel printed inputs" (p. 130), "a task functionally equivalent to nonword reading" (Protopapas et al. 2012, p. 218). And after the repeated derivation of appropriate phonological representations from unfamiliar letter strings, direct lexical access, i.e. fast and accurate word recognition will eventually be acquired. Such automatic word recognition can free up one's cognitive resources in the complex reading process, and thereby allows to direct active attention to more sophisticated comprehension tasks such as making inferences and recalling details, etc.

In a word, this study lends support to previous studies that find phonological decoding to be a crucial element in learning to read in English. And it seems to apply to L2 children too even children who learn to read a typologically and orthographically unrelated language to their L1.

A further exploration of how phonological decoding skills relate to reading ability focuses on the three most advanced readers (PS5, SQ15, SQ14) and the three least advanced readers (JZ12, PS9, JZ6). By focusing on a few of the most advanced and least advanced readers, a detailed qualitative analysis can be carried out to gain some insight into what exactly they do differently. Table 4.7 provides the information concerning their use of different vowel decoding strategies, and performance on different graphemic units. Table 4.8 reports each of the 6 participants' error rate involving graphemic units of different complexity.

Table 4.7 The vowel decoding strategies used by top 3 and bottom 3 readers

Top 3 and bottom 3 readers		Whole word	Decoding (Total)	Decoding – MAGPC-SR	Decoding – MAGPC-IR	Decoding – MAGPC-NR	Decoding – MIGPC	Others	Nonword test (%)	Reading comprehension test (%)	Real word test (%)
1st lowest	JZ12	18	9	0	4	4	1	9	2.4	20.6	30.7
2nd lowest	PS9	7	13	1	7	3	2	16	11.9	38.2	37.3
3rd lowest	JZ6	16	12	3	5	2	2	8	4.8	35.3	47.3
3rd highest	SQ14	5	29	13	4	12	0	2	54.8	85.3	94.0
2nd highest	SQ15	4	32	13	4	14	1	0	64.3	85.3	98.0
1st highest	PS5	4	30	14	3	11	2	2	57.1	94.1	97.3

Table 4.8 The performance on graphemic units of different complexity among top 3 and bottom 3 readers

Top 3 and bottom 3 readers		Consonant errors								Vowel errors							
		Total (Max. = 94)		SC errors (Max. = 63)		CC errors (Max. = 21)		CD errors (Max. = 10)		Total (Max. = 48)		SV errors (Max. = 36)		VC errors (Max. = 8)		Split VD errors (Max. = 4)	
		F	P (%)	F	P (%)	F	P (%)	F	P (%)	F	P (%)	F	P (%)	F	P (%)	F	P (%)
1st lowest	JZ12	53	56.4	29	46	16	76	8	80	32	67	23	64	6	75	3	75
2nd lowest	PS9	27	28.7	7	11	15	71	5	50	38	79	30	83	5	63	3	75
3rd lowest	JZ6	33	35.1	16	25	15	71	2	20	31	65	23	64	5	63	3	75
3rd highest	SQ14	7	7.4	2	3	3	14	2	20	15	31	7	19	4	50	4	100
2nd highest	SQ15	4	4.3	1	2	2	10	1	10	12	25	9	25	1	13	2	50
1st highest	PS5	8	8.5	4	6	4	19	0	0	15	31	12	33	2	25	1	25

Note F frequency of error occurrence, *P* percentage, *SC* single consonant, *CC* consonant cluster, *CD* consonant diagraph, *SV* single vowel letter (e.g. *a*), *VC* non-split letter combination representing vowel (e.g. *oi*), *Split VD* split vowel digraph (e.g. *a-e*)

JZ12 scored the lowest in the nonword reading test, the real word reading test, and the reading comprehension test. His number of consonant errors was the greatest, and the number of his vowel errors ranked 10th among the 54 participants. He performed particularly badly in converting consonant letters or letter strings into corresponding sounds. 53 out of the 94 consonant orthographic units were decoded inaccurately. His deficiency in decoding consonant orthographic units was revealed particularly in decoding consonant orthographic units involving two or more letters, i.e. consonant clusters and consonant digraphs. Only 5 out of 21 consonant clusters were decoded successfully and only 2 out of 10 consonant digraphs were mapped correctly onto their sounds. His performance on single consonant letter-sound relations was also rather poor—almost half of them were incorrect (29 single consonant errors out of the total possible of 63). Such poor performance on decoding consonant graphemes of different complexity, combined with his total insensitivity to rime units when decoding vowel graphemes, indicates that JZ12 had not completed Ehri's partial-alphabetic phase of learning to read in English (1992, 1999, 2005a). Moreover, he most often read the nonwords as real words (18 out of 42 nonword test items). For example, *lun* was misread as *lunch*, *yat* as *rat*, *knud* as *kid*, *plaf* as *pan*, and *haif* as *half*, etc. It seemed that he might still be at the pre-alphabetic phase, where according to Ehri's (1992, 1999, 2005a) phase model, L1 children lack knowledge of letter sounds and read words logographically, focusing on the shape or length of the word, learning words by rote, and guessing words from context. The visual-analysis dominant method of learning to read Chinese characters might reinforce this phase. An alternative explanation is that he was still stuck at the partial-alphabetic phase of learning to read in English, processing only partial letter-sound relations, i.e. mapping only initial and/or final letters to their sounds and overlooking other letters and their corresponding sounds. In addition, he only used a decoding strategy with 9 out of 36 monosyllabic nonwords. His reliance on whole-word visual reading strategy and poor decoding skills explain his very low score on the reading comprehension and real word reading test. He probably tended to use a more word-specific mechanism than a decoding mechanism, i.e. behaved more like a Chinese reader than a Phoenician reader (Baron 1979; Bowey 2008; Gough and Walsh 1991). According to Baron (1979), Bowey (2008) and Gough and Walsh (1991), skilled readers require both mechanisms, i.e. a more balanced word reading profile. Gough and Walsh (1991) suggested that there are semi-skilled readers who might be called Phoenician, but there is no Chinese counterpart. If a child does not have the ciphers, s/he can only be a poor reader. However, it is obvious that JZ12 used the whole word visual mechanism much more often than the orthographic mechanism. Such an imbalanced use of the two mechanisms may explain his poor reading ability. He probably needs to receive extra instruction in phonological decoding skills and to be trained to process letters in words more thoroughly. Or he might need to learn more English, e.g. acquiring English phonology and accumulating more oral vocabulary. Otherwise, he might have great difficulty in moving on to the full-alphabetic phase of decoding English words.

PS9 scored the second lowest in terms of average score on the real word and reading comprehension tests. Compared with JZ12, who obtained 46% incorrect in decoding single consonant graphemes, PS9 performed much better and scored 11% incorrect in decoding single consonant graphemes. However, in decoding consonant clusters and vowel graphemes, like JZ12, PS9 also made many mistakes (71% incorrect in decoding consonant clusters; 50% incorrect in decoding consonant digraphs; 79% incorrect in decoding vowel graphemes). It seems that he possessed the working knowledge of the major grapheme-phoneme correspondences of single consonants, but not of more complex consonant orthographic units and vowel graphemes. In terms of vowel decoding strategy use, similarly to JZ12, he only decoded vowel graphemes with sensitivity to rime units once. This may be due to his lack of knowledge of rime spelling patterns consolidated out of the grapheme-phoneme correspondence of the vowel letter(s) that recur in words. All this evidence suggests that PS9 had not entered the full-alphabetic phase of learning to read, which is characterised by the working knowledge of more complex consonant orthographic units (consonant clusters and consonant digraphs) and vowel orthographic units (single vowel letters and vowel digraphs) (Ehri 1992, 1999, 2005a). Although he did not show the same pattern of relying on a whole word visual reading strategy as JZ12 did, PS9 used other strategies, probably guessing, more often. This suggests that PS9 tended to be more like a Phoenician reader although his phonological decoding skills are still underdeveloped so that he had to use guessing strategies on many occasions to compensate for his lack of GPC knowledge.

JZ6 scored the third lowest in terms of average score in the real word and reading comprehension tests. He made many fewer mistakes with single consonant graphemes (25% incorrect) than JZ12 (46% incorrect), but more than PS9 (11% incorrect). Yet in decoding consonant digraphs, JZ6 (20% incorrect) made fewer mistakes than PS9 (50% incorrect), and performed the same as P9 (29% incorrect) in decoding consonant clusters. The vowel graphemes were decoded with a similar low accuracy rate (JZ6: 65% incorrect; PS9: 79% incorrect; JZ12: 67% incorrect). Like PS9, JZ6 also rarely decoded vowel graphemes with sensitivity to rime units (3 out of 36 monosyllabic nonwords). Such performance on graphemic units of different complexity and the rare use of rime strategy suggest that PS9 was probably at the same partial alphabetic phase as PS9 and may be a little further within that stage. But different from PS9 who tended to be more like a Phoenician reader and relied much on guessing strategy, JZ6 relied more on whole word visual strategy than on graphophonic analysis, as JZ12 did. Therefore, without sufficient working knowledge of major GPC knowledge and proper decoding strategies, he could not move from the partial alphabetic to the full alphabetic phase, which is a critical prerequisite for children to accumulate more and more sight words and develop their reading ability.

Compared with the three least advanced readers, the three most advanced readers performed much better in decoding orthographic unis, with error rates of consonant decoding of 8.5% (PS5), 4.3% (SQ15) and 7.4% (SQ14), and error rates of vowel decoding of 31% (PS5), 25% (SQ15) and 31% (SQ14). All of them showed a good knowledge of the letter sound relations of consonant graphemes. But their error rates of decoding single vowel graphemes and non-split vowel digraphs seem to suggest that they had not reached the end of the full alphabetic phase. One reason could be that they acquired a working knowledge of GPCs but were not skillful enough at applying their GPC knowledge consistently, and thereby might need more practice in applying this knowledge, especially of vowel graphemes, in word decoding. Another reason could be that their GPC knowledge is developing and is still incomplete. Or despite their sufficient knowledge of major GPCs introduced in their phonics lessons, they might not be familiar with some basic rules (e.g. a vowel letter usually has its short sound in a stressed and closed syllable), and therefore might map an inappropriate sound to the vowel letter. But PS5, who ranked first in terms of reading ability, was able to decode 3 out of 4 split vowel digraphs hierarchically, which is a feature of the consolidated alphabetic phase (Ehri 1992, 1999, 2005a). In that sense, PS5 might be near the end point of the full alphabetic phase. Moreover, all of the three most advanced readers used decoding strategies with most of the 36 monosyllabic nonwords, showed sensitivity to rime units with 2/3 of the nonwords that have rime-level base words, and used the Chinese readers' word-specific mechanism with only 4 to 5 nonwords. They tended to be much more like Phoenician readers than Chinese readers. Their greater ability in phonological decoding might enable them to learn to read English words more efficiently and more accurately than other learners and therefore score the highest in reading comprehension test and real word test. Or it could be the other way round. As their English is better, they are better at reading and comprehending and therefore have a stronger base to develop their phonological decoding skills.

To sum up, the three most advanced readers had more knowledge of grapheme-phoneme correspondences than the three least advanced readers, and tended to be more like Phoenician readers, who apply graphophonic analysis with more sensitivity to rime units in reading words, than like Chinese readers, who apply a whole word visual strategy to read words. Such evidence supports the positive correlation between phonological decoding and reading ability.

4.4 Summary

In general, there are some specific types of orthographic units that cause more problems than others in decoding tasks, such as vowels in general, consonant clusters, less common consonant digraphs, and the consonant orthographic units in final position. Accordingly, although children might be able to overcome phonological difficulties and eventually associate correct sounds to the difficult graphemes on their own and with more exposure to English, teachers should be aware that these orthographic units may cause particular difficulties to their students in learning to decode English words and some children may not be developmentally ready to deal with them.

Good readers tend to use more decoding strategies and fewer whole word reading strategies. They tend to have a better knowledge of major grapheme-phoneme correspondences and rely more on rime units when decoding vowel graphemes. This implies that phonics instruction may complement the teaching of major grapheme-phoneme correspondences with the introduction of rime units, in which the sounds of vowel graphemes are more stable. More importantly, in teaching children to decode words that contain regular GPCs, the decoding strategy and a thorough analysis should be modelled, instead of using the whole word visual strategy to introduce word sound, so that non-analytic children can be encouraged to become more so. But it should be noted that the effectiveness of the teaching of phonological decoding may depend on whether children have built up their working knowledge of English sounds, English phonological system and whether they have accumulated sufficient English vocabulary. Without these foundations in place, phonics instruction could be confusing and ineffective.

Finally, Chinese children's phonological decoding ability strongly correlates with their reading ability and follows similar developmental stages as L1 children. None of the participants seemed to have reached the full alphabetic phase. Participants also varied widely in the extent to which their knowledge and skills of phonological decoding were developed. Some participants were still stuck at the earlier phase of partial alphabetic phase, while some were near the end point of the full alphabetic phase.

The next chapter will describe, interpret and to some extent evaluate the teaching of phonological decoding that the participants received, to enable the tentative exploration of the links between their English phonological decoding ability and the phonological decoding instruction they received in the English classroom.

References

Adams, M. J. (1990). *Beginning to read: Thinking and learning about print*. Urbana-Champaign, IL: Center for the Study of Reading.

Baron, J. (1979). Orthographic and word-specific mechanisms in children's reading of words. *Child Development, 50*(1), 60–72.

Bowey, J. A. (2008). Is a "Phoenician" reading style superior to a "Chinese" reading style? Evidence from fourth graders. *Journal of Experimental Child Psychology, 100*(3), 186–214.

Bryson, S. E., & Werker, J. F. (1989). Toward understanding the problem in severely disabled readers. Part I: Vowel errors. *Applied Psycholinguistics, 10*(1), 1–12.

Byrne, B., Freebody, P., & Gates, A. (1992). Longitudinal data on the relations of word-reading strategies to comprehension, reading time, and phonemic awareness. *Reading Research Quarterly, 27*(2), 141–151.

Cain, K. (2010). *Reading development and difficulties* (Vol. 8). Chichester: J. Wiley & Sons.

Chen, R., & Vellutino, F. R. (1997). Prediction of reading ability: A cross-validation study of the simple view of reading. *Journal of Literacy Research, 29*(1), 1–24.

Chu, H. (2002). Beginning EFL learners' decoding skill and word reading ability. *Taipei Municipal Teachers College Journal, 33*, 471–484.

Davis, C., & Bryant, P. (2006). Causal connections in the acquisition of an orthographic rule: A test of Uta Frith's developmental hypothesis. *Journal of Child Psychology and Psychiatry, 47*(8), 849–856.

Ehri, L. C. (1992). Reconceptualizing the development of sight word reading and its relationship to recoding. In P. Gough, L. Ehri, & R. Treiman (Eds.), *Reading acquisition* (pp. 107–143). Hillsdale, NJ: Lawrence Erlbaum Associates.

Ehri, L. C. (1999). Phases of development in learning to read words. In J. Oakhill & R. Beard (Eds.), *Reading development and the teaching of reading* (pp. 79–108). Oxford: Blackwell publishers.

Ehri, L. C., & McCormick, S. (1998). Phases of word learning: Implications for instruction with delayed and disabled readers. *Reading & Writing Quarterly, 14*(2), 135–163.

Ehri, L. C. (2005a). *Development of sight word reading: Phases and findings.* Oxford: Blackwell Publishing Ltd.

Ehri, L. C. (2005b). Learning to read words: Theory, findings, and issues. *Scientific Studies of Reading, 9*(2), 167–188.

Gough, P. B., & Walsh, M. A. (1991). Chinese, phoenicians, and the orthographic cipher of English. In S. A. Brady & D. P. Shankweiler (Eds.), *Phonological processes in literacy: A tribute to Isabelle Y. Liberman* (pp. 199–209). Hillsdale, NJ: Lawrence Erlbaum Associates.

Hamada, M., & Koda, K. (2010). The role of phonological decoding in second language word-meaning inference. *Applied linguistics, 31*(4), 513–531.

Hoover, W. A., & Gough, P. B. (1990). The simple view of reading. *Reading and Writing, 2*(2), 127–160.

Huang, H., & Hanley, J. (1995). Phonological awareness and visual skills in learning to read Chinese and English. *Cognition, 54*(1), 73–98.

Laxon, V., Gallagher, A., & Masterson, J. (2002). The effects of familiarity, orthographic neighbourhood density, letter-length and graphemic complexity on children's reading accuracy. *British Journal of Psychology, 93*(2), 269–287.

Locke, J. L. (1983). *Phonological acquisition and change.* New York: Academic Press.

McLeod, S., van Doorn, J., & Reed, V. A. (2001). Normal acquisition of consonant clusters. *American Journal of Speech-Language Pathology, 10*(2), 99–110.

Ohala, D. K. (2008). Phonological acquisition in a first language. In J. G. H. Edwards & M. L. Zampini (Eds.), *Phonology and second language acquisition* (pp. 19–39). Amsterdam, Philadelphia: John Benjamins Publishing.

Peng, P., & Tao, S. (2009). Native Chinese-speaking children learning to read English: The role of decoding, English language comprehension and general cognitive ability. *Foreign Language Teaching and Research, 41*(1), 30–37.

Protopapas, A., Simos, P. G., Sideridis, G. D., & Mouzaki, A. (2012). The components of the simple view of reading: A confirmatory factor analysis. *Reading Psychology, 33*(3), 217–240.

Rixon, S. (2011). *Beyond ABC: Investigating current rationales and systems for the teaching of early reading to young learners of English.* (Unpublished PhD thesis). University of Warwick.

Roberts, T. A. (2005). Articulation accuracy and vocabulary size contributions to phonemic awareness and word reading in English language learners. *Journal of Educational Psychology, 97*(4), 601–616.

Seymour, P. H. K., Bunce, F., & Evans, H. M. (1992). A framework for orthographic assessment and remediation. In C. M. Sterling & C. Robson (Eds.), *Psychology, spelling and education* (pp. 224–249). Clevedon, England: Multilingual Matters.

Share, D. L. (1995). Phonological recoding and self-teaching: Sine qua non of reading acquisition. *Cognition, 55*(2), 151–218.

Smit, A. B., Hand, L., Freilinger, J. J., Bernthal, J. E., & Bird, A. (1990). The Iowa articulation norms project and its Nebraska replication. *Journal of Speech and Hearing Disorders, 55*(4), 779–798.

Tal, N. F., & Siegel, L. S. (1996). Pseudoword reading errors of poor, dyslexic, and normally achieving readers on multisyllable pseudowords. *Applied Psycholinguistics, 17*(2), 215–232.

Treiman, R., Mullennix, J., Bijeljac-Babic, R., & Richmond-Welty, E. D. (1995). The special role of rimes in the description, use, and acquisition of English orthography. *Journal of Experimental Psychology: General, 124*(2), 107.

Vandervelden, M. C., & Siegel, L. S. (1995). Phonological recoding and phoneme awareness in early literacy: A developmental approach. *Reading Research Quarterly, 30*(4), 854–875.

Vellutino, F. R., Scanlon, D. M., & Spearing, D. (1995). Semantic and phonological coding in poor and normal readers. *Journal of Experimental Child Psychology, 59*(1), 76–123.

Wang, Y., Lin, C., & Yu, G. (2002). Relationship between phonological skill and reading comprehension ability among poor English learners. *Acta Psychologica Sincia, 34*(3), 279–283.

Yin, L., Anderson, R. C., & Zhu, J. (2007). Stages in Chinese children's reading of English words. *Journal of Educational Psychology, 99*(4), 852–866.

Zhao, D. (1995). *English phonetics and phonology: As compared with Chinese features.* Qingdao, China: Qingdao Ocean University Press.

Chapter 5
The Teaching of Phonological Decoding

This chapter reports findings and provides discussion of both qualitative and quantitative analyses of the data collected from the teaching materials for phonological decoding, and the actual classroom teaching of phonological decoding.

5.1 Phonological Decoding Teaching Materials

This section reports results and provides discussion of the analyses of the textbook, students' workbook and teacher's books pertaining to the teaching of phonological decoding, with a view of addressing research questions 4, 5 and 6. Results of the interview with textbook writer are also used to supplement and triangulate the data collected from the teaching materials. Answers to these research questions are concerned with the scope and sequence of the component knowledge and skills of phonological decoding as reflected in the textbook, the relevant practice presented in the teaching materials, and the extent to which the letter sound relations are taught for sounding out the words in each phonics section, and in the textbook vocabulary.

5.1.1 Scope and Sequence

The scope and sequence of the knowledge and skills related to phonological decoding are summarised below, based on the textbook and teacher's book (Table 5.1).

K. Hua, *The Learning and Teaching of Phonological Decoding in Chinese EFL Children*, https://doi.org/10.1007/978-981-97-6891-2_5

Table 5.1 Syllabus of the teaching of letters and sounds

Textbook	Teaching objectives	Letters and sounds	Rime patterns
1A & 1B[1]	/	/	/
2A	Learn the names and shapes of letters a-z	Aa Bb Cc Dd Ee Ff Gg Hh Ii Jj Kk Ll Mm Nn Oo Pp Qq Rr Ss Tt Uu Vv Ww Xx Yy Zz	/
2B	Identify and pronounce the sounds of single consonant letters correctly in words	p, b ;[2] t, d ┊ k, g ┊ h ┊ f, v ┊ s, z ┊ m, n ┊ l, r	/
3A	Identify and pronounce the sounds of single vowel letters correctly in words	a (table) ┊ a (jam) ┊ e (he) ┊ e (ten) ┊ i (kite) ┊ i (pig) ┊ o (photo) ┊ o (dog) ┊ u (pupil) ┊ u (sun)	/
3B	Identify and pronounce the sounds of consonant digraphs and clusters correctly in words (to be continued)	ch ┊ sh ┊ wh ┊ <u>ck</u>[3] ┊ <u>ll</u> ┊ <u>ss</u> ┊ <u>ff</u> ┊ <u>cl</u>, <u>pl</u>, <u>gl</u> ┊ <u>bl</u>, <u>fl</u>, <u>sl</u>	/
4A	Identify and pronounce the sounds of consonant digraphs and clusters correctly in words	<u>-sk</u> ┊ <u>-sp</u> ┊ <u>-st</u> ┊ sh ┊ dr, <u>pr</u> ┊ <u>br</u>, <u>cr</u> ┊ <u>fr, gr</u>, tr ┊ <u>sl</u>, <u>sn</u>, <u>sw</u> ┊ <u>sm</u>-, <u>sp</u>-, <u>st</u>- ┊ <u>sc</u>-, <u>sk</u>- ┊ th (this) ┊ th- (thin), -th (path)	/
4B	Identify and pronounce the sounds of letter combinations representing vowels correctly in words	ar, <u>ue</u>, oo ┊ ir, ur, au, oor ┊ ee, ea, eer, ear ┊ ie ┊ <u>oe</u>, oa ┊ oy, oi ┊ <u>are</u>, ear, air ┊ ou, ow ┊ ay, ai	/
5A	Learn International phonetic alphabet (IPA) symbols for phonemes	/iː/[4] (e, e_e*,[5] ee, ea), /ɪ/ (i, y) ┊ /ɛ/ (e, a*, ea*), /æ/ (a) ┊ /p/ (p), /b/ (b), /t/ (t), /d/ (d), /k/ (k, c*, ck), /g/ (g) ┊ /ɑː/ (a*, ar), /ʌ/ (u, o*) ┊ /uː/ (u*, oo), /ʊ/ (u*, oo*) ┊ /f/ (f), /v/ (v), /θ/ (th), /ð/ (th) ┊ /s/ (s, c*), /z/ (z, s*), /ts/ (ts*), /dz/ (ds*) ┊ /ɔː/ (or*, al*, au, oor) ┊ /ɒ/ (o, a*) /ɜː/ (er*, ir, ur, or*) ┊ /ə/ (er*, a*) ┊ /ʧ/ (ch), /ʤ/ (g*, j*), /ʃ/ (sh), /ʒ/ (s*) ┊ /tr/ (tr), /dr/ (dr)	/

(continued)

Table 5.1 (continued)

Textbook	Teaching objectives	Letters and sounds	Rime patterns
5B	Learn International phonetic alphabet (IPA) symbols for phonemes	/eɪ/ (a, a-e*, ai, ay, eigh*), /aɪ/ (i, i-e*, y*, igh*, ie) ⋮ /ɪə/ (ear, ere*, eer), /eə/ (air, ere*, ear) ⋮ /ɔɪ/ (oy, oi), /ʊə/ (ure*, our*, oor*) ⋮ /əʊ/ (o, o-e*, ow*, oa) ⋮ /aʊ/ (ou, ow) ⋮ /m/ (m), /n/ (n), /ŋ/ (ng*, n(k)*, n(g))* ⋮ /j/ (y*), /h/ (h, wh*), /w/ (w*, wh) ⋮ /l/ (l), /r/ (r) ⋮ /θ/ (th), /ð/ (th)	/

[1] 1A represents the first semester of primary grade 1. 1B represents the second semester of primary grade 1
[2] ⋮ separates each unit
[3] Letters that are underlined represent the ones that are not revisited in the textbooks 5A and 5B
[4] Symbols in // represent the phonemic symbols following the conventions of the International Phonetic Alphabet (abbreviated as IPA)
[5] Letters that are marked with asterisks represent the alternative spellings for the phonemes that are not covered in grades 2, 3, and 4

5.1.1.1 Phonological Awareness

No explicit phonological awareness training is identified in the first grade, namely before the teaching of letters and sounds begins in grade 2. However, some phonological awareness training may be embedded in the section "Listen and enjoy"[1] across the textbook for all grades, because reading and listening to the nursery rhymes or songs in that section may allow students to notice the rimes or alliterations. Such practice of implicit phonological awareness training before the teaching of letter sounds is different from the phonics programme "Letters and Sounds" developed in the UK Primary National Strategy (Department for Education and Skills 2007b), which assigns the very first phase of its phonics programme to the explicit training of children's phonological awareness, e.g. producing rhyming words, identifying alliterations, blending and segmenting phonemes orally. It is hoped that phonological awareness training can pave the way for L1 children to make a good and quick start in learning to decode English words using letter-sound relations. However, for Chinese EFL children who are at the very beginning of learning English, the implicit phonological awareness training may be more beneficial at the early stage of learning to read because their working knowledge of English sounds is still limited.

From grade 2 on, the training of phoneme identification skill is explicitly stated in the textbook phonics syllabus. Each unit of the teacher's books (except those for grade 1) states one of the teaching objectives for listening skills as "identifying the

---

[1] "Listen and enjoy" is a section that can be found in each unit of the textbook *English (Oxford Shanghai Edition)* (abbreviated as OE). It has a nursery rhyme or a song that reviews the topic of the unit.

sounds of letter(s) (e.g. <ch>) in words (e.g. *chair*, *chick*)". The different positions of single consonant letters and consonant letter combinations within words also allow children to practise identifying phonemes in initial, medial and final positions. For example, in OE 2B, single consonant letters are introduced usually at both initial and final positions (e.g. *pig*, *skip*), except <b>, <v> and <r>, which are introduced at initial and medial positions (e.g. *bag*, *table*). In that sense, phoneme identification skill, which as discussed in Sect. 2.2.1 is the most rudimentary phonemic awareness skill strongly related to early phonological decoding ability, is explicitly taught along with the instruction of letter sounds in the OE syllabus. This is in line with the results of some studies (Ball and Blachman 1991; Chen 2003; National Reading Panel 2000; Piasta and Wagner 2010; Qiu 2007; Stuart 1999) indicating that training in phonological awareness is most beneficial when combined with the teaching of letters.

In addition, the training of phoneme articulation and phoneme discrimination is also explicitly incorporated in the syllabus for teaching letters and sounds. Each unit of the teacher's books (except those for grade 1) explicitly states one of the teaching objectives for the section "Learn the sounds" as "pronouncing the sounds of letters (e.g. <ch>) correctly in words (e.g. *chair*, *chick*)". Phoneme discrimination training is also embedded in the teaching of letter sounds. For example, the introduction of single consonant letters in the form of consonant minimal pairs (e.g. <p>/<b>, <t>/<d>) in OE 2B draws children's attention to the sound difference between the pair of consonants. And in the "listen and circle" task in OE 5A and 5B, which requires children to choose the word they hear, between two words that are usually minimal pairs (e.g. *bean/bin*, *share/chair*), children's skill in discriminating between phonemes is explicitly trained.

The importance attached to phoneme articulation and discrimination in the OE syllabus is noteworthy and echoes some researchers' (Birch 2007; Rixon 2011; Verhoeven 2000; Wade-Woolley and Geva 2000) views about the teaching of phonological decoding to EFL children, to whom full and reliable access to the whole English phoneme repertoire and the ability to discriminate the phonemic contrasts specific to English are required for the acquisition of English grapheme-phoneme correspondences (see details in Sect. 2.5.3.1). Accordingly, the explicit training in articulating and discriminating phonemes in OE enables children to acquire English sounds, which is essential for developing phonological decoding skills.

In contrast, the development of phoneme blending skill is not explicitly included as one of the teaching objectives at primary level. Neither are teaching and learning tasks in the textbooks explicitly designed to help children develop oral blending of the sounds of spoken words, whether at the level of larger sub-word units (syllables, rimes), or at the phoneme level. However, we concede that the teaching of consonant blends may involve training in phoneme blending. This is different from the practice of the UK PNS phonics programme, which attaches great importance to the explicit training in blending phonemes. As discussed in Sect. 2.5.2, although Pinyin instruction in grade 1 allows children to practise blending phoneme onset and rime (Shu et al. 2008), the blending of medial and final phonemes is not involved in teaching Pinyin. Therefore, Chinese children need some explicit training in blending the phonemes within rime structure, i.e. medial vowel and final consonant, in learning to read in English, despite the possibility that rich experience with printed words may allow children to develop such ability on their own.

5.1.1.2 Letters and Sounds

The knowledge and skills related to phonological decoding explicitly covered in the primary textbooks in the present study include the names and shapes of 26 letters in both uppercase and lowercase, and the sounds of single letters and letter combinations. This finding is consistent with the textbook writer's description of the textbook design for developing children's ability to use phonics rules to sound out words:

> The teaching of knowledge and skills required for children to apply phonics rules to sound out words is presented in the section "Learn the letters" in OE 2A, and "Learn the sounds" in the textbook for the following grades. Children are required to be able to sound out the letter or letter combination. (TW)

The instruction of letter-sound relations focuses on the smaller size of sub-word units, i.e. graphemes, rather than larger word segments, i.e. rime patterns, e.g. <at>, <ock>. No phonic generalizations (e.g. when there is one <e> in a word that ends in a consonant, the letter <e> usually has a short sound) are explicitly stated in the textbooks or teacher's books.

The teaching of letters and sounds starts from grade 2. In the first semester of grade 2, the teaching of letters focuses on the letter names and shapes in both upper and lower cases. As each letter is accompanied with an example word that usually starts with the letter, children may also be aware that a letter can represent a sound in a word (e.g. <n> for *net*). It is obvious that the instruction of letter-sound relations is incremental from grade 2 through grade 4, progressing from the simple to the relatively more complex, i.e. from single consonant letters (2B) to single vowel letters (3A), to letter combinations representing consonants (3B & 4A), and to letter combinations representing vowels (4B). In grade 5, the focus of phonics instruction shifts to the International Phonetic Alphabet (IPA) symbols for the 44 English phonemes and 4 blends of sounds (e.g. /æ/ for the sound of <a> in *cat*; /ts/ for the sound of <ts> in *lights*). All 44 English phonemes have already been covered in the previous grades 1 to 4, except 3 new phonemes (/ʊ/, /ə/, /ʊə/), and 2 new blends of sounds (/ts/ and /dz/). Meanwhile, common graphemes for the 44 phonemes and 4 blends of sounds are also listed under the corresponding IPA symbols, e.g. <i>, <i-e>, <y>, <igh> and <ie> for /aɪ/, <dr> for /dr/. Among the 96 correspondences between letters and sounds covered in textbooks 5A and 5B, 42 are newly introduced (see Table 5.1). For instance, <igh>, <i-e> and <y> are newly included for /aɪ/, in addition to previously taught <i> and <ie>. The remaining 54 correspondences in textbooks 5A and 5B are the ones that have been covered in the previous textbooks. In that sense, although the teaching objective of "Learn the sounds" in grade 5 is to teach the IPA symbols, new letter-sound relations are introduced and some relations are revisited. But it should be noted that 28 correspondences are not revisited in grade 5 textbooks. 21 of them are consonant clusters, 3 consonant digraphs, 3 letter combinations representing vowels, and 1 single vowel letter.

Letter names and shapes are intended to be taught before letter-sound relations in OE. According to some studies (Cardoso-Martins et al. 2011; Piasta and Wagner 2010; Share 2004), letter names can facilitate the learning of letter-sound relations when some letter names contain their sounds (e.g. <t> named *tea* contains /t/). Moreover, the knowledge of letter names can be conducive to the teaching of the sounds of letter combinations, as it may be misleading to refer to the graphemes <aw> as /æ/-/ w/, <sh> as /s/-/h/, without reference to the letter names (Department for Education and Skills 2007a).

The sequence of introducing letter-sound relations in OE is similar to the general incremental sequence often recommended for L1 children according to Peregoy and Boyle (2012)—single consonants, followed by short and long vowels, and then letter combinations, despite the absence of instruction in rime patterns and syllabication. The explanation given by the textbook writer of OE for the sequence behind the introduction of letter sounds in the textbook corroborates the findings from the material analysis:

> The criteria for the sequence of introducing letter sounds mainly is to start from what our students find easier to what they find more difficult. For example, the sound of single consonant letters is relatively simpler for our students while the letter combinations are more difficult. (TW)

The grapheme-phoneme correspondences of single consonant letters are more consistent and therefore easier than those of single vowel letters, and blends of letters are more complicated than single letters (National Reading Panel 2000). But the sequence in OE is different from that in "Letters and Sounds" programme suggested by the UK Primary National Strategy at least in two respects. Firstly, the PNS introduces single vowel letters along with single consonant letters (e.g. <s>, <a>, <t>, <p>, <i>, <n>) while OE separates the instruction of the two types of single letters (e.g. single consonant letters in 2B, followed by single vowel letters in 3A). *Jolly Phonics* (Lloyd 1992) also arranges the sequence of introducing letter-sound correspondences in a similar manner as the UK Primary National Strategy. A possible interpretation can be that OE may not adopt a synthetic approach in teaching phonics, at least at an early stage. To L1 children, who usually possess a substantial bank of oral vocabulary, the synthetic approach is of immediate effect on their learning to read. For example, with the knowledge of the sounds of <s>, <a>, <t>, <p>, <i>, <n>, and blending skills, they can sound out the words like *sit, is, it, sat, at, pin, pan, pat, nap, nip*, and get access to the meaning in their mental lexicon. Chinese children, however, have a very limited oral vocabulary size and the synthetic approach may not produce the same effect on learning to read English words as it does for L1 children. On the contrary, as Rixon (2011) argued, "analytic phonics, which works by encouraging learners to observe and compare the sound and symbol correspondences in words with which they are already familiar aurally and orally, seems to have more prospect of usefulness for EYL" (p. 90). In addition, the introduction of the long sounds for single vowel letters is postponed until some digraphs and consonant clusters are covered in the PNS; however, the short and long sounds for single vowel letters are simultaneously introduced in OE (3A). One consequent concern with the simultaneous instruction of short and long vowel sounds is that children might feel confused about the choice of sounds for single vowel letters if neither phonic generalisations nor rime patterns are provided for clarification.

No phonic generalisations are explicitly incorporated in the OE scheme for teaching letter-sound relations. The absence of phonic generalisations in the OE textbooks and teacher's books may be in keeping with the widely held belief in the L1 context that asking children to recite or state phonic generalisations is a less effective teaching technique, although phonic generalisations can be used by teachers to explain certain aspects of the word that is under decoding analysis (Ehri 2003; Stahl et al. 1998). The major argument is that some generalisations may be too abstract and complex for children to understand and being able to state a phonic generalisation does not mean being able to use it. Thereby, as Ehri (2003) and Stahl (1992) indicated, a more effective approach is to have children recognise the patterns of letters by reading words that exhibit the generalisation and children will then begin to internalise the generalisations about these words. The UK Primary National Strategy seems to hold the same belief as Ehri (2003) and Stahl (1992), and thereby does not state any phonic generalisations in its "Letters and Sounds" programme, but embeds the generalisations in letter-sound correspondences. For example, instead of teaching the generalisation "when <c> and <h> are next to each other, they make only one sound", it may be more effective to teach the sound of the letter pattern <ch> with following sufficient practice of sounding it out in words. This is in keeping with the design of the phonics syllabus in the textbooks in this study. In OE, some generalisations are also found to be embedded in certain letter patterns. For instance, the letter patterns <a-e>, <e-e>, <i-e>, <o-e> and their corresponding sounds /eɪ/, /iː/, /aɪ/, /əʊ/ are introduced, which actually conveys the generalisation "when there are two vowels, one of which is final <e>, the first vowel is long and the <e> is silent". Also, the generalisations "the first vowel is usually long and the second silent in the digraphs <ai>, <ea>, and <oa>", "words having double <e> usually have the long <e> sound" or "when two of the same consonants are side by side only one is heard", are embedded in the teaching of the sounds of individual graphemes, e.g. <ai> sounded out as /eɪ/, <ea> as /iː/, <oa> as /əʊ/, <ee> as /iː/. It is hoped that with repeated exposure to the patterns, the generalisations can be internalised and the children are saved from the tedious task of memorising those generalisations and understanding them.

However, most of the patterns conveying the phonic generalisations that are presented in the textbooks are limited to the patterns of letter combinations representing vowels or consonants, such as <ch>, <ck>, <ss>, <ai>, <ea>, <ee>, etc. The rime patterns (vowel graphemes followed by final consonants, e.g. <op>, <ot>, <old>) are not included in the teaching scheme. As discussed in Sect. 2.2.3, vowels tend to be more stable within the context of rime patterns. In that sense, rime patterns can be an alternative to teaching phonic generalisations of vowels, which are much less reliable than those of consonants. For example, the rule "when a vowel is in the middle of a one-syllable word, the vowel is short" is applicable to *nod*, rather than *hold*. In this case, the introduction of rime patterns (e.g. <od>, <old>) can be an alternative to the teaching of abstract and broad phonic generalisations and thereby makes additional contribution to decoding beyond letter-sound knowledge (Ehri 2003; Goswami 1999; Johnston 2001; Savage et al. 2003; Stahl et al. 1998).

To recap, OE includes phoneme identification skills explicitly and the awareness of rhymes and alliterations implicitly in its syllabus, while phoneme blending and segmenting skills are not specified. As blending and segmenting in the Pinyin system usually happens at the level of onset and rime, some explicit training in blending and segmenting the phoneme components within rime structure in English may be worthwhile for Chinese children. The training in articulating and discriminating English phonemes runs alongside the teaching of letter-sound relations, to equip Chinese EFL children with full and reliable access to the English phoneme repertoire and phoneme discrimination ability. Following the instruction of letter names and shapes, the knowledge of letter-sound relations are taught in an incremental sequence. The sequence of the letter-sound relations throughout the textbook suggested the analytic phonics approach, at least at the initial stage of learning to read. Two thirds of the graphemes covered in grades 2–4 are revisited in grade 5, and most of those that are not revisited are consonant clusters, which do not exist in Chinese. In addition, neither phonic generalisations nor spelling-sound correspondences at the larger sub-word level of rimes are included as a supplement to the teaching of letter sounds. The concern is that some children might be too overwhelmed by the complexity of sounding out a vowel grapheme, particularly a vowel grapheme that represents a variety of sounds (e.g. <o> can be sounded out as /ɒ/ in *hot*, /əʊ/ in *hold*). Gradually, they may lose interest and confidence in learning and applying phonic knowledge and skills to word decoding. However, it has to be admitted that some children may be able to deduce and extract the generalisations and rime patterns without explicit instruction when they accumulate a sufficiently large vocabulary.

5.1.2 Practice Presented in the Textbook Materials

In this section, the textbook and students' workbook will be examined to find out whether they provide any practice for developing phonological awareness, knowledge of letter names, letter shapes and letter-sound relations, and applying the knowledge and skills in decoding word sound. The teacher's books will also be examined to find out whether any guidance on teaching the above-mentioned knowledge and skills is provided. In addition, the results of the interviews with teachers and the textbook writer provide supplementary explanation and triangulation for the data collected from the analysis of teaching materials, in terms of the practice provided in the textbook materials.

5.1.2.1 Textbook Materials (1A and 1B)

As grade 1 focuses on developing children's listening and speaking skills, the teaching and learning tasks are primarily in the form of songs, rhymes, games and conversations. According to the English version of the materials description in the teacher's books (1A-1B), songs and rhymes are used to review the topic of the unit. Its Chinese version provides a more detailed description of the objective of teaching songs and rhymes, which is translated as follows:

> "Listen and enjoy" contains a rhyme or a song that is related to the topic of the unit. Its main purpose is to create an enjoyable classroom atmosphere through using audio-visual materials, activities such as singing songs and reading nursery rhymes, and in the mean time to develop children's feeling for the English language. The new words and sentence patterns are not the focus of teaching in this part, and children only need to know the general meaning of the rhyme or song. (pii)

In the teacher's books for grade 1, different types of activities pertaining to this section are suggested as below:

(1) listening to the nursery rhyme or song and repeating after it
(2) acting it out
(3) substituting words with other key words in the unit
(4) teacher asking questions using key patterns and students answering the questions.

The use of nursery rhymes and songs has been widely acknowledged as a common technique in developing children's interest in the language (Jarvis 2013). Children's vocabulary and phonological sensitivity (sensitivity to rhyming words, alliterations) can also be developed at the same time. As the nursery rhymes and songs are presented in the textbooks, children therefore might be encouraged to notice the connections between letters and sounds when they listen to them alongside the printed texts. This can pave the way for the development of early partial letter-sound recognition mechanism, as Vandervelden and Siegel (1995) suggested. But it is interesting to note that neither textbooks nor teacher's books draw children's attention directly to the phonological elements. This is probably because at this stage, they are just trying to get the children to get used to hearing English and get a feel for it, instead of explicitly teaching the phonological elements.

5.1.2.2 Textbook Materials (2A)

The teaching of early reading starts from 2A, where letter names and shapes are introduced in a new section "Learn the letters". The teaching of the 26 English letters in both upper and lower cases is spread among the 12 units of 2A. Each letter is accompanied with an example word that usually starts with the letter and a picture to convey the word meaning (e.g. *A, a, apple*; *B, b, bag*). At the end of this section in each unit, a nursery rhyme is provided for practice.

In the students' workbook, there is an exercise related to letter learning that appears in each unit, i.e. saying the letter name and writing the letter, in both upper and lower cases. There are also other exercises available for students to practice, e.g. listening and circling the letter whose name(s) you hear, recognising the letters in both upper and lower cases by colouring the letters, matching the capital letter with its small counterpart.

According to the materials description in the teacher's book (2A), this new section is aimed to teach the letters. The objective is to enable students to identify the letters by listening to their names, pronounce their names correctly, and write them correctly. Nursery rhymes that have the words containing the target letters and pictures are designed to establish a lively classroom atmosphere for learning the letters. And audio-visual materials can also be used to teach the letters.

The majority of activities suggested for teaching the 26 letters are listed as below:

(1) using flashcards to elicit and teach the letters within words
(2) having children listen to the recording and read alongside the recording
(3) having children listen to the recording and then read the letters, words, and rhymes by themselves
(4) writing the letters in both upper and lower cases
(5) matching capital letters with the corresponding small letters.

The guidance that can be found on teaching the letters in the teacher's book mainly relates to pronouncing letter names, and recognising and writing the letters. Despite the above-mentioned limited teaching objective, children are likely to notice that besides the letter name, a letter can also represent a sound in a word, and its name and sound can be similar or different, when learning to read the nursery rhymes.

5.1.2.3   Textbook Materials (2B-4B)

After the introduction of the 26 English letters, the sounds of letters are gradually taught in the new section "Learn the sounds" from 2B through 4B. According to the materials description in the teacher's books (2B-4B), "Learn the sounds" contains "the sounds that help students get to know the pronunciation of different letters in words, including consonant letters, vowel letters, and letter combinations". Details of the types of letters can be found in Table 5.1. In the textbooks, each letter-sound relation is provided with example word(s). In addition, there are pictures to illustrate the meaning of each example word in the textbooks. Additional words containing the target letter-sound relations together with some example words are incorporated within the context of a nursery rhyme for further practice in each unit of textbooks 3A-4B, but not 2B. No exercises are found in the students' workbooks (2B-4B) designed specifically for practicing the letter sounds or applying the taught letter-sound relations to decode words.

The activities suggested in the teacher's books for teaching the sounds of letters are listed as below:

(1) showing children some cards/pictures with letter, word and picture on them, and asking children to repeat the words containing the letter-sound relations after the teacher, until they can correctly pronounce the sounds
(2) having children listen to the recording and repeat
(3) having children listen to the recording and then practise on their own (in groups) the sounds of letters, words, (and rhymes in 3A-4B), for example, *p*, /p/, *pig*
(4) encouraging children to say more words that contain the target letter-sound relations, which can be organised in the form of a competition
(5) the teacher saying more words containing the target sound and writing them on the blackboard for students to practise
(6) the teacher showing more cards of the words with the target sounds and asking students to respond/say them aloud quickly

The majority of activities suggested for teaching the sounds of letters fall into the first four categories. "Learn the sounds" section seems to focus on pronouncing the sounds of individual letters or letter combinations correctly by repeating after the teacher or the recording. However, it is interesting to note that little effort is found to be made in either the textbook or the teacher's book to encourage children to independently decode printed words using their knowledge of taught letter-sound relations, although the National English Curriculum (Ministry of Education 2001, 2011) specifies "being able to sound out simple words based on phonic rules" as one of the descriptors for reading skills that are required to be developed at primary school level. All the activities suggested with the nursery rhyme that contains additional words for practice are either repeating after the recording or practising reading it after listening to the rhyme. Only the sixth activity, which the teacher's book suggests in one unit, provides students with word building activities, i.e. translating letters to sounds and assembling the sounds to form the word. In that sense, children may most of the time just respond while teachers take an active role, if teachers follow the teacher's books. In other words, children may not be given enough opportunities to learn how the letter-sound system works through problem solving.

Moreover, all four teacher interviewees thought the words provided in the phonics section were insufficient for helping children to have a good grasp of the letter-sound relations and to apply what they have learnt in word decoding.

> Most students will still be unable to decode word sound at the end of primary schooling, because there is a lack of systematic learning. Usually only a couple of words are provided for practising the sound of a letter or letter combination in each unit in the textbook. Therefore, if the students do not practice word decoding after class, they still cannot develop their decoding ability very well. (PM)

> There are only several words on the page of "Learn the sounds". We simply read those words aloud several times. That's it. There are not enough additional materials for us to use. And when teaching new words, I sometimes decode some letters while sometimes not. (JZ)

This was congruent with the comments by the textbook writer.

> Because of the limited class hours, the reading materials for practicing phonics knowledge and skills included in the textbook are simple. (TW)

Two teacher interviewees specifically pointed out that some nursery rhymes are not very conducive to practicing phonic knowledge because they contain too many new words and are too long for children to practice reading and recite. For example, in the nursery rhyme presented below, almost every line contains at least one new word.

Mr Bee is having **tea**

   With his friend Miss **Deer**.

Suddenly he falls into the tea,

   And Miss Deer **cries** in **fear**.

'Don't worry,' says Mr Bee.

   'I can **even** swim in **beer**.'

Miss Deer says, 'You **scared** me!'

   And then she **bursts** into **tears**.

(From the textbook 4B)

Notes: Words underlined are new. The target letter combinations are <ee>, <ea>, <eer> and <ear>.

I think the nursery rhymes in the phonics section contain too many words but only several practice words that contain the target letter-sound associations. Some nursery rhymes contain new words. If the words in the rhyme are simple and familiar to the students, they would like to read the rhyme. But if the nursery rhyme is long and contains more than 3 new words, the student will be discouraged from reading aloud and reciting it, because they think it is too difficult and boring to remember new words and the letter sound at the same time. Moreover, they have already had plenty of knowledge to remember within a unit. So I think short captions or sentences are better for our children to practice the taught letter-sound relations. (HL)

Some nursery rhymes are ok while some are very difficult. Perhaps the writer wants to keep the nursery rhymes meaningful. Some are difficult to pronounce and awkward to read... I used to ask children to recite the nursery rhymes in "Learn the sounds" after class and then recite them in the following lessons, but children seemed unable to recite the nursery rhymes vey fluently and I therefore did not make such attempt any more. (PM)

Two teachers (PM and SQ) mentioned that in order to create more opportunities for children to practice the taught phonics knowledge, they would add some exercises.

Except the words and nursery rhymes in the textbook, there are no related exercises in students' workbook for students to practice the taught phonics knowledge and skills. We have to provide some supplementary materials. (PM)

Such supplementary exercises mentioned by the teacher interviewees are either in the same form as in the test papers, i.e. judging whether the underlined graphemes usually in a pair of words share the same sound, or listing some words that contain the same target sound. This resonates with the findings from the classroom observations, pertaining to the phonics activities based on supplementary materials (see details in Sect. 5.2.1.3). And this is also in line with the activities suggested in the teachers' books. It seemed that no additional text materials are provided for children to consolidate their decoding skills.

5.1.2.4 Textbook Materials (5A and 5B)

The section "Learn the sounds" is still there in grade 5 textbooks, but its major objective is to "help students learn the International Phonetic Alphabet" (pii). Here, only the letters and the words containing the letter-sound relations are listed under the corresponding IPA symbol, without pictures to illustrate the meaning. For example, / i:/: <e>, *she, me*; <e_e>, *these, Chinese*; <ee>, *bee, sweet*; <ea>, *sea, read*. In addition, a task "Listen and circle" is provided on the same page for further practice. In this task, children are required to choose the word they hear. No exercises found in the students' workbooks (5A-5B) are designed specifically for practising the letter sounds or applying the taught letter-sound relations to decode words.

The activities suggested in the teacher's books for teaching the sounds of letters are listed as follows:

(1) show the phonetic symbol cards for the sounds, e.g. /i:/ and /ɪ/.
(2) have students read the words in "Learn the sounds" after teacher until they can pronounce the sounds correctly. For example, <e>, /i:/, *she, me*; <e_e>, /i:/, *these, Chinese*; <ee>, /i:/, *bee, sweet*; <ea>, /i:/, *sea, read*.
(3) play the recording and ask the students to repeat after the recording.
(4) ask students to think of more words with the sounds.
(5) ask the students to do the "Listen and circle" exercise in the textbook.
(6) invite some students to read the words in this part after practice.
(7) give students more exercises to practise and compare the sounds they have learnt (see Table 5.2).
(8) Write six words with several sounds on the blackboard (e.g. *it, sleep, cool, book, arm, duck*). Put more flashcards of words containing these sounds at random on the blackboard (e.g. *big, this, happy*; *leaf, sweet, eat*; *moon, school, tooth*; *cook, look, put, full*; *park, sharp, father*; *touch, mother, colour, club*). Ask the students to group the words with the same sounds. Finally, ask them to read the words together*1.
(9) In the last unit of 5A, review all the phonetic symbol cards for the sounds that the students have learnt in the previous units and ask the students to read them. Then ask them to read the words*1.
(10) In the middle of 5B, show the phonetic flashcards for the sounds the students have learnt in the previous units. Have them read together. Have the students play a game. Put the pile of phonetic flashcards on the desk. Ask the students to take turns to read them out. They may collect and give a word with that sound. The student who has the most cards at the end wins the game*1.

Table 5.2 Activities for practising and comparing the sounds that have been learnt

Activity types	Listen and circle the word that is heard *2[a]	Listen and judge whether the printed word is the word they hear *1	Read and circle the word whose underlined part sounds different *3	Listen and write/ complete the spelling of the word that is heard *5
Examples	1. *bed, dad, did*; 2. *bean bin Ben* (Words that are heard: 1. *dad*, 2. *bin*)	1. *read* (False); 2. *big* (False) (Words that are heard: 1. *red*, 2. *bag*)	1. *first nurse water* 2. *door doctor what* 3. *noisy toy boat* (Words that are heard: 1. *water*, 2. *Door*, 3. *boat*)	*a u tumn g i r l h o r se*

[a]The number after * represents the number of units where a certain type of activity is suggested; There are a total of 21 units that contain the section "Learn the sounds" in textbooks 5A and 5B

The majority of suggested activities fall into the first five categories, which serve as routine practice in each unit. Although the major objective of this section is to teach the IPA for English sounds, the list of choices of graphemes under the IPA symbols suggest phoneme-to-grapheme mapping, which is needed for spelling (Department for Education and Skills 2007b), and reading printed example words can also enable children to map phonemes to graphemes. Some previously taught letter-sound relations are also revisited and some additional graphemes for the sounds are introduced. There are a greater variety of activities suggested for teacher's use in this grade compared with the previous grades. For example, more listening activities aim to help children discriminate sounds and convert sounds into letters. However, similar to what is found in the previous textbooks and teacher's books, few word building activities (assembling sounds to make words) are found in this grade for children to practice decoding word sound on their own, e.g. "Read and circle" in activity 7, activity 8 and the 9.

The teacher's books were also examined to find out whether a phonological decoding approach is suggested in teaching vocabulary. In the teacher's books throughout all grades, the sounds of words are suggested to be taught by means of a whole word approach, i.e. using flashcards and asking children to repeat after teacher. For example,

T   (Show the flashcard for underground) Underground. U-N-D-E-R-G-R-O-U-N-D,[2] underground.

SSS   Underground. U-N-D-E-R-G-R-O-U-N-D, underground.

        (The spelling part is skipped in grades 1 and 2 because this is not required until children enter grade 3.)

The teacher's books do not provide any suggestions on using taught phonic knowledge and skills to decode word sounds in vocabulary teaching.

---

[2] The capital letter represents the name of each letter.

Table 5.3 The numbers of letter-sound relations embedded in the OE vocabulary

	Total number	Number (Percentage)—taught
High-frequency letter-sound relations embedded in OE vocabulary	52	46 (88.5%)
Non-high-frequency letter-sound relations embedded in OE vocabulary	203	70 (34.5%)
Total	255	116 (45.5%)

In summary, little explicit training in phonological awareness can be found in the textbook, students' workbooks and teacher's books of early grades. However, phonological awareness may have been implicitly taught through the rhymes and alliterations in the activities involving nursery rhymes, right from the beginning of English learning, i.e. grade 1. And training on the perception, articulation and discrimination of phonemes is integrated into the teaching of letter-sound relations. It cannot be denied that phonological awareness can be developed with the increasing experience of learning to read. Most activities suggested for the teaching of phonological decoding focus on the perception and pronunciation of the letter sounds. There is a noticeable lack of practice in applying the taught letter-sound relations to decode words. Most of the time, the activities suggested to teach the sounds start with repeating the letter sounds in the context of words, after the teacher or the recording. And what is most surprising is that despite the instruction of letter-sound correspondences, the teacher's book still suggests a whole word approach in teaching word sound.

5.1.3 The Coverage of the Letter-Sound Relations

Appendix G presents the letter-sound relations embedded in the primary textbook vocabulary, grouped by different types (single consonant letters, single vowel letters, letter combinations representing vowels, consonant digraphs/trigraphs, consonant clusters, others) and, within each type, ranked in order of the total number of occurrences of the letter-sound relations. Table 5.3 lists the total number of letter-sound relations embedded in the complete vocabulary pool of OE, including high-frequency[3] ones and non-high-frequency[4] ones, as well as the number and percentage of those embedded letter-sound relations that are covered in the textbook phonics syllabus.

---

[3] High-frequency correspondences refer to the ones that are embedded in no less than 20 words in the OE vocabulary list.

[4] Non-high-frequency correspondences refer to the ones that are embedded in less than 20 words in the OE vocabulary list.

As displayed in Table 5.3, nearly half of the letter-sound relations that are embedded in the primary textbook vocabulary are covered in the phonics syllabus. This is in line with the results of the textbook analysis conducted by Kuo (2011), who reported that the percentage of correspondences governing the basic words at primary level that are covered in phonics syllabus ranges from 21.3 to 41.3% among 6 different textbooks in Taiwan. Considering the limited class hours allocated for English teaching, however, it is understandable that not all correspondences required for sounding out all the OE words are covered. In addition, it might be counter-productive to teach correspondences that are infrequent, and therefore making word decoding not very productive. Moreover, it cannot be denied that the untaught corre-spondences between letter(s) and sound(s) may be deduced and learnt by some chil-dren with their increasing experience of printed words. Anyhow, one way to maximise the possibility of decoding words with phonic knowledge and skills is to include as many high-frequency correspondences as possible in the teaching syllabus. The results of textbook analysis showed that 46 out of 52 high-frequency letter-sound relations are covered. OE covers a higher percentage of high-frequency letter-sound relations (88.5%) than the textbooks (Kuo 2011) studied (ranging from 59 to 73%). It seems that the OE textbook writers have tried to include as many high-frequency letter-sound relations as possible in the textbook.

Table 5.4 presents the results of the analysis of the letter-sound relations that are embedded in the monosyllabic vocabulary pool of OE. The textbook phonics syllabus covers 58.1% of the letter-sound relations embedded in the OE monosyllabic words, whereas the high-frequency letter-sound relations embedded in the OE monosyllabic words are all covered in the phonics syllabus. This to some extent indicates that the design of the OE phonics syllabus may focus more on the letter-sound relations required for decoding monosyllabic words, as the national curriculum standards suggests.

Table 5.5 presents the summary of the percentage of decodable words used for practising the target letter-sound relations in the section "Learn the sounds" in the textbook for each semester (see an example in Appendix H). As the section "Learn the sounds" in OE (2B) only includes the sounds of single consonant letters and no vowel sounds are introduced, none of the practice words are fully decodable in OE (2B). With the introduction of the sounds of vowel letters in 3A, the percentage of decodable words increases. It is obvious from Table 5.5 that the percentage of the practice words

Table 5.4 The numbers of letter-sound relations that are embedded in OE monosyllabic vocabulary and of the relations that are taught

	Total number	Number (Percentage)—taught
High-frequency letter-sound relations embedded in OE monosyllabic vocabulary	26	26 (100%)
Non-high-frequency letter-sound relations embedded in OE monosyllabic vocabulary	160	82 (51.3%)
Total	186	108 (58.1%)

that can be fully decoded by using previously taught letter-sound relations is low in lower grades, even for monosyllabic practice words. It is then doubtful whether children would have enough successful experience of sounding out the practice words by fully decoding them and would thereby regard phonological decoding as the prime approach to sounding out words. Additionally, the low percentage of fully decodable words for practice may also suggest that teachers may focus mainly on the target letter-sound relations, without analysing the component letter-sound associations within a word thoroughly and then blending all the sounds to form the word sound.

Considering that the ultimate aim of teaching the sounds of letters is to apply them in decoding word sound, the proportion of the vocabulary that can be sounded out using taught letter-sound relations in each unit of each grade will now be examined. It is hoped that this can reveal a clearer picture of the extent to which children can practise decoding strategies using the phonic knowledge and skills they have been taught.

Table 5.6 presents the percentage of fully decodable words in the vocabulary list for each unit. The percentage of words that can be fully decoded by applying taught letter-sound relations increases with grades, reaching up to 54.3% in the textbook for the last semester of primary schooling. The analysis with monosyllabic words shows the same pattern, except that the percentage of decodable monosyllabic words was a bit higher, but likewise it did not reach a very satisfactory level. Appendix I gives an example of the words that can be fully decoded with reliance on taught letter-sound associations in each unit of OE (4B).

As the teaching of letter-sound relations is incremental from grade 2 through grade 5, it is understandable that there are a very limited number of words that can be sounded out by means of phonological decoding in early grades. If teachers do not demonstrate how to apply phonic knowledge and skills as the prime approach to reading to ensure that their pupils adopt the same primary approach, as indicated in the UK Primary National Strategy (Department for Education and Skills 2007a), children might resort to other strategies, like whole word strategy, as their primary approach to sounding out words, even if the words can be sounded out using taught letter-sound relations.

Table 5.5 The percentage of fully decodable words for practising letter-sound relations in the section "Learn the sounds"

Textbook	Percentage (%) of decodable words for practice (%)	Percentage (%) of decodable monosyllabic words for practice (%)
1A-2B	0	0
3A	38	48
3B	26	30
4A	20	23
4B	67	73
5A	70	74
5B	83	89

Table 5.6 The number and percentage of fully decodable words in the vocabulary list for each unit in different grades

Textbook	Mono and polysyllabic words		Monosyllabic words	
	Mono and polysyllabic words (N)	Decodable mono and polysyllabic words (N (%))	Monosyllabic words (N)	Decodable monosyllabic words (N (%))
1A-2A	138	0 (0%)	99	0 (0%)
2B	58	0 (0%)	35	0 (0%)
3A	245	17 (6.9%)	184	17 (9.2%)
3B	196	19 (9.7%)	123	18 (14.6%)
4A	296	42 (14.2%)	174	38 (21.8%)
4B	302	62 (20.5%)	180	56 (31.1%)
5A	237	92 (38.8%)	148	77 (52.0%)
5B	280	152 (54.3%)	149	106 (71.1%)

To conclude, although around half of the letter-sound relations embedded in the textbook vocabulary are not taught in the textbook, most high-frequency letter-sound relations embedded in the complete vocabulary pool of OE and all the high-frequency letter-sound relations embedded in the monosyllabic vocabulary pool of OE are taught. However, a very small percentage of words for practising letter-sound associations in the section "Learn the sounds" in grades before 4B are fully decodable. This may lead to the emphasis solely on the target letter sounds instead of decoding word sound during the phonics lessons in those grades. Moreover, a small proportion of the textbook vocabulary that can be fully decoded using taught letter-sound relations, particularly at early grades, might persuade teachers and children to sound out a word as a whole most of the time, and therefore hinder children from developing their phonological decoding skills at primary school level. This may also explain why the whole word approach is suggested for teaching word sound throughout the teacher's books.

5.2   The Classroom Teaching of Phonological Decoding

This section reports and discusses the results pertaining to the classroom teaching of phonological decoding. Although the national curriculum incorporates phonological decoding as an approach to sounding out words and the textbook embodies the syllabus for teaching phonological decoding, provides input for classroom lessons, and offers guidance to teachers in planning lessons, it is the teachers who carry the role of executing the syllabus. Therefore, in order to gain a clearer and more comprehensive picture of the teaching of phonological decoding, classroom observations were conducted to investigate research questions 7, 8 and 9, along with the supplementary data collected from teacher interviews. Answers to these research questions are concerned with the phonics instruction in the classroom, the application of phonological decoding in teaching word sound, and the text-level reading activities that may provide opportunities for children to practise phonological decoding.

5.2.1 Phonics Instruction

All four teachers who were interviewed held the belief that phonics instruction is conducive to decoding word sound.

> It is helpful for students to learn to read words. At least they know the sounds of letters, such as <p>, and then they can decode some simple words... Although they might extract a totally wrong sound, they are aware of this method that they can use to read words. (HL)

> It can help students to learn to read words. But children are actually very lazy. With an unfamiliar word, they would directly ask the teacher or just skip it. (JZ)

All the four teacher interviewees pointed out that letter sounds are not the focus of their teaching. Not much attention was drawn to "Learn the sounds" section, which usually takes 10 to 15 min within a unit and a unit usually takes 5–6 sessions of 35 min each.

> There is only one part in the final examination that is related to this section. That test part only contains 5 items (5 pairs of words whose component letters are underlined for students to judge whether the underlined parts share the same sound) and its total score is not high. Therefore, teachers would not pay much attention to the related teaching. (PM)

> We start teaching letters and sounds from grade 2. But meanwhile, we also need to teach vocabulary, texts, and sentence patterns. We can only cover a bit of phonics every week. (JZ)

> There is too much to teach students within a unit, like sentence patterns, vocabulary. We also need to do exercises and prepare for exams, etc. You cannot spend a lot of time on the phonics section. Moreover, this part seems not to be the focus of our teaching; therefore we just cover it. (JZ)

The textbook writer, who was at the same time a teacher trainer, corroborated this dilemma.

> Children cannot grasp all the letter-sound relations because of limited class hours. For 4th grade English classes, there are 5 sessions per week, and each session lasts for 35 minutes. It is impossible for our teachers to pay equally close attention to each section. So this section (phonics section) is not the teaching focus, and students do not necessarily need to be able to sound out <oy>. They just need to feel this. This is not an important section. (TW)

The textbook writer also suggested in the interview spending 5 to 10 min in every lesson on phonics instruction or on the revision of previously taught phonics knowledge and skills.

> Teachers should have a plan of what letter sound relations to be focused on in each lesson during a week and regularly revisit the alphabetic knowledge that has been taught. If they simply cover the letter-sound associations that coincidentally appear in each unit, students will not be able to have a reliable knowledge of letter sounds. (TW)

Teacher PM held the same belief on the revision of phonics but meanwhile she did admit that the regular revision of phonics knowledge and skills could not be ensured, partly because vocabulary and grammar teaching were of overriding importance.

> Phonics instruction would not be effective in helping children to decode words if you just deliver the lesson on letter sound once a week. It is necessary to incorporate the phonics knowledge and skills in every lesson, and frequently revisit them. I sometimes revisit the previously taught phonics content, but sometimes when I am busy with other things, I will forget. For example, these days we are teaching the present progressive tense. As children tend to confuse it with the simple present tense, we spend more time on the teaching of tense... I cannot revisit the previously taught phonics content very regularly. (PM)

The teaching of letter-sound relations was found in three out of four 4th grade English classrooms observed, except school JZ.[5] Similar to the section "Learn the sounds" positioned at the end of each unit[6] in the textbook, phonics instruction also happened after the teaching of all the other sections within the unit. Although all four teacher interviewees reported picking out some graphemes and mapping sounds onto them when teaching new vocabulary, three teachers felt that the phonics section was taught separately and bore no connection to the other sections within the same unit.

> The letter-sound relations appear only once, at the end of a unit. They bear no relations to the previous teaching content within the unit. Moreover, they cannot necessarily be applied in the teaching of next unit. Only when teaching new words, some letter-sound relations can be referred to from time to time. This is because each module (3 units) involves a specific theme, and has little connection with the phonics content. Moreover, the size of vocabulary is small and there are not many opportunities to apply the phonics knowledge taught. So I think the phonics section has little connection with the previous content within a unit, and students forget quickly the letter-sound relations they have just learned. (HL)

Table 5.7 lists the basic information about the phonics instruction in the four primary schools. Further details about how the previously taught phonics knowledge and skills were revisited, and how new letter-sound relations were presented and practised, will be described in Sects. 5.2.1.1, 5.2.1.2 and 5.2.1.3 respectively.

5.2.1.1 Revision of Previous Phonics Lessons

Three out of four teachers (the teachers from schools SQ, HL and PM, abbreviated as teacher SQ, teacher HL, teacher PM) were observed to revisit the previously taught phonics knowledge.

---

[5] The teacher from JZ claimed afterwards in the interview that she usually spent 10 to 15 min teaching the section "Learn the sounds". The missing phonics lesson in the observed JZ class may be due to the loss of a lesson because of a school outing. In order to catch up with the teaching schedule, the teacher skipped that section, which contains one untaught letter-sound correspondence (<ie>) and a taught one (<i>), accompanied with related words and nursery rhyme.

[6] In OE, each textbook consists of 4 modules and each module is composed of 3 units. A unit usually takes 5 to 6 lessons and each lesson takes 35 min. When this study was conducted, 4th graders in Shanghai had 5 lessons per week.

Table 5.7   The overall information about the phonics session in four classes

	SQ	PM	JZ	HL
Number of lessons observed for a whole unit (minutes)	5 lessons (175 min)	5 lessons (175 min)	5 lessons (175 min)	6 lessons (210 min)
Duration of the phonics session within the whole unit	Approx. 25 min (at the end of the unit)	Approx. 10 min (at the end of the unit)	/	Approx. 15 min (at the end of the unit)
Revision of previous phonics lessons	Approx. 7 min	Approx. 1 min	/	Approx. 2 min
Presentation of new letter-sound relations	✓	✓	/	✓
Practice of new letter-sound relations	✓	✓	/	✓

Teacher SQ asked students to judge whether the underlined vowel letters in 10 pairs of words share the same sound (1. p_ar_k, f_a_ther; 2. sch_oo_l, g_oo_d; 3. sk_ir_t, p_ur_se; 4. fl_oo_r, _o_ffice; 5. t_ea_, m_e_; 6. f_i_ve, p_i_g; 7. b_oa_t, h_o_le; 8. n_oi_se, sh_or_t; 9. d_ear_, t_ear_; 10. h_ear_, b_ear_). Additionally, students were asked to write the IPA symbol for each vowel letter on the blackboard, and to repeat the vowel sound and word sound after the teacher. All the vowel letter combinations were taught in the previous units in textbook 4B.

Teacher HL revisited the vowel letter combinations taught in the previous unit, mainly through oral activities, although the example words were written on the blackboard. Students were asked to recognise and pronounce the shared sounds of two words, and to repeat the sounds of letters and words after the teacher. They were also asked to recall the IPA symbols for the sounds. For instance,

T (HL)	The second pair. They also share the same sound. Listen carefully.
Ss (volunteers)	Blue.
T (HL)	Listen, blue.
SSS	Blue.
T (HL)	School.
SSS	School.
Ss (volunteers)	/uː/
T (HL)	Good job. They all have /uː/. Follow me. /uː/
SSS	/uː/
…	
T (HL)	U-E, /uː/

SSS	U-E /uː/

...

T (HL)	O-O /uː/
SSS	O-O /uː/
T (HL)	Ok. Do you remember, how to write?
Ss (volunteers)	\<u plus two dots\> /uː/ /uː/ /uː/

Teacher PM did not revisit the previous phonics lessons in as detailed a way as the other two teachers. She simply included pairs of words *wheel, bell, hear* (as comparison with *hair*) and *deer* (as comparison with *pear*) in an exercise, which required students to read the two words and judge whether the underlined letter combinations share the same sound. In this way, student's knowledge of the sounds of letters \<ee\>, \<l\>, \<e\>, \<ll\>, \<ear\> (as /ɪə/), and \<eer\> was reinforced. But this exercise could be confusing for the children if they had not fully assimilated these letter-sound relations.

5.2.1.2   Presentation of Letter-Sound Relations

Table 5.8 briefly summarises the approaches used by the teachers when presenting new letter-sound relations to their students in the phonics sessions observed.

Both teachers HL and PM always elicited the sounds of letters from word sounds, when the words had been taught before. For example,

T (PM)	Look at the screen. Tell me what shape is it? It's a ...
SS	Square.
T (PM)	Yes, it is a square. Follow me. Square.
SSS	Square.
T (PM)	A-R-E...
SSV	/eə/

Teacher SQ, however, tended to combine both whole-to-part analytic approach and part-to-whole synthetic approach, when presenting the target letter-sound relations. Among the three target letter-sound correspondences (e.g. \<are\> -/eə/; \<ear\> -/eə/; \<air\> -/eə/), the teacher only extracted the sound of \<ear\> from *bear*, although all the three example words, *square, bear, hair*, were all taught before.

T (SQ)	Now, A-R-E is pronounced /eə/. Follow me. A-R-E, /eə/.
SSS	A-R-E, /eə/.
...	
T (SQ)	Square.
SSS	Square.

Table 5.8 Presentation of new letter-sound relations in the phonics session

Activities involved	New letter-sound relations			
	SQ	PM	JZ	HL
	<are> (*square*); <ear> (*bear*); <air> (*hair*)		/	<ir> (*skirt*); <ur> (*purse*)*; <au> (*Laura*)*; <oor> (*floor*)
Eliciting letter sound from known words (from whole to part)	<ear> (*bear*)	<are> (*square*); <ear> (*bear*); <air> (*hair*)	/	<ir> (*skirt*); <oor> (*floor*)
Directly telling students letter sound before sounding out the word (from part to whole)	<are> (*square*); <air> (*hair*)	/	/	<ur> (*purse*)*; <au> (*Laura*)*
Providing the IPA symbol	√	√	/	√
Teaching mouth gesture	/	/	/	√

Note* represents that the word is a new word

On the other hand, when the example words were new (e.g. *purse* and *Laura*), teacher PM directly told the sounds of <ur> and <au> to students before eliciting the word sounds. However, as all the example words in the unit observed in schools SQ and PM were taught before, there was no clue as to how teachers SQ and PM would present the letter sound when the example word is untaught.

> T (PM)   And let me tell you, U-R is pronounced as /ɜ:/ too. Listen, U-R is pronounced as /
> ɜ:/. So who can read this new word purse?

It should be noted that although the IPA symbols were not introduced until fifth-grade textbooks, all the teachers introduced the IPA symbols to their students here in grade 4, along with the letter sound. For instance, /eə/ for <are>, and /ɜ:/ for <ur>.

Only teacher HL directed students' attention to the mouth gesture for articulating the sound correctly. When initially introducing the sounds of letters, she asked students to look at her mouth or reminded students "If you mouth shape is not right, your pronunciation will not be standard".

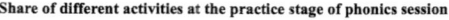

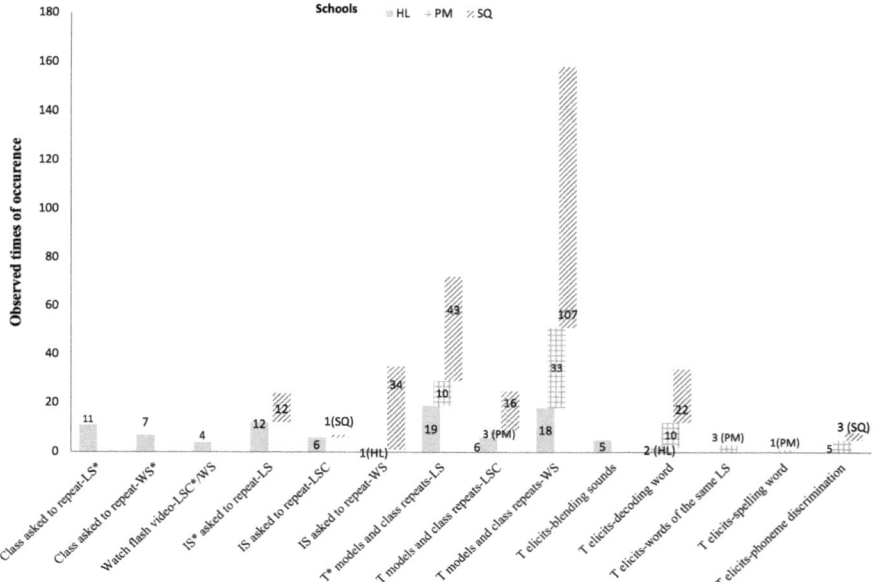

Fig. 5.1   Share of different activities at the practice stage of phonics sessions in 3 schools (HL, PM, SQ). *Note LS* letter sound (e.g. the sound of <ur>), *WS* word sound, *LSC* letter-sound correspondence (e.g. firstly the letter names, <ur>, and then the sound /ɜ:/), *IS* individual student, *T* teacher

5.2.1.3   Practice of Phonics Knowledge and Skills

The activities used to practise phonics knowledge and skills in the observed English classes mainly involved the sub-word or word level (see Fig. 5.1) or were integrated within the context of the nursery rhyme in "Learn the sounds" (see Sect. 5.2.1.3.2).

Practice at Sub-Word and Word Level

As the time spent on the phonics session was different among the three classes, the percentage of different activities observed at the sub-word and word level in different classes was calculated in Table 5.9.

It is obvious from the graph above that in all three classes, the two most frequent activities used to practice phonics knowledge and skills are teacher modelling and then asking the whole class to repeat the letter sound (see code "T models and class repeats-LS") or word sound (see code "T models and class repeats-WS"). Another two activities that were found in all three classes are teacher modelling and asking the whole class to repeat the letter name and sound (see code "T models and

Table 5.9 Percentage of different activities at the practice stage of phonics sessions in 3 schools (HL, PM, SQ)

	HL	PM	SQ	JZ
Class asked to repeat-LS*	12%	/	/	/
Class asked to repeat-WS*	8%	/	/	/
Watch flash video-LSC*/WS	4%	/	/	/
IS* asked to repeat-LS	13%	/	5%	/
IS asked to repeat-LSC	7%	/	0.4%	/
IS asked to repeat-WS	1%	/	14%	/
T* models and class repeats-LS	21%	15%	18%	/
T models and class repeats-LSC	7%	5%	7%	/
T models and class repeats-WS	20%	51%	45%	/
T elicits-blending sounds	5%	/	/	/
T elicits-decoding word	2%	15%	9%	/
T elicits-words of the same LS	/	5%	/	/
T elicits-spelling word	/	2%	/	/
T elicits-phoneme discrimination	/	8%	1%	/

Note LS letter sound (e.g. the sound of <ur>), *WS* word sound, *LSC* letter-sound correspondence (e.g. firstly the letter names, <ur>, and then the sound /ɜː/), *IS* individual student, *T* teacher

class repeats-LSC"), and children being asked to decode words (see code "T elicits-decoding word"). However, Table 5.9 reveals that children in class HL were asked to repeat word sound after the teacher, strikingly less frequently than the children in class SQ and PM, who tended to repeat after the teacher the word sound much more frequently than the letter sound. Additionally, teachers SQ and PM also encouraged their students to decode word sounds more frequently than teacher HL.

The frequency of the remaining activities varies among different teachers. It is interesting to note that teachers SQ and HL both asked individual students to repeat the letter sound and word sound, while teacher PM did not. Teacher HL was also found to ask the whole class to repeat the letter sound and word sound.

Besides, teachers SQ and PM drew children's attention to the discrimination of phonemes, i.e. /ɪə/ and /eə/, by requiring students to read and judge whether the underlined vowel letters in pairs of words share the same sound, e.g. *hear* and *hair*; *pair* and *deer*, while teacher HL did not. Moreover, only teacher PM encouraged students to say some words that share the same sound as the target letter sound, for example, *pear* for /eə/ in *bear*.

To recap, all teachers frequently got students to notice and repeat the letter sound and word sound, as a whole class for the most part. Teachers HL and SQ were found to ask individual students to repeat the letter sound and word sound, probably for the purpose of checking whether students had grasped the letter sound or not, whilst teacher PM was not found to do so in the observed lessons. All teachers did encourage students to decode words using taught letter-sound relations, though teacher HL did so much less frequently in relation to teacher PM and SQ. And only teacher PM and SQ drew children's attention to distinguishing minimal pairs. It seems that compared with the other two teachers, teacher SQ covered a more comprehensive range of activities related to phonological decoding.

The Use of Nursery Rhymes

After the practice of decoding at sub-word and word level as discussed in Sect. 5.2.1.3.1, both teachers HL and PM conducted the activities around the nursery rhyme provided in the textbook section "Learn the sound" for further practice. Teachers HL, PM and SQ had already picked out all the words containing the target letter-sound relations in the nursery rhymes for students to practise decoding at sub-word and word level. The nursery rhymes usually include the example words used to introduce and illustrate the target letter-sound relations (e.g. *square, bear, hair*) and additional words that contain the target letter sounds (e.g. *Clare, pear*) (see an example of the nursery rhymes below).

Don't go near that **square**, Clare!

I can see a **bear**.

Can you see the **bear, Clare**?

It has long, brown **hair**.

And it's eating a yellow **pear**.

Clare, don't go near that **bear!**

(From the textbook 4B)

Both teachers HL and PM firstly asked some oral questions to students, based on the pictures beside the nursery rhymes, thus encouraging the children to say the example words that had just been taught. Children were also given some background information about the content of the rhyme. Then common activities were asking the whole class to read aloud the nursery rhyme in unison together, either with the teacher or without the teacher, and asking individual students to read it aloud. However, although the flash video was a supplementary material accessible to all teachers, it was only used in teacher HL's phonics session. In teacher HL's class, students were required to watch the flash video of the nursery rhyme with scripts and sound on. The video was paused after each sentence for the whole class and sometimes individual pupils to repeat it in unison.

Next, the results relevant to the classroom phonics instruction presented above will be discussed. Phonics instruction was generally believed by all teacher interviewees to be beneficial to children in decoding words. However, as the teachers taught very much with the exam in mind, the phonics decoding was a very minor part of the exam and therefore a very minor part of the teaching. Because of that, although teachers reported the lack of sufficient phonics material for children's practice and the inappropriateness of some nursery rhymes (see Sect. 5.1.2), it is doubtful that if more phonics material was provided, they would use it.

This also explains why phonics instruction does not seem to be the focus of teaching in the observed primary English classrooms. The most surprising finding was that teacher SQ skipped phonics instruction, although she claimed in the interview that she usually spent 10 min teaching the phonics section, and the reason she gave was making up for the lost session caused by a school outing. However, it is interesting that she did not skip any other sections in the unit. This may echo teachers' perception of phonics instruction as a minor part of the teaching.

The time spent on phonics instruction in classrooms varied among teachers. Among the three teachers who were observed to deliver phonics teaching, teacher SQ spent approximately double the time on phonics instruction than teacher PM and teacher HL. The time factor has been generally regarded as crucial for instructional effectiveness, and was found to be the only classroom variable explaining pupils' scores for listening, reading and vocabulary, when controlling for socio-economic background (Edelenbos 1990, cited in Blondin et al. 1998). In that sense, the amount of time teachers spent on phonics instruction may impact the development of their students' phonological decoding ability.

Although three of the teachers were observed teaching phonics, the extent to which they revisited the previous phonics lessons varied. Teacher SQ and HL revisited previously taught phonics knowledge in a much more detailed and systematic way than teacher PM.

When presenting the new target letter-sound relations, teachers seemed to mix the synthetic and analytic approaches of phonics instruction. The choice between synthetic approach and analytic approach might lie in whether the word containing the target letter-sound correspondence had been taught before or not. Teachers tended to adopt a whole-to-part analytic approach to teach the sound of letters if the word had been taught before (e.g. *skirt*, *bear*), although they still needed to offer help with the word sound if some pupils failed to recall it (e.g. *floor*). But with the sounds of letters embedded in new words (e.g. *purse*, *Laura*), a part-to-whole approach tended to be used, i.e. directly telling pupils the sound of letter combinations before eliciting their attempt to decode the word sound. In the context of the acquisition of L1 reading skills, the jury is still out whether a synthetic or analytic approach is more effective. Although the explicit synthetic approach of phonics instruction was held more effective in the UK Primary National Strategy (Department for Education and Skills 2007a) and the longitudinal studies on L1 children by Johnston et al. (2012), Johnston and Watson (2005), the review by Torgerson et al. (2006) revealed that synthetic and analytic approaches did not appear to differ significantly in the effectiveness of promoting substantial growth in L1 children's reading ability, and the report by US National Reading Panel (2000) did not address this issue. In the context of L2 reading, Rixon (2011) has pointed out that for most EFL children who lack a large oral vocabulary as a basis for synthetic phonics approach to lead to the recognition of the blended phonemes mapped onto the graphemes, the analytic phonics approach might "have more prospect of usefulness" (p. 90), by encouraging students to observe and compare the letter-sound correspondences in words they know by sight. Cameron (2001) also presented similar arguments in favour of using words the children can recognise as the context for work on letters and sounds. For L1 children, who have already acquired a good level of English phonology and oral vocabulary before learning to read, once a printed word is decoded and gets matched with its phonological representation stored in the mental lexicon, its meaning can thereby be retrieved and the word is recognised. This is probably why phonics has been favoured as an effective and accelerated way to teach L1 children to read in English. For L2 children, however, especially the Chinese children in the present study, who begin learning to read in English with a very limited size of oral vocabulary, synthetic phonics would not be so effective in helping them to activate the word meaning even if the spelling-sound connection of the word can be worked out in a similar way. On the other hand, with the analytic phonics approach, L2 children can work on letter sounds in the context of familiar words, and thereby construct their learning process on a meaningful basis. Moreover, familiar vocabulary can facilitate the acquisition of the phonological representations of the letters (Roberts 2005).

In addition, it is notable that when presenting the sounds of letters, the teacher also presented their IPA symbols alongside. No experimental studies have been found to compare the effectiveness of phonics instruction with the IPA and without the IPA. Therefore, it cannot be confirmed whether the teaching of IPA symbols adds extra support to the teaching of phonics to EFL children. My intuition, through observing the children in these classes, is that the teaching of the IPA might help some students, while for other students the IPA symbols might be too abstract and difficult to associate with letters, and therefore learning the system might overburden the students while they are still trying to grasp letter-sound relations, as implied in Chen's (2011) training study, in which children receiving the instruction of the IPA showed a more negative attitude towards learning to read English words, finding it difficult and boring to memorise English words and intimidating to decode unfamiliar words.

Another interesting finding is that children's attention was drawn to their mouth gesture when pronouncing letter sounds in teacher HL's class and phoneme discrimination was incorporated in the activities of teacher SQ's and PM's classes. In addition, in order to consolidate children's perception and articulation of phonemes, all three teachers, in the phonics sessions observed, modelled the letter sound either in the context of words or in isolation and then asked the whole class to repeat it after her. Unlike L1 children, who already have a grasp of English oral language as the basis for learning letter-sound relations, many English phonemes are new to Chinese EFL children, who therefore need to develop a good operational command of the complete phoneme system of the language (Rixon 2011). Repetition and imitation of the sounds after the teacher, either within a word or in isolation, can certainly help children identify and articulate the English phonemes. And when teachers HL and SQ asked individual students to repeat the phonemes, they can identify students' problems in pronouncing them and offer immediate feedback. Moreover, the repetition drills can also reinforce the connections between letters and sounds in children's memory.

Although the repetition drills account for the largest proportion of activities used at the practice stage of phonics sessions, teachers HL, PM and SQ all incorporate varying amounts of word decoding activities. The important differences between teachers' frequency in the use of a range of word decoding activities may be partially due to the fact that both teachers SQ and PM introduced additional words containing the target letter-sound relation for practice, while teacher HL stuck to the words provided in "Learn the sound" section of the textbook. As Ehri (2003) pointed out, research shows that students will not apply their phonics knowledge if they do not use it to read. This underlines the importance of applying phonics knowledge in decoding words. The next section will further investigate whether phonological decoding was used in teaching vocabulary.

5.2.2 The Place of Phonological Decoding in Vocabulary Teaching

All teacher interviewees reported applying letter-sound relations to teach word sound in vocabulary instruction in higher grades, although the whole word approach is the dominant method of teaching children to sound out words in lower grades.

Words in the vocabulary list of the observed unit and additional words supplemented in the 4 grade 4 classes, together with the information relating to whether the words involved phonological decoding (mapping sounds to graphemes or larger letter sequences) are presented in Appendix K, for each class respectively. The units observed in classes SQ and PM are the same. However, although the textbook vocabulary list drawn from that unit is the same, supplementary words from the two classes are not identical. Therefore, not only the number of words that involved different approaches but also the percentage was calculated (see Fig. 5.2).

It is obvious from the bar graph that the vocabulary instruction in all the 4 classes involved a certain degree of phonological decoding, although the whole word approach appeared to be preferred. With the 4 classes taken as a whole, 42 out of 70 monosyllabic words (60%) did not involve any decoding of the sound of sub-word units (e.g. rime or grapheme), blending or segmenting of word parts. For instance, teacher HL told pupils the word sound of *lost* directly and asked the whole class to repeat after her the word as a whole.

T (HL)	Do you know lost? Do you know lost? lT wrote *lost-property* on blackboard.l Follow me, lost.
SSS	Lost.
T (HL)	Lost.
SSS	Lost.
T (HL)	Lost means they can't find it. Follow me, lost.

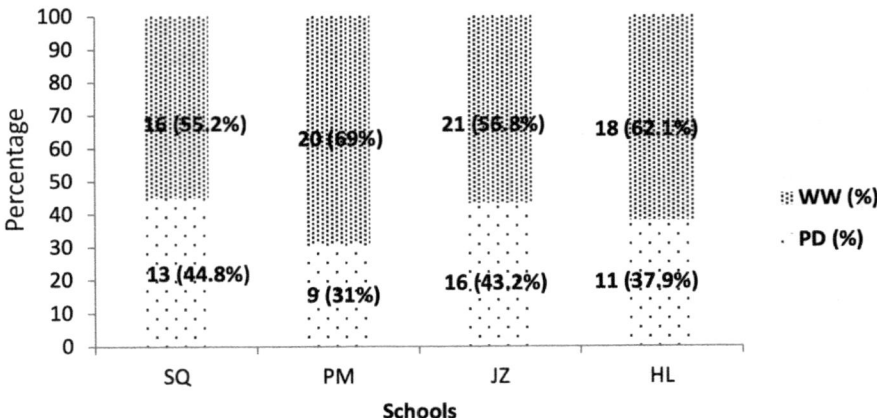

Fig. 5.2 Percentage of the words sounded out with different approaches in 4 schools. *Note WW* whole word approach, *PD* phonological decoding approach

SSS	Lost.
T (HL)	Lost.
SSS	Lost.

33 out of 54 (61.1%) multisyllabic words were taught to be read aloud as a whole, without analysis of the sound at any sub-word level, e.g. graphemes, rimes or syllables. Even syllable segmentation was not involved. For example,

T (PM)	Crayons. These are crayons. But they are old crayons. They are old. And they are used. Follow me. Crayons.
SSS	Crayons.
T (PM)	Crayons.
SSS	Crayons.

Although the whole word approach seemed to be preferred by teachers, it should be noted that 4 out of the 16 words sounded out as a whole in class SQ were words that had appeared in the previous units, 4 out of 20 in class PM, 9 out of 21 in class JZ, and 10 out of 18 in class HL. Therefore, with some words that have been taught in textbooks 2B and 3B before (e.g. *smooth* and *soft* in class HL), teachers might take it for granted that children are already familiar with the sound of these words or already know the sound mapped onto individual letters and therefore simply revisited these words as sight words. However, it is possible that some of these words might not have involved any sound analysis, or thorough analysis when taught in the previous units, where some letter-sound correspondences had not been covered in the phonics section yet. Take the word *smooth*, which was taught with the whole word approach in the second semester of grade 4, as an example. The sounds of its letter components, <sm>, <oo>, and <th> were covered in "Learn the sounds" section initially in the textbook 4A. The word was taught to be sounded out as a whole in the grade 2 class observed, and again as a whole in 4B in class HL, whereas we have no evidence showing whether the teacher decoded the constituent letters later in grade 3. As for the new words that were taught with the whole word approach (e.g. *lost*, *knife*, *hobby*, *cry*, *nap*, *later*, *television*), although most of them contained highly consistent letter-sound correspondences (e.g. <l>, <o>, <st>, <i-e>, <f>, <cr>, <n>, <a>, <p>, etc.) and therefore were decodable, the teachers chose to teach them as a whole. Teacher's choice of the whole-word approach may be due to the possibility that some letter-sound correspondences (e.g. <kn>, <er>, <y>) had not been taught yet or some words, like *television*, contained some inconsistent letter-sound relations.

Further investigation of the words involving phonological decoding was carried out to find out which sub-word units were decoded and which were not (see Appendix L). Generally speaking, as shown in Table 5.10, among the monosyllabic words, 34.7% of the vowel letter or letter combinations were taught to be converted to phonemes. For example:

T (SQ) |points at the word *loud* on the screen| Follow me. Loud.

SSS   Loud.

T (SQ)   How to pronounce O-U? ##, you try.

S   /aʊ/.

T (SQ)   O-U, /aʊ/, loud.

SSS   O-U, /aʊ/, loud.

In contrast, on very few occasions were larger spelling patterns of rimes used to decode words. Teachers PM, JZ and HL each used the rime pattern with one monosyllabic word (<ell> in *bell*, <alk> in *talk*, <ind> in *blind*), and teacher SQ only decoded one of the vowels in a disyllabic word (*awake*) within the context of rime pattern (<ake>).

Additionally, the decoding of consonant letters in monosyllabic words did not draw much attention in the observed classes. Among the monosyllabic words, 7 out of 68 (10.3%) consonant letters or letter combinations at the initial position were decoded, and 2 out of 60 (3.3%) consonant letters or letter combinations at the final position were sounded out. A closer look at the different types of consonant letters and letter combinations at both positions (see Table 5.11) revealed that no attempt was made to decode final consonant clusters and single initial consonant letters, and only one single final consonant letter and one final consonant digraph were found to be sounded out.

It is not surprising that teachers would skip the decoding of almost all single consonant letters at both initial and final positions (e.g. <b> in *bell*, <d> in *hard*), which are generally considered much easier and straightforward, and the teachers thereby might decide to save the time for other relatively more complex sub-word components or other teaching content. What is truly surprising, however, is that the decoding of final consonant clusters and final consonant digraphs received extremely little attention. But caution should be taken here, because the monosyllabic words contain a limited number of final consonant clusters, most of which are from class HL.

Table 5.10 Share of focal sub-word units in words in 4 classes

	SQ		PM		JZ		HL		4 classes in total	
	Focal sub-word units*/Total	Focal sub-word units (%)	Focal sub-word units/Total	Focal sub-word units (%)	Focal sub-word units/Total	Focal sub-word units (%)	Focal sub-word units/Total	Focal sub-word units (%)	Focal sub-word units/Total	Focal sub-word units (%)
Monosyllabic words (PD* & WW*)										
Initial consonant	0/17	0%	1/16	6%	0/15	0%	6/20	30.0%	7/68	10.3%
Vowel	7/17	41%	6/16	38%	5/17	29%	7/22	31.8%	25/72	34.7%
Final consonant	0/14	0%	0/13	0%	0/14	0%	2/19	10.5%	2/60	3.3%
Rime (vowel + final consonant)	0/14	0%	1/13	8%	1/14	7%	1/19	5.3%	3/60	5.0%
Multisyllabic words (PD & WW)										
1st syllable	6/13	46%	1/14	7%	6/20	30%	2/7	29%	15/54	27.8%
2nd syllable	2/13	15%	0/14	0%	4/20	20%	2/7	29%	7/54	13.0%
3rd syllable	0/2	0%	0/3	0%	1/6	17%	1/3	33%	2/14	14.3%
4th syllable	0/1	0%	0/1	0%	/*	/	/	/	0/2	0.0%
1st vowel	3/13	23%	2/14	14%	8/20	40%	0/7	0%	13/53	24.5%
2nd vowel	2 (1 rime)/13	33%	0/14	0%	3/20	15%	0/7	0%	5/53	9.4%
3rd vowel	0/2	0%	0/3	0%	0/6	0%	0/3	0%	0/16	0.0%
4th vowel	0/1	0%	0/1	0%	/	/	/	/	0/2	0.0%

Notes Focal sub-word units represent the sub-word units (e.g. initial consonant; 1st syllable) that were decoded; *words (PD)* represent the words that involved phonological decoding in vocabulary instruction; *words (WW)* represent the words that involved whole word approach; *"/"* means quadrisyllabic words did not appear in the observed classes

Table 5.11 Share of the different types of consonant letters that were decoded in monosyllabic words in 4 classes

	SQ		PM		JZ		HL		4 classes in total	
	Focal sub-word units/Total	Focal sub-word units (%)	Focal sub-word units/Total	Focal sub-word units (%)	Focal sub-word units/Total	Focal sub-word units (%)	Focal sub-word units/Total	Focal sub-word units (%)	Focal sub-word units/Total	Focal sub-word units (%)
SIC*	0/11	0%	0/11	0%	0/11	0%	0/10	0%	0/43	0.0%
ICC*	0/5	0%	1/5	20%	0/4	0%	3/5	60%	4/19	21.1%
ICD*	0/1	0%	/	/	/	/	3/5	60%	3/6	50.0%
SFC*	0/8	0%	0/7	0%	0/11	0%	1/9	13%	1/35	2.9%
FCC*	0/1	0%	0/1	0%	0/1	0%	0/5	0%	1/8	0.0%
FCD/FCT*	0/5	0%	0/5	0%	0/1	0%	1/5	20%	1/16	6.3%

Note SIC single initial consonant letter, ICC initial consonant cluster, ICD/ICT initial consonant digraph, SFC single final consonant letter, FCC final consonant cluster, FCD/FCT final consonant digraph/ trigraph (e.g. < tch >)

As for the multisyllabic words, the first syllables (27.8%) generally tended to receive much more attention than the second syllable (13%), the third (14.3%) and the fourth (0%). But it should be noted that only one four-syllable word (*television*) was observed to be taught in classes SQ and PM, and none of the syllables got attention. It is similar in the case of individual vowel letters in different syllables (see Table 5.10). It is obvious from the example below that when teaching the sound of the disyllabic word *tennis*, teacher JZ only focused on the first vowel, without attention allocated for any syllabic units or the other graphemic units.

T (JZ)	IT writes tennis on the blackboard.I Look, this is tennis. Tennis.
SSS	Tennis.
T (JZ)	Tennis.
SSS	Tennis.
T (JZ)	Tennis.
SSS	Tennis.
T (JZ)	Tennis.
SSS	Tennis.
T (JZ)	E, /ɛ/.
SSS	E, /ɛ/.
T (JZ)	E, /ɛ/.
SSS	E, /ɛ/.
T (JZ)	E, /ɛ/, tennis.
SSS	E, /ɛ/, tennis.

To recap, teachers seemed to mix the whole word approach with the phonological decoding approach in teaching children to sound out words. And when decoding a monosyllabic word, the emphasis was usually placed on vowel graphemes instead of decoding all the component graphemes and blending them to form the word sound. Moreover, rime patterns were very rarely used in teaching children to decode vowel graphemes. In addition, the first syllable or the first vowel tended to draw more attention than the other syllables or vowels. In other words, very rarely were teachers or students observed to decode a word thoroughly and blend the individual sounds to form the word sound.

5.2.3   Text-Level Reading Practice

Table 5.12 shows that the teachers spent between 18 and 27% of the observed class time on text reading activities. Teacher SQ spent the most time on reading activities at the text level, i.e. beyond the word level, for example, in the context of sentences, chants and stories. However, teacher HL spent the lowest proportion, considering her lesson was 35 min longer than the other classes, and she spent roughly the same amount of time during the lesson as the other teachers.

Table 5.12 Time allotment to reading at the text level in 4 classrooms

	SQ	PM	JZ	HL
Amount of time (Minutes) spent reading texts	46.52	39.46	36.98	38.53
Amount of time (Minutes) spent on the whole observed unit	175	175	175	210
Proportion of time spent reading texts	26.6%	22.5%	21.1%	18.3%

Table 5.13 shows that among the different types of reading activities, rereading constitutes the majority (81% in classroom SQ, 60% in PM, 69% in JZ, 59% in HL). Rereading took a variety of forms, such as role play reading, whole class or group reading aloud in unison, practising reading aloud individually, in pairs or in groups. However, the reading activities used at the first encounter with the texts varied among different classrooms. Teacher SQ tended to encourage students to try to read the texts individually on their own most of the time, which was also found in the classroom of PM. In contrast, individual reading activities were rarely used in the classrooms of JZ and HL. In addition, listening to the teacher or to characters in the flash videos reading aloud the new texts was found to be least frequently used in classroom SQ (4%)), compared to classroom PM (13%), JZ (19%), and HL (23%).

What is striking is that teacher SQ did not ask her students to read aloud the new texts in unison. Instead, she required her students to finger point to words when listening to the multimedia, while the other teachers did not. In this way, children's attention can be drawn to the printed words and letter components on one hand, and on the other hand, students might be noticing the letter-sound associations when listening to the multimedia.

As for the source of reading materials, teachers SQ, JZ and HL spent most of the time on textbook materials (83% for SQ; 86% for JZ; 87% for HL), while teacher PM spent a much smaller proportion of time on textbook materials (42%). However, teacher PM spent a much greater proportion of time on supplementary materials (58%) compared to the other three teachers (17% for SQ; 14% for JZ; 13% for HL). The proportion of time allocated for nursery rhymes or songs and reading other texts such as passages and sentences varied among the four classes. Teacher PM seemed to spend a similar proportion of time on the two types of supplementary materials and even incorporated additional flash videos for children to practice reading. It should be noted that in the process of data analysis, only the flash videos with transcriptions displayed on the screen were counted as reading materials. A larger proportion of time was spent on supplementary nursery rhymes than other types of supplementary texts in classroom SQ while classrooms JZ and HL exhibited an opposite trend.

It should be noted that according to one of the teacher interviewees, either the supplementary reading texts or textbook materials are mainly used for practising the key vocabulary and grammar. However, although students were not explicitly required to apply their decoding skills in those reading activities, it cannot be denied that these text reading activities provided children with the opportunities to consolidate their phonics knowledge and skills, although we are not sure about how much

Table 5.13 Time allotment to different reading activities and materials in 4 classrooms

	Minutes (%) – SQ	Minutes (%) – PM	Minutes (%) – JZ	Minutes (%) – HL
1. Reading activities at the first encounter with the text				
(1) Individual reading*	4.97 (11%)	5.37 (14%)	2.67 (7%)	1.63 (4%)
(2) Listening to teacher reading aloud	0.54 (1%)	1.48 (4%)	6.79 (18%)	7.91 (21%)
(3) Watching flash videos	1.51 (3%)	3.48 (9%)	0.22 (1%)	0.7 (2%)
(4) Choral reading*	–	5.3 (13%)	1.78 (5%)	5.6 (15%)
(5) Finger-point reading while listening to the flash*	1.71 (4%)	–	–	–
2. Reading activities after the first encounter with the text				
Rereading*	37.79 (81%)	23.83 (60%)	25.52 (69%	22.69 (59%)
Total	46.52	39.46	36.98	38.53
3. Reading materials				
(1) Materials in the textbook	38.5 (83%)	16.46 (42%)	31.73 (86%)	33.43(87%)
(2) Supplementary materials	8.02 (17%)	23 (58%)	5.25 (14%)	5.1 (13%)
– Supplementary flash videos	–	2.67 (7%)	–	–
– Supplementary nursery rhymes/ songs	5.5 (12%)	11.19 (28%)	–	0.53 (1%)
– Other supplementary texts*	2.52 (5%)	9.14 (23%)	5.25 (14%)	4.57 (12%)
Total	46.52	39.46	36.98	38.53

Notes Individual reading included silent reading, and as it occurred very rarely and for very short amount of time, the amount of time spent on silent reading is included in the counting
Choral reading: whole class or groups read aloud a piece of text in union, along with or without the teacher or the multimedia
Rereading: children read aloud the text again after the first encounter with the text
Other supplementary texts include passages and sentences

attention children devoted to the letter-sound associations embedded in words when they were reading those texts.

In conclusion, similar amount of time was spent on the reading activities beyond word level in the four classes. The majority of time was spent on repeating reading aloud the texts after the first encounter in all four classes. On one hand, reading fluency can be facilitated. On the other hand, children may attend to the constituent letter-sound relations in words and decode the words when they try to read aloud the texts.

However, students' neglect of oral reading after class was mentioned by teachers HL and JZ. Those teachers believed that reading aloud was important for children to grasp the sounds of letters.

> The students read very little English. The only source of input for them is the 35-minute English lesson per day. After school, they simply finish the written homework. Even if you ask them to read aloud, say 5 times, they would not do it. (HL)

> They lack practice after class. For example, I asked students to repeat reading the letter sounds, word sounds and nursery rhymes in "Learn the sounds" section after class. But to them, such oral reading assignment is not actually homework. Last time, I asked the whole class to read aloud that section after school, but there were only three students who did it... Oral homework is greatly ignored. This really needs parents' cooperation... (JZ)

They also pointed out that part of the reason why some students cannot learn the letter sounds very well is related to the limited aural input.

> Different from L1 children, who have had much aural input before learning phonics, our students have very little experience with English. It would be a very long process for them to learn to pronounce the sounds correctly, and to progress from grasping the alphabetic knowledge to applying the knowledge in decoding words. Although I told him <a> in rabbit is sounded out as /æ/, he would still sound out the vowel differently. When he enters grade 4 or 5, he would notice that each letter has its sound in a word and you have to pronounce the sounds correctly. In the lower grades, they would not pay much attention to this. (HL)

> It is difficult to teach pronunciation. You cannot tell children any rules. For example, when I taught them to sound out quarter, they kept sounding it as /kɔːtə/. Some sounds are difficult for them to pronounce correctly, like /ð/. The sounds of ear (/ɪə/) and air (/eə/) are difficult for the students to distinguish. The students had little listening and speaking practice. (JZ)

However, it should be noted that some teachers did try to encourage their students to read extracurricular materials. For example, teacher PM recommended reading lists to students to read during summer and winter vacation, although no follow-up check was carried out. Teacher JZ asked her students to subscribe to domestic primary school students English newspapers but only 6 children did. Teacher HL asked all of her students to buy a book composed of 60 short passages with exercises for each passage and the topic of each passage is in alignment with the topic of each unit in the textbook. But besides asking students to read the passages, teacher HL also focused on the grammatical points in the reading materials. She admitted that students thought such exercises were useless and she gave it up.

And teacher SQ also mentioned that there were some parents who would encourage their children to read English aloud after school, although very few. Such phenomenon was also described by the textbook writer, who thought this was caused by some parents' misconception of learning English.

> Most parents would rather send their children to out-of-school classes for passing standardised tests to get certificates. Few of them would really spend time developing children's interest of reading in English because the effects could not be immediately reflected in the exam results. (TW)

However, interestingly and understandably, the textbook writer pointed out that in primary schools with focus of the specialty area on English and some key schools, teachers and parents would attach more importance to children's exposure to English, both in spoken and written form.

> In a key primary school, a teacher allocates 5 minutes before class for a child to report the story he/she read. (TW)

The interview with teacher PM supported the textbook writer's observation above.

> My son is studying in a foreign language primary school. As far as I know, his classmate's parent would play the CDs of audio stories when driving the child to school in the morning. (PM)

But it should be noted that this type of primary schools was not included in this study.

5.3 Summary

The description and analysis of the materials for teaching phonological decoding and the actual classroom teaching of phonological decoding reveals that the teaching of phonological decoding in OE incorporates the explicit instruction in phoneme identification, phoneme articulation, phoneme discrimination, letter names and shapes, letter-sound relations, and the IPA. But neither spelling-sound correspondences at the rime level nor phonics generalisations are included in the syllabus. The sequence of introducing letter-sound associations is incremental, from the simple to the relatively more complex. Most of the letter-sound relations covered in the textbook 2B-4B are revisited when the IPA is introduced in the textbook for grade 5, except consonant clusters. Around half of the letter-sound relations embedded in OE vocabulary are covered in the phonics syllabus. But it should be noted that a very high percentage of the high frequency letter-sound relations embedded in OE vocabulary and all the high-frequency letter-sound relations embedded in monosyllabic words are covered. This may maximise the possibility of decoding words with taught letter-sound relations.

Although a high proportion of high-frequency letter-sound relations are covered in the phonics syllabus, it is not until the second semester of grade 5 that the introduction of all these high-frequency ones is completed. This is probably part of the reasons why a large proportion of the words used for practising target letter-sound relations in OE phonics section (particularly in OE 2B-4A) are not fully decodable, which may lead to the teaching emphasis on letter sounds and teachers' modelling of partial decoding of word sound. Similarly, a large proportion of textbook vocabulary is not fully decodable using the taught letter-sound relations, particularly in lower grades, which may discourage students from employing the phonological decoding approach to sound out words or from decoding words thoroughly, if teachers do not model using phonological decoding approach as the prime method of sounding out words and performing complete graphophonic analyses on words wherever possible.

It is interesting to note that although phonics instruction is generally believed to be conducive to decoding words, it is a minor part of teaching because it is a minor part of the examination system. Because of that, although teachers reported the lack of sufficient phonics material for children's practice and the inappropriateness of some nursery rhymes, it is doubtful that if more phonics material was provided, they would use it. Moreover, phonics instruction is treated as a section separate from the other teaching content within a unit, and always taught at the end of each unit. The activities suggested for phonics instruction in the teachers' books mainly involves phoneme identification and articulation, e.g. repetition of the letter sounds in isolation or within the context of words. In contrast, there is a perceptible lack of word decoding activities suggested in the teachers' books. This marked preference of repetition drills on the sounds of letters and words over word building activities was also found in the actual classroom teaching context.

In vocabulary instruction, the phonological decoding approach was adopted in teaching children to sound out words while the whole word approach appeared to be preferred. Moreover, graphophonic analyses tended to focus on the constituent vowel graphemes in monosyllabic words, and the orthographic units associated with the first syllable the first vowel sound in disyllabic words. Consonant orthographic units, like single consonant letters and consonant letter combinations, particularly final consonant clusters, were greatly neglected. Moreover, on very few occasions did the phonological decoding of words occur at the rime level.

Although teachers assign some out-of-class listening and oral reading practice to their students, this type of homework was usually ignored by many children and their parents, although few children and parents did not. Then there is the possibility that the children who get more exposure to English oral/aural input and written language would have more chance of reinforcing the phonics knowledge and skills taught in class and their decoding ability would therefore surpass their peers who had little exposure to English after school.

References

Ball, E. W., & Blachman, B. A. (1991). Does phoneme awareness training in kindergarten make a difference in early word recognition and developmental spelling? *Reading Research Quarterly, 26*(1), 49–66.

Birch, B. M. (2007). *English L2 reading: getting to the bottom*. Mahwah, N.J.: Lawrence Erlbaum Associates.

Blondin, C., Candelier, M., Edelenbos, P., Johnstone, R., Kubaneck, A., & Taeschner, T. (1998). *Foreign languages in primary and pre-school education: A review of recent research within the European Union.* London: Centre for Information on Language Teaching.

Cameron, L. (2001). *Teaching languages to young learners.* Cambridge: Cambridge University Press.

Cardoso-Martins, C., Mesquita, T. C. L., & Ehri, L. C. (2011). Letter names and phonological awareness help children to learn letter–sound relations. *Journal of Experimental Child Psychology, 109*(1), 25–38.

Chen, Y. (2003). *The effects of phonological decoding training on English word recognition skills in Taiwanese EFL children.* (Unpublished Master dissertaion). National Taipei University of Education.

Chen, Y. (2011). *Research on the practice of phonics in primary school English teaching.* (Unpublished Master dissertation). Xihua University.

Department for Education and Skills. (2007a). *Letters and Sounds: Notes of guidance for practitioners and teachers.* Retrieved September 2, 2011, from http://nationalstrategies.standards. dcsf.gov.uk/node/84969.

Department for Education and Skills. (2007b). *Letters and Sounds: Principles and practice of high quality phonics.* Retrieved September 2, 2011, from http://nationalstrategies.standards.dcsf.gov. uk/node/84969.

Ehri, L. C. (2003). *Systematic phonics instruction: Findings of the National Reading Panel.* Retrieved October 2, 2011, from http://www.standards.dfes.gov.uk/pdf/literacy/lehri_phonics. pdf.

Goswami, U. (1999). Causal connections in beginning reading: The importance of rhyme. *Journal of Research in Reading, 22*(3), 217–240.

Jarvis, S. (2013). How effective is it to teach a foreign language in the Foundation Stage through songs and rhymes? *Education 3–13, 41*(1), 47–54.

Johnston, F. P. (2001). The utility of phonic generalizations: Let's take another look at Clymer's conclusions. *The Reading Teacher, 55*(2), 132–143.

Johnston, R. S., McGeown, S., & Watson, J. E. (2012). Long-term effects of synthetic versus analytic phonics teaching on the reading and spelling ability of 10 year old boys and girls. *Reading and Writing, 25*(6), 1365–1384.

Johnston, R. S., & Watson, J. E. (2005). *The effects of synthetic phonics teaching on reading and spelling attainment: A seven year longitudinal study.* Ediburgh, Scotland: Scottish Executive Education Department.

Kuo, L. (2011). *The role and efficacy of phonics instruction in the early literacy development of young Taiwanese EFL learners.* (Unpublished PhD thesis). University of Warwick.

Lloyd, S. (1992). *The phonics handbook.* Chigwell, UK: Jolly Learning.

Ministry of Education, China. (2001). *National English curriculum standards for nine-year compulsory education and senior high schools (Piloting Edition).* Beijing: Beijing Normal University Press.

Ministry of Education, China. (2011). *English curriculum standards for compulsory education.* Beijing: Beijing Normal University Press.

National Reading Panel. (2000). *Teaching children to read: An evidence-based assessment of the scientific research literature on reading and its implications for reading instruction (Reports of the subgroups).* Retrieved November 16, 2010, from http://www.nationalreadingpanel.org/pub lications/subgroups.htm.

Peregoy, S. F., & Boyle, O. F. (2012). *Reading, writing, and learning in ESL: A resource book for K-12 teachers* (6th ed.). Boston: Pearson Education.

Piasta, S. B., & Wagner, R. K. (2010). Learning letter names and sounds: Effects of instruction, letter type, and phonological processing skill. *Journal of Experimental Child Psychology, 105*(4), 324–344.

Qiu, J. (2007). An experimental study on phonics instruction. *Journal of Basic English Education, 9*(1), 29–33.

Rixon, S. (2011). *Beyond ABC: Investigating current rationales and systems for the teaching of early reading to young learners of English.* (Unpublished PhD thesis). University of Warwick.

Roberts, T. A. (2005). Articulation accuracy and vocabulary size contributions to phonemic awareness and word reading in English language learners. *Journal of Educational Psychology, 97*(4), 601–616.

Savage, R., Carless, S., & Stuart, M. (2003). The effects of rime- and phoneme-based teaching delivered by learning support assistants. *Journal of Research in Reading, 26*(3), 211–233.

Share, D. L. (2004). Knowing letter names and learning letter sounds: A causal connection. *Journal of Experimental Child Psychology, 88*(3), 213–233.

Shu, H., Peng, H., & McBride-Chang, C. (2008). Phonological awareness in young Chinese children. *Developmental Science, 11*(1), 171–181.

Stahl, S. A. (1992). Saying the "p" word: Nine guidelines for exemplary phonics instruction. *The Reading Teacher, 45*(8), 618–625.

Stahl, S. A., Duffy-Hester, A. M., & Stahl, K. A. D. (1998). Everything you wanted to know about phonics (but were afraid to ask). *Reading Research Quarterly, 33*(3), 338–355.

Stuart, M. (1999). Getting ready for reading: Early phoneme awareness and phonics teaching improves reading and spelling in inner-city second language learners. *British Journal of Educational Psychology, 69*(4), 587–605.

Torgerson, C., Brooks, G., & Hall, J. (2006). *A systematic review of the research literature on the use of phonics in the teaching of reading and spelling.* London: Department for Education and Skills.

Vandervelden, M. C., & Siegel, L. S. (1995). Phonological recoding and phoneme awareness in early literacy: A developmental approach. *Reading Research Quarterly, 30*(4), 854–875.

Verhoeven, L. (2000). Components in early second language reading and spelling. *Scientific Studies of Reading, 4*(4), 313–330.

Wade-Woolley, L., & Geva, E. (2000). Processing novel phonemic contrasts in the acquisition of L2 word reading. *Scientific Studies of Reading, 4*(4), 295–311.

Chapter 6
Conclusion

This chapter begins with the recapitulation of the key findings concerning the phonological decoding ability of Chinese EFL children and the teaching of phonological decoding. Based on the overall findings, the interrelationship between textbook design, classroom teaching and the decoding ability of Chinese children is explored. The subsequent sections present the contribution and implications of the study, followed by the discussion of its limitations and suggestions for future research.

6.1 Recapitulation of the Main Findings

This study aimed to describe, interpret and evaluate the learning and teaching of phonological decoding in the Chinese primary EFL context. Children's phonological decoding ability was investigated through a battery of tests in order to provide insight into the effect of different types of orthographic units on children's decoding performance, the different strategies adopted by children of different levels of reading ability in sounding out vowel graphemes, and children's phonological decoding ability in relation to their reading ability. In addition, the teaching materials used by the student participants were described and analysed in order to reveal whether they provide an explicit and systematic programme in teaching phonological decoding. Finally, the actual classroom teaching was explored to discover how teachers deliver the instruction in phonological decoding. The main findings for the present study are reported as following.

6.1.1 Chinese Children's Phonological Decoding Ability

- **Performance in Decoding Different Types of Orthographic Units**

K. Hua, *The Learning and Teaching of Phonological Decoding in Chinese EFL Children*, https://doi.org/10.1007/978-981-97-6891-2_6

RQ 1: How is children's phonological decoding accuracy affected by different types of orthographic units?

The investigation of Chinese children's phonological decoding ability by means of a nonword reading test showed that they were generally more capable of decoding consonant orthographic units than vowel orthographic units. To be more specific, participants were more proficient at decoding single consonant letters than consonant digraphs and consonant clusters, and more proficient at decoding single vowel letters than complex vowel orthographic units, among which the split vowel digraphs were more problematic than the non-split letter combinations representing vowels. This finding is consistent with what previous studies found about L1 children's developmental sequence of acquiring the decoding of English orthographic units (Laxon et al. 2002; Seymour et al. 1992). This also adds support to Yin and her colleagues' (2007) findings that Chinese EFL children learn to decode English words in a sequence similar to their L1 counterparts.

Additionally, it is interesting to find that most children struggled with the decoding of the orthographic units that are not covered in the textbook phonics syllabus (e.g. <wr>, <kn>), but some children were able to decode them correctly (8 out of 54 decoded <kn> correctly; 18 out of 54 decoded <wr> correctly). This suggests that some analytic children may be able to derive the letter-sound relations embedded in the words on their own, once they have got a large vocabulary.

In terms of the orthographic units in different positions, the medial consonant orthographic units and the second vowel graphemes in disyllabic nonwords posed the biggest problem to the participants, compared with initial or final consonant orthographic units and the first vowel graphemes. This can be due to the great cognitive demand of the task, requiring more developed working memory and syllabification skills compared with decoding monosyllables. In addition, participants performed better in decoding the initial consonant orthographic units than the final consonant orthographic units. This is probably attributable to the salience of the initial graphemes. Additionally, due to the predominance of CV syllables in Chinese, Chinese children have not had much experience with decoding the final consonant graphemes in their L1 literacy learning experience, which may also explain their poorer performance in decoding final consonant orthographic units.

- **Strategies of Sounding Out Vowel Graphemes in the Nonword Reading Test**

RQ2: What strategies do children at different levels of reading ability employ in sounding out vowel graphemes?

No participants employed the whole word strategy in sounding out every nonword test item, which suggests that all of them have passed beyond the pre-partial alphabetic phase, which is characterised by the absence of letter-sound relations even for single consonant letters and hence heavy reliance on the non-alphabetic visual cues. However, children in the present study demonstrated great disparity in their use of different strategies to sound out vowel graphemes. Above-average readers tend to use significantly more decoding strategies and less the whole word strategies to sound out vowel orthographic units, compared with average and below-average readers. More-over, in using different decoding strategies, above-average readers demonstrated significantly more reliance on major grapheme-phoneme correspondences and more sensitivity to rime patterns than average and below-average readers.

- **Phonological Decoding Ability in Relation to Reading Ability**

RQ3: How does Chinese children's phonological decoding ability relate to their reading ability?

Children's phonological decoding ability correlated highly with their reading ability, as assessed in the real word reading test and reading comprehension test. Although all children received similar phonics instruction, their phonological decoding ability varied widely across individuals. Considering that their reading ability also varied widely, we can speculate that the above average readers' greater decoding skills may give them an advantage when reading. But we have to acknowledge that it could be the other way round. That is to say, the above average readers' greater reading ability may lay a solid foundation for them to develop phonological decoding skills.

6.1.2 The Teaching of Phonological Decoding

- **Phonological Decoding in the Teaching Materials**

RQ4: What is the scope and sequence of the component knowledge and skills of phonological decoding as reflected in the textbook?

Phonological decoding in the teaching materials consists of the explicit teaching of the component knowledge and skills of phonological decoding, namely phoneme identification skill, letter names and shapes, letter-sound relations. However, the teaching of phonological decoding in the context of Shanghai gets its own interpre-tations from textbook writers and teachers. Phoneme articulation, phoneme discrim-ination and the International Phonetic Alphabet are also included in the textbook phonics syllabus. This conflation of instruction in English phonology and phonics is resonated in Rixon's (2011) findings, which suggested that L2 phonics instruction needs to combine the teaching of English phonology and the teaching of letter-sound relations. Phonological decoding implicates the access to the phonemic reper-toire of the target language, which is mapped onto the letters for further assembly into words. Unlike L1 children, who have already acquired English sounds before learning to decode words, L2 children have to construct their repertoire of English phonemes and of English words in order to establish the reliable link between letters and the corresponding sounds. The perception and articulation of English sounds, the operational knowledge of English phonology are believed to be related to L2 chil-dren's performance in phonological decoding (Roberts 2005; Wade-Woolley and Geva 2000).

The letter-sound relations are introduced in a systematic and incremental way, from single consonant letters (2B), to single vowel letters (3A), to consonant digraphs and consonant clusters (3B and 4A), and to letter combinations representing vowels (4B). But one concern is that the simultaneous introduction of the short and long sound of the vowel letter may confuse young learners. In grade 5, taught graphemes and letter combinations, together with newly introduced ones, are grouped under each of the 44 English phonemes. In this way, almost all the letter-sound relations taught before grade 5 are revisited, except the consonant clusters, which tend to pose more problems to Chinese children compared with single consonant letter and consonant digraphs. The letter-sound relations in the phonics syllabus do not include rime-level spelling-to-sound correspondences. The instructional sequence of letter sounds adopted in the textbook implies the implicit underpinning approach in analytic phonics. Phonics is contained in a separate section at the end of each unit in the textbook.

RQ5: Is practice provided for developing phonological decoding skills in the textbook materials for different grades? If yes, what kind of practice?

In terms of the practice suggested for the phonics section in the teachers' books, there is a marked preference of activities for training in phoneme identification, phoneme articulation, and repetition drills on the letter sounds in isolation or within words over word decoding activities. This is consistent with Kuo's (2011) findings about phonics instruction in Taiwan, which also lays much less emphasis on word building as phonics instruction in the L1 context does. This may be due to the difference between L1 children and L2 children in preexisting phonological skills and vocabulary knowledge before learning to read in English. For L1 children, phonics instruction allows children to retrieve the meaning of an unfamiliar word in the mental lexicon by working out its sound representations based on their phonics knowledge and skills. In that sense, word building is an indispensable first step for L1 children to learn to read. However, in the L2 context, phonics instruction allows children to derive the sound representations of an unfamiliar word from its printed form, but not necessarily its meaning, if the word is not yet in their mental lexicon. And L2 children usually have a limited vocabulary size at the very early stage of learning the language. Even if they assemble the sounds of letters and build the word, they may not be able to activate its meaning. That is probably why textbook writers and teachers in the present study mainly attend to individual component letters or letter combinations, and do not engage with many word building activities, which involve the thorough analysis of all the letters within a word and the assembly of sounds. Nevertheless, this is not to say that L2 children should not be engaged in word building activities. Such activities are also of value to develop children's self-teaching ability and confidence with decoding unfamiliar words on their own (Kuo 2011; Share 1995; Woore 2009). In addition, they can also be made aware of the importance of the thorough analysis of component spelling-sound associations within words in forming strong and reliable connections for sight word learning.

In addition, teachers reported the lack of sufficient phonics materials for children's practice and the inappropriateness of some nursery rhymes. Moreover, although the

2011 English Curriculum Standards (Ministry of Education 2011) state that primary children should acquire the ability to decode English words by applying their phonics knowledge and skills, the approach to teaching vocabulary suggested in the teachers' books is still the whole word approach.

RQ6: To what extent are the letter sound relations taught for sounding out the words in each phonics section, and in the textbook vocabulary?

Although 42.1% of the 186 letter-sound relations embedded in the monosyllabic words are not included in the syllabus, all the 26 high-frequency letter-sound relations embedded in the monosyllabic words are covered in the phonics syllabus. This reflects the fact that the textbook design takes into account how to maximise the possibility of decoding simple words with taught letter-sound associations under the constraint of class hours. A large proportion of the words used for practising target letter-sound relations in the phonics section of OE (particularly 2B-4A) are not fully decodable. This may encourage the partial decoding of word sounds, instead of the thorough analysis of the constituent letter-sound associations within a word. In addition, a large proportion of textbook vocabulary is not fully decodable using the taught letter-sound relations, even in the higher grades such as the first semester of grade 5. This may discourage the application of the phonological decoding approach to perform complete graphophonic analyses on words.

- **The Classroom Teaching of Phonological Decoding**

RQ7: Is phonics taught in the classroom? If so, how?

Although teachers in general recognised the importance of phonics in helping children learn to decode English words, teachers tended to neglect phonics instruction, which is a very minor part of the examination system and concentrate on what they perceived as core skills for exams. Hence, phonics instruction constitutes a minor part of the teaching. This may explain why a phonics session was skipped by one of the teachers when the teaching schedule was tight.

The observations of actual classroom teaching showed how phonological decoding is taught in primary English classes. Time allocated for phonics instruction varied among teachers varied (teacher SQ spent about 25 min, teacher PM about 10 min, teacher HL about 15 min, and teacher JZ skipped it). It was carried out after all the other content within the unit was covered, as implied by its "end-piece" location in the textbook. Phonics instruction was reported not to be well integrated with the main lessons on vocabulary and reading. The letter-sound relations were taught at the graphemic level as prescribed in the textbook syllabus, and no rime patterns were introduced. Teachers adopted the synthetic and analytic phonics approaches flexibly when presenting the target letter sounds. They tended to use the synthetic approach with unfamiliar words and the analytic approach with familiar words.

The most frequently used activities for practising the phonics knowledge are teacher modelling and asking the whole class to repeat the target letter sound and word sound. This implies that all teachers gave relatively more attention to the perception and articulation of the English phonemes than word decoding activities. Although all teachers involved children in applying the taught phonics knowledge to decode words independently, this type of activity accounted only for a very small proportion of the range of activities used to practise the taught phonics knowledge and skills. Not all teachers revisited the previously taught phonics knowledge systematically.

RQ8: To what extent is phonological decoding applied in vocabulary teaching?

In vocabulary teaching, both the whole word approach and the phonological decoding approach were adopted in teaching children to sound out words. It is notable that no words were decoded thoroughly, i.e. letter by letter. And if decoding was involved, the emphasis was usually placed on the letter(s) representing the vowel in a mono-syllabic word, and the first syllable or the first vowel in a multi-syllabic word. In contrast, the constituent consonant letters or letter combinations received much less attention, including final consonant clusters and final consonant digraphs. On very few occasions were larger spelling patterns of rimes used to decode words.

RQ9: Are text-level reading activities used in the classroom? If so, what activities?

Teachers allocated a similar amount of time (approximately one fifth of the total amount of time spent on a whole unit) for reading activities beyond word level, among which rereading the text after the first time of hearing or reading it, was found to be the most frequently used. However, all teachers reported that most students and their parents neglected the out-of-class oral or aural homework and extracurricular reading.

6.2   Overall Discussion

The overall findings obtained from each of the research tools enable the present research to triangulate and explore the interrelationship between the design of the textbook, classroom teaching, teachers' beliefs, and young learners' decoding ability. The results of the textbook analysis and the teacher/textbook writer interviews allow detection of how the design of the textbook may influence the instructional practice with respect to phonological decoding. The investigation of how the knowledge and skills related to phonological decoding are presented in the textbook and taught in the actual classroom also provides explanations for children's phonological decoding ability reflected in the nonword reading test. The combined results enable a comprehensive description, interpretation and evaluation of the teaching of phonological decoding to young Chinese EFL learners.

- **The influence of textbook design on the instructional practice**

The design of the textbook has a huge impact on teachers' instructional practice because teachers work through the lessons in the textbook and refer to the objectives that are expected to be achieved in each part of the textbook. Teachers implemented phonics instruction, bearing in mind the overriding objective of the phonics programme stated in teachers' books, i.e. to identify and pronounce the letter sounds.

However, there is no direction or indication in the teacher's book of how and when to apply the phonics knowledge in relevant vocabulary and reading instruction. The phonics programme as an end-piece is not designed to be well integrated with the other parts of teaching. During the phonics session, teachers spent a majority of the time sounding out letters either in isolation or within words, whilst only a small proportion of time was allocated for word decoding activities. There is also an absence of exercises designed to practise phonics knowledge in the students' workbooks. Similarly, in vocabulary instruction, if any decoding attempt was made, it occurred only at the level of component letters. In other words, no thorough letter-by-letter decoding was involved in teaching vocabulary. Teachers' neglect of applying letter-sound relations in decoding words may be ascribed to the simplified teaching objective specified for the phonics programme. The inadequate teachers' modelling and students' practicing of the thorough decoding of words based on taught phonics knowledge suggest to the children that they are not expected to apply the letter-sound relations in sounding out words. This seems to contradict the official curriculum objectives for phonics, i.e. to work out the sound representations of a simple word based on taught phonics knowledge.

Although the present study shares similar findings about the lack of word building practice in phonics programme with Kuo's (2011) study on the phonics programmes for Taiwanese children, the teachers in this study do not regard phonics exclusively as a pronunciation system, as the teachers in Kuo's study did. The phonics programme in this study was indeed used to facilitate children in acquiring English phonology, but although word decoding activities were observed in phonics sessions, such activities remained limited. As revealed in the teachers' interviews, they acknowledged the importance of phonics instruction in teaching children to decode words; however, they admitted not spending enough time on it, because this is only a very minor part of the exams and therefore a minor part of the teaching. The limited instruction time, combined with the lack of regular revision and sufficient practice, may diminish the effectiveness of phonics instruction.

- **The link between phonological decoding ability and its teaching**

The distinct advantage of the children in school SQ over the children in school JZ in the nonword reading tasks may be linked to the fact that teacher SQ spent more time teaching phonological decoding and covered a more comprehensive range of decoding activities while teacher JZ skipped the phonics session. This suggests that phonics instruction is more conducive to developing L2 learners' decoding skills compared to non-phonics instruction, as reported by Chen (2003), Qiu (2007), and Stuart (1999) (see Sect. 2.5.4.2). But caution should be taken here because other variables (e.g. the time children spent learning English after class, children's abilities, etc.) were not controlled.

As suggested by Felton (1993), Foorman et al. (1998), and McGeown and Medford (2014), instructional approaches may shape the skills children draw upon when learning to read and may explain their different performance on decoding.

The results of the nonword reading test showed that all Chinese children have passed the pre-alphabetic phase of learning to decode English words and all of them can decode a certain number of single consonant letters. This may be attributed to the teaching of phonological decoding they received in class. This is congruent with the findings of previous research that showed the positive effect of phonics instruction on EFL/L2 learners (Chu et al. 2007; Stuart 1999). Participants' movement from the pre-partial alphabetic phase into the partial alphabetic phase may also be due to their accumulating experience of learning English, which may familiarise them with the relationship between the simplest orthographic unit and the corresponding sound.

Although the introduction of the letter-sound relations in the OE phonics programme is incremental and covers all the high-frequency letter-sound relations embedded in the textbook monosyllabic vocabulary, children performed poorly in consonant clusters and vowels in general. Even if the sounds of single vowel letters and vowel digraphs are covered in textbooks 3A and 4B and then revisited in textbooks 5A and 5B, most children are still struggling in decoding them. One explanation is that these more difficult orthographic units are usually acquired at a later phase of learning to decode English words, namely the full alphabetic phase of decoding. Some children may not be developmentally ready to acquire them. The lack of consonant clusters in Chinese and the straightforward one-to-one relationship for vowels in the Pinyin system may exacerbate the difficulty for Chinese EFL children to learn to decode consonant clusters and vowel orthographic units. In addition, some limitations in terms of the teaching materials and teaching practice may also explain children's particular difficulty with consonant clusters and vowels in general. Consonant clusters received little attention when graphophonic analyses were performed on words in vocabulary instruction and most of the letter-sound relations that are never revisited in in grade 5 are consonant clusters. In introducing the sounds of single vowel letters, the long sound and short sound of a vowel letter are presented simultaneously, which may be confusing to children and therefore counterproductive for children to master the more frequent sounds of single vowel letters (i.e. the short sounds) before the less frequent sounds of single vowel letters (i.e. the long sounds). Moreover, no rime patterns are included in the phonics syllabus or introduced in the phonics sessions, in spite of the fact that it has been found helpful.

Most Chinese children had difficulty decoding the orthographic units which are not included in the textbook phonics syllabus, with only a few children able to decode them correctly. This resonates with Adam's (2004) suggestion that the explicit teaching of letter-sound relations is necessary for most children, especially those who are not analytic learners. This also suggests that some analytic children can derive the letter-sound relations embedded in words on their own, if they have accumulated many sight words.

When decoding nonword test items, all participants employed the whole word approach to a varying degree. When using the whole word strategy, they assign the nonword with the sound of the real word that shares some constituent letters, usually the boundary consonant letters of its nonword counterpart. Below average readers used the whole word strategy significantly more frequently than average readers, who used it significantly more than above average readers. This suggests the developmental phases of learning to decode English words, from the partial alphabetic phase, where decoding relies on the boundary consonant orthographic units and the whole word substitution may thereby happen, to the full alphabetic phase, where children perform thorough analyses on the constituent letter-sound relations, including the vowel graphemes. Teachers' use of the whole word approach to sound out new words, in conjunction with the absence of thorough decoding in vocabulary instruction, may not set a good model for thorough decoding for the children, who therefore may not pay close attention to all the component graphemes, particularly the medial letters or letter combinations representing vowels, which are less salient to beginning readers. In addition, the dominant role of visual analysis and rote learning in their L1 literacy acquisition may aggravate some Chinese children's reliance on the whole word strategy.

When decoding nonword test items, all participants employed the phonological decoding approach to varying degrees. Above average readers tend to use more decoding strategies relying on the taught grapheme-phoneme correspondences than average and below average readers. This again suggests these children are following the developmental stages of learning to decode English words, in which children are developing their knowledge of the major grapheme-phoneme correspondences. The explicit and systematic teaching of phonological decoding is crucial to facilitate children in developing their decoding skills. The teaching materials introduce the high-frequency grapheme-phoneme correspondences as many as possible in a systematic and incremental way. Moreover, the enabling skills for English language learners to acquire phonological decoding, such as phoneme identification, articulation, and discrimination skills are also included in the syllabus. However, the limitations inherent in the teaching materials combined with the classroom teaching may weaken the instructional effects, for example, the limited time allocated for the instruction in phonological decoding, the preference for repetition drills over word decoding activities, the insufficient practice provided in the teaching materials, the large proportion of practice words that are not fully decodable, the secondary role of the phonological decoding approach in vocabulary instruction, the lack of complete graphophonic analyses on words, and the neglect of out-of-class oral reading homework and extracurricular reading by most children and parents. For some capable children who are analytic learners, the phonological decoding instruction described in the present study may be sufficient in helping them develop their decoding knowledge and skills at this early stage. But for some children who are not analytic learners, more explicit instruction in phonological decoding and more practice in applying taught phonics knowledge to decode words thoroughly might be helpful.

Participants in general did not show a high frequency of using the rime-based decoding strategy. This is because the sensitivity to the rime patterns develops with the accumulating knowledge of grapheme-phoneme correspondences and the growing vocabulary size, and is the specific characteristics of the advanced stage of learning to decode English words (Ehri 1992, 1999, 2005). The participants in the present study were still at the early stage of learning English. Their underdeveloped knowledge of major grapheme-phoneme correspondences and small vocabulary size may not have prepared the children well enough for developing their knowledge of the rime patterns and further applying this knowledge in decoding tasks. Moreover, the rime patterns in which vowels tend to be stable are not included in the phonics syllabus.

Students may therefore not be made aware of the larger sub-word units of rimes, which can facilitate the selection of the sound mappings for ambiguous vowel letters and letter combinations in a more hierarchical and more context-dependent way (for example, <ea> tends to sounded out as /i:/ in the rime patterns of <eam> and <ean>) (Ehri and McCormick 1998; Woore 2014). In terms of relying on rime patterns in the decoding process, above average readers again showed their advantage over the average readers, who were superior to the below average readers. Although no rime patterns are introduced in the textbook syllabus or the classroom teaching of phonics, and only on very few occasions is the phonological decoding approach involved with rime patterns in vocabulary instruction, good readers tend to be more reliant on rime patterns compared with less proficient readers, because of their better knowledge of major grapheme-phoneme correspondences and larger vocabulary size.

In general, the results obtained from the present study clearly show the effectiveness of phonics instruction in developing Chinese children's phonological decoding ability, although caution should be taken that some capable young readers may acquire phonological decoding skills eventually without receiving phonics instruction (Ehri 1994) but this process may be "too lengthy and uneven in its results" (Woore 2007, p. 177). Children's phonological decoding skills and use of decoding strategies may be influenced by instructional factors. Their varying phonological decoding abilities suggest that some other factors may be interplaying with the impact of teaching, such as children's different levels of L2 phonological skills, children's English vocabulary size, and children's abilities.

6.3   Contribution of the Study

The methods of teaching phonological decoding, children's acquisition of phonological decoding skills, and the interaction between teaching and learning have been widely researched and debated in the L1 context. However, it was not until the beginning of the 21st century that instruction in phonological decoding was first proposed and introduced in China. There has not been much research investigating and evaluating the teaching and learning of phonological decoding among Chinese young learners. The contribution of the present study can be approached from two angles.

Firstly, the study contributes to a better understanding of the teaching of early English reading to young learners in China. The findings obtained from the combined methods of textbook analysis, classroom observation, and teacher interviews depict a comprehensive picture of how phonological decoding is taught in Shanghai primary schools. It thus provides valuable information with regard to the EFL decoding instruction in China which is useful for policymakers, curriculum developers, textbook writers and teachers (see implications in Sect. 6.4), and it is believed that it will lead to improvement in curriculum and textbook design, and in teaching practice.

Secondly, the findings of the present study also contribute to the research field of the learning and teaching of phonological decoding in the EFL/L2 context. While a substantial body of research has been accumulated on EFL/L2 literacy acquisition in recent years, most of the literature addresses higher level reading or its subcomponents (e.g. vocabulary, grammar). The present study adds supporting evidence to the literature suggesting that Chinese EFL children go through the similar developmental phases of phonological decoding as L1 children (Yin et al. 2007) and their phonological decoding strongly correlates with their reading performance (Chu 2002). It is hoped that by revealing the important role of phonological decoding in Chinese EFL children's early English literacy acquisition, more attention will be drawn to decoding instruction. In addition, the findings with respect to the difference in strategy use among children at different levels of reading ability also contribute to our understanding of Chinese EFL children's use of different strategies at different developmental phases of phonological decoding.

6.4 Implications of the Study

6.4.1 Implications for Policymakers and Curriculum Developers

English Curriculum Standards for Compulsory Education (Ministry of Education 2011) specified "sounding out simple words by drawing on phonics rules" as one of the reading skills to be acquired by the end of the primary school. However, as Ma and Feng (2011) have argued, the 2011 ECS does not give clear or detailed explanations about what specific phonics knowledge and what level of proficiency in decoding skills are required at different grades, and where or how the phonological decoding skills can be applied. As a consequence it is unclear in the 2011 ECS what expectations are held for phonics instruction. The lack of clearly defined objectives is reflected in the design of textbook materials and the classroom teaching, which, as the present study revealed, demonstrated little attempt at integrating phonics instruction with vocabulary and reading instruction. It is worth mentioning that the 2022 ECS (Ministry of Education 2022) puts forward clearer objectives for phonological decoding, with the lower primary grades working towards the grasp of 26 English letter names, the perception of the letter sounds within words, and the perception of simple phonics rules, while higher grades towards decoding English words by drawing on phonics rules. Nevertheless, neither the 2011 ECS nor the 2022 version specifies what spelling-sound relations are required to be taught and learnt at different phases.

Moreover, there are no sample lesson plans or detailed guidelines on phonics instruction provided in the 2011 ECS, and in the latest version. This indicates that despite the educational authorities' recognition of the place of phonological decoding in early literacy instruction, its teaching does not receive as much attention as the other skills in the curriculum.

The contradiction between teachers' belief and teaching practice may lie in the lack of understanding of Chinese children's English literacy acquisition and effective approaches for phonics instruction in the Chinese EFL context. There is a pressing need for the MoE to encourage more research on Chinese children's acquisition of English decoding skills and optimal phonics instructional approaches for Chinese EFL children. The curriculum needs to be more research-based in order to produce guidelines which make the most of Chinese children's decoding ability.

Generally speaking, policymakers and curriculum developers need to recognize that the national English curriculum standards should specify clearly defined objectives and content for phonics instruction. Meanwhile, there should be adequate support for curriculum implementation with various curriculum resources and a research base about issues of phonics instruction and English literacy acquisition among Chinese EFL children. Without sufficiently and effectively addressing these challenges, it will be difficult for the early start of English instruction to achieve its expected goals.

6.4.2 Implications for Textbook Writers

As specified in the national English curriculum standards, it is of vital importance to revisit important language knowledge throughout the textbook. The revision scheme of phonics knowledge in the textbook does not cover consonant clusters, which turns out to be the most problematic consonant graphemic type. Accordingly, it is advisable to revisit consonant clusters at some point in the textbook.

The spelling-sound relations included in the present phonics programme are all at the graphemic level, rather than at the level of larger sub-word units, namely rime patterns. It may be beneficial to include the common rime spelling patterns embedded in the textbook vocabulary, which may help students to be more accurate in decoding vowel letters and letter combinations. But more research is needed with regard to when and how to introduce the common rime spelling patterns, and the effectiveness of teaching rime spelling patterns as supplement to GPCs among children at different phases of development in phonological decoding.

Few exercises and activities for practicing word decoding were detected in the textbook analysis. The ultimate aim of phonics instruction, namely working out the sound of words based on spelling-sound associations, necessitates exercises for applying the taught letter-sound relations in decoding words. Moreover, the types of phonics activities in the textbook should be more diversified. For example, all the taught words containing the target letter-sound association can be presented in segmented forms, namely the letters representing onset, vowel and coda, so that students can be required to assemble the letters, translate them to sounds and assemble the sounds to form the word. Unfamiliar words can also be used for students' practice, with pictures to illustrate their meaning. The UK Department for Education and Skills (2007) includes a variety of phonics activities, which the textbook writers could refer to. In addition, considering that some nursery rhymes were reported to be difficult and lengthy for children to read and memorise, and a teacher simply picked out the words containing the target letter-sound relations without using the nursery rhyme, it may be worth including some captions or short sentences composed of one or more high-frequency words and words containing the target letter-sound associations. Of course, the effectiveness of using captions or short sentences in the instruction of decoding awaits research.

The present study also has some implications for the structure of the phonics content in the textbook. There should be more links between the taught letter-sound relations and the teaching of other sections, especially vocabulary and reading instruction. Firstly, the textbook writer can sequence the teaching of letter sounds, taking account of the frequency of the occurrence of letter-sound links in the vocabulary list. For example, the most common vowel letter-sound associations (the short sound of <a>, <e>, <i>, <o>, <u> can be introduced in the first phonics lessons, together with the most common consonant letter-sound relations, most of which are existent in Chinese and thus would be easy to learn. Teaching the most common phonics content first could allow more key vocabulary to be decoded with taught letter sounds in lower grades, which hence may allow phonological decoding to play a more significant role in the teaching process earlier and reduce the probability of students resorting to other less efficient strategies, like whole word strategy. Secondly, more practice of phonics should be integrated into the main lessons. Decodable words can be deliberately built into the reading texts to consolidate students' newly learnt phonics rules. And corresponding guides should be provided in teachers' books to ensure teachers know how and where to use these words for practicing decoding skills. With more experience of successful decoding, children can develop a sense of the utility of phonics knowledge.

6.4.3 Implications for Teachers

The present study revealed teachers' relative neglect of decoding instruction although they recognise its place in children's early reading acquisition. Teachers may need to cleverly arrange their limited class hours and allocate time for students to practice and revisit the taught letter-sound relations, despite the fact that phonological decoding is only a very minor part in the examination system.

The textbook does not integrate the instruction in decoding closely with vocabulary instruction and literacy instruction, so it may be challenging for teachers to plan themselves the integration of decoding instruction into daily teaching, but it should nonetheless be possible. Teachers could model or engage students in the thorough decoding of component letters in a word wherever it is applicable. Children can thereby develop the awareness that learning a word entails the careful and full decoding of all the constituent letters. In the meantime, children can also be made aware of the utility of the letter-sound relations that they have learnt.

The nonword reading test demonstrated children's problems with certain types of orthographic units. Accordingly, teachers may need to bear in mind those aspects that pose particular difficulty to their students (e.g. consonant clusters and vowel digraphs), treat them with more care when teaching phonological decoding, and understand that some children may need more time and more exposure to the English language before acquiring them. Children's progress in learning the sounds of those graphemes should be monitored. There are some children who still had a lot of difficulties in decoding consonant letters and letter combinations, and appeared to be stuck in the partial alphabetic phase, thus requiring prompt identification and appropriate intervention.

According to Ehri and McCormick (1998), appropriate and sufficient instruction at different phases of learning to decode are necessary. In order to promote learning in the full-alphabetic phase, students' attention could be directed to common rime spelling patterns at grade 5, after the introduction of most major grapheme-phoneme correspondences. Also, as Stahl (1992) suggested, teachers could point out some rules to help children see the spelling patterns but not ask students to state or memorise the rules.

6.4.4 Implications for Teacher Educators

Teacher educators should provide teachers with sufficient training on teaching phonological decoding. None of the teachers in the present study received any specific training on phonics instruction and how to integrate it into their daily teaching. During the training, teacher educators can use relevant research to make teachers aware of the necessity and importance of implementing systematic instruction in decoding, and the application of the taught phonics knowledge in daily teaching. Teacher educators should also take the responsibility of suggesting a good variety of activities to teachers, who can refer to the pool of recommended activities when planning their phonics lessons.

Teachers should be trained in their subject knowledge of decoding instruction, if teachers lack such knowledge. Teachers should at least have some knowledge of English phonology, especially the letter sounds that may cause particular problems for Chinese young EFL children, and some basic phonics rules or common rime spelling patterns, which they can use to explain the choice of a sound mapping for the letter(s) that permit(s) several optional sound representations.

6.5 Limitations of the Study and Suggestions for Future Research

With the use of five methods of data collection, and the involvement of four schools, the findings from this investigation could reasonably be argued to be a true reflection of the learning and teaching of phonological decoding in the primary schools in

Shanghai and that this in turn gives these findings a claim to credibility, weight and trustworthiness. However, some limitations of the study are worth pointing out and discussing along with suggestions for future research to address these issues.

Firstly, given the relatively small sample size of 54 children and 4 primary schools in Shanghai, a metropolitan city in China, the findings must be treated with caution as they might not be generalizable to the whole context of China or other wider contexts. Therefore, future research could be carried out in the broader context of China, including both cities and rural areas. A large-scale nationwide survey and follow-up interviews and classroom observations can be used to explore the teaching and learning of phonological decoding in both urban and rural primary schools in China. This would provide a more comprehensive and better understanding of the teaching and learning of phonological decoding at primary level in China.

Secondly, the present study did not assess children's knowledge and skills in English phonology, i.e. phonological awareness, auditory discrimination, and phoneme production, as variables. Thus, those variables were not analysed in relation to participants' phonological decoding ability. Future research could hence assess these variables to further explore their role in children's phonological decoding.

Thirdly, there may be some other strategies the participants used to decode the nonword items in the present study. Future study could use verbal report protocol, e.g. think-aloud method, to elicit participants' report on their use of different strategies in decoding nonwords, and gain deeper insight into what is going on inside the young learners' minds, even if the self-report procedure may influence and change their decoding performance in the process of reflection and report on each test item.

Finally, this study provides an investigation and evaluation of the effectiveness of a specific instructional programme on phonological decoding skills among Chinese young children, but did not involve any intervention. Further longitudinal empirical work is required on the effectiveness of different approaches to decoding instruction in developing the decoding skills of Chinese EFL children. It would also be interesting to investigate how children of different levels of reading ability, or at different primary grades, would respond to the same method of decoding instruction. And it would also be worthwhile to conduct a systematic investigation of the links between decoding abilities and other skills, such as working memory, vocabulary size, phonological awareness skills, the grasp of English phonology, listening comprehension ability, and language input, with a view of understanding why some children are much better than others at decoding English words.

References

Chen, Y. (2003). *The effects of phonological decoding training on English word recognition skills in Taiwanese EFL children.* (Unpublished Master dissertaion). National Taipei University of Education.

Chu, H. (2002). Beginning EFL learners' decoding skill and word reading ability. *Taipei Municipal Teachers College Journal, 33*, 471–484.

Chu, H., Yu, Y., Chang, H., Ting, L., Yu, C., & Hu, C. F. (2007). Effectiveness of phonological remediation for children with poor English word reading abilities. *English Teaching & Learning, 31*(4), 85–125.

Department for Education and Skills. (2007). *Letters and Sounds: Notes of guidance for practitioners and teachers.* Retrieved September 2, 2011, from http://nationalstrategies.standards. dcsf.gov.uk/node/84969.

Ehri, L. C. (1992). Reconceptualizing the development of sight word reading and its relationship to recoding. In P. Gough, L. Ehri, & R. Treiman (Eds.), *Reading acquisition* (pp. 107–143). Hillsdale, NJ: Lawrence Erlbaum Associates.

Ehri, L. C. (1999). Phases of development in learning to read words. In J. Oakhill & R. Beard (Eds.), *Reading development and the teaching of reading* (pp. 79–108). Oxford: Blackwell publishers.

Ehri, L. C. (2005). *Development of sight word reading: Phases and findings.* Oxford: Blackwell Publishing Ltd.

Ehri, L. C., & McCormick, S. (1998). Phases of word learning: Implications for instruction with delayed and disabled readers. *Reading & Writing Quarterly, 14*(2), 135–163.

Ehri, L. C. (1994). Development of the ability to read words: Update. In R. B. Ruddell, Ruddell, M. R., Singer, H. (Ed.), *Theoretical models and processes of reading* (4th ed., pp. 323–358). Newark, DE: International Reading Association.

Felton, R. H. (1993). Effects of instruction on the decoding skills of children with phonological-processing problems. *Journal Of Learning Disabilities, 26*(9), 583–589.

Foorman, B. R., Francis, D. J., Fletcher, J. M., Schatschneider, C., & Mehta, P. (1998). The role of instruction in learning to read: Preventing reading failure in at-risk children. *Journal of Educational Psychology, 90*(1), 37–55.

Kuo, L. (2011). *The role and efficacy of phonics instruction in the early literacy development of young Taiwanese EFL learners.* (Unpublished PhD thesis). University of Warwick.

Laxon, V., Gallagher, A., & Masterson, J. (2002). The effects of familiarity, orthographic neighbourhood density, letter-length and graphemic complexity on children's reading accuracy. *British Journal of Psychology, 93*(2), 269–287.

Lin, Y. (2004). *Taiwanese university students' word decoding skills with the knowledge of letter-sound correspondences: The context of biotechnology and chemical engineering department students.* (Unpublished Master dissertation). Southern Taiwan University of Technology.

Ma, Z., & Feng, X. (2011). The imperfection on English curriculum standard: The analysis on the issue of English phonology during the basic education. *Journal of Northeast Normal University (Philosophy and Social Sciences), 4,* 211–214.

McGeown, S., & Medford, E. (2014). Using method of instruction to predict the skills supporting initial reading development: insight from a synthetic phonics approach. *Reading and Writing, 27*(3), 591–608.

Ministry of Education, China. (2011). *English curriculum standards for compulsory education.* Beijing: Beijing Normal University Press.

Ministry of Education, China. (2022). *English curriculum standards for compulsory education.* Beijing: Beijing Normal University Press.

Qiu, J. (2007). An experimental study on phonics instruction. *Journal of Basic English Education, 9*(1), 29–33.

Rixon, S. (2011). *Beyond ABC: Investigating current rationales and systems for the teaching of early reading to young learners of English.* (Unpublished PhD thesis). University of Warwick.

Roberts, T. A. (2005). Articulation accuracy and vocabulary size contributions to phonemic awareness and word reading in English language learners. *Journal of Educational Psychology, 97*(4), 601–616.

Seymour, P. H. K., Bunce, F., & Evans, H. M. (1992). A framework for orthographic assessment and remediation. In C. M. Sterling & C. Robson (Eds.), *Psychology, spelling and education* (pp. 224–249). Clevedon, England: Multilingual Matters.

Share, D. L. (1995). Phonological recoding and self-teaching: Sine qua non of reading acquisition. *Cognition, 55*(2), 151–218.

Stahl, S. A. (1992). Saying the "p" word: Nine guidelines for exemplary phonics instruction. *The Reading Teacher, 45*(8), 618–625.

Stuart, M. (1999). Getting ready for reading: Early phoneme awareness and phonics teaching improves reading and spelling in inner-city second language learners. *British Journal of Educational Psychology, 69*(4), 587–605.

Wade-Woolley, L., & Geva, E. (2000). Processing novel phonemic contrasts in the acquisition of L2 word reading. *Scientific Studies of Reading, 4*(4), 295–311.

Woore, R. (2007). 'Weisse Maus in meinem Haus': Using poems and learner strategies to help learners decode the sounds of the L2. *The Language Learning Journal, 35*(2), 175–188.

Woore, R. (2009). Beginners' progress in decoding L2 French: Some longitudinal evidence from English modern foreign languages classrooms. *The Language Learning Journal, 37*(1), 3–18.

Woore, R. (2014). Beginner learners' progress in decoding L2 French: Transfer effects in typologically similar L1-L2 writing systems. *Writing Systems Research, 6*(2), 167–189.

Yin, L., Anderson, R. C., & Zhu, J. (2007). Stages in Chinese children's reading of English words. *Journal of Educational Psychology, 99*(4), 852–866.

Appendix A
List of Acceptable Pronunciations for Nonword Test Items

	Nonwords	IPA		
1	lun	lʌn		
2	fod	fɒd		
3	lik	lɪk		
4	tep	tɛp		
5	rel	rɛl		
6	juf	dʒʌf		
7	yat	jæt		
8	nop	nɒp		
9	fote	fəʊt		
10	kile	kaɪl		
11	bage	beɪdʒ		
12	hime	haɪm		
13	whik	wɪk		
14	shos	ʃɒs		
15	knud	nʌd		
16	wret	rɛt		
17	vock	vɒk		
18	muth	mʌθ	muːθ	
19	zess	zɛs		
20	toch	tɒtʃ		
21	haif	heɪf	haɪf	
22	soin	sɔɪn		
23	galk	gɔːk		
24	cight	saɪt		

(continued)

Appendix A: List of Acceptable Pronunciations for Nonword Test Items

(continued)

	Nonwords	IPA		
25	grop	grɒp		
26	plaf	plɑ:f	plæf	
27	snet	snɛt		
28	prug	prʌg		
29	wect	wekt		
30	selt	sɛlt		
31	lext	lɛkst		
32	zelp	zɛlp		
33	cleals	kli:ls		
34	stount	staʊnt		
35	twesk	twɛsk		
36	snump	snʌmp		
37	floket	flɒkɪt	flɒkət	
38	zaycred	zeɪkred	zeɪkrəd	
39	malras	mælræs; mɑ:lræs; mɔ:lræs	mælrəs; mɑ:lrəs; mɔ:lrəs	mælrɑ:s; mɑ:lrɑ:s; mɔ:lrɑ:s
40	fraklenk	fræklɛŋk; frækləŋk	frɑ:klɛŋk; frɑ:kləŋk	
41	chensert	tʃɛnsɜ:t		
42	shemslip	ʃɛmslɪp		

Appendix B
List of the Test Words that Share with the Nonwords the Same Rime-Level Sub-word Units

	Nonwords	Monosyllabic words containing the same rime-level graphemic patterns
1	lun	Run, Sun
2	fod	Nod
3	lik	
4	tep	
5	rel	
6	juf	
7	yat	Cat, Fat, Hat, Sat, What, That, At
8	nop	Hop, Shop, Stop
9	fote	
10	kile	While, Smile
11	bage	Age
12	hime	Time
13	whik	
14	shos	
15	knud	Bud
16	wret	Get, Wet
17	vock	Clock, Sock
18	muth	
19	zess	Chess, Dress
20	toch	
21	haif	
22	soin	Join
23	galk	Talk, Walk
24	cight	Night, Light

(continued)

K. Hua, *The Learning and Teaching of Phonological Decoding in Chinese EFL Children*, https://doi.org/10.1007/978-981-97-6891-2

(continued)

	Nonwords	Monosyllabic words containing the same rime-level graphemic patterns
25	grop	See *Nop*
26	plaf	
27	snet	See *Wret*
28	prug	Hug
29	wect	
30	selt	
31	lext	Next
32	zelp	Help
33	cleals	
34	stount	Count
35	twesk	Desk
36	snump	Jump

Appendix C
Real Word Reading Test

	Textbook	Real words		Textbook	Real words
1	1A	Nose	37	2A	Run
2	1A	Short	38	2A	Swing
3	1A	Duck	39	2A	Plate
4	1A	Chick	40	2A	Sun
5	1A	Thin	41	2A	Fox
6	1A	Tall	42	2A	Seesaw
7	1A	Mouth	43	2A	Chopsticks
8	1A	Green	44	2A	Desk
9	1A	Peach	45	2A	Ten
10	1A	Pie	46	2B	Brown
11	1A	Rubber	47	2B	Black
12	1A	Five	48	2B	Smooth
13	1A	Six	49	2B	Soft
14	1A	Fat	50	2B	Train
15	1A	Blue	51	2B	Van
16	1B	Kite	52	2B	Skate
17	1B	Sheep	53	2B	Snake
18	1B	Frog	54	2B	Fish
19	1B	Bird	55	2B	Cold
20	1B	Hen	56	2B	Wait
21	1B	Dress	57	2B	Light
22	1B	Cream	58	2B	Thirsty
23	1B	Blouse	59	2B	Hop
24	1B	Sweet	60	2B	Stop

(continued)

K. Hua, *The Learning and Teaching of Phonological Decoding in Chinese EFL Children*, https://doi.org/10.1007/978-981-97-6891-2

(continued)

	Textbook	Real words		Textbook	Real words
25	1B	Cat	61	3A	Bud
26	1B	Ride	62	3A	Count
27	1B	Gift	63	3A	Dream
28	1B	Card	64	3A	What
29	1B	Rabbit	65	3A	That
30	1B	Farmer	66	3A	Shop
31	2A	Small	67	3A	Tail
32	2A	Night	68	3A	Trunk
33	2A	Write	69	3A	Get
34	2A	Slide	70	3A	Fold
35	2A	Spoon	71	3A	Jam
36	2A	Swim	72	3A	Leaf
73	3A	Wet	112	4B	Lawn
74	3A	Nine	113	4B	Plum
75	3A	Well	114	4B	Vine
76	3B	Boil	115	4B	Chess
77	3B	Jump	116	4B	Cartoon
78	3B	Sock	117	4B	Dumpling
79	3B	Turn	118	4B	Kitchen
80	3B	Fun	119	4B	Dinner
81	3B	March	120	4B	Back
82	3B	Shape	121	5A	Age
83	3B	Smell	122	5A	Hug
84	3B	Whale	123	5A	Talk
85	3B	Circle	124	5A	Match
86	3B	Jacket	125	5A	Nod
87	3B	Hat	126	5A	Bank
88	3B	Help	127	5A	Fifteen
89	3B	Fifth	128	5A	Button
90	3B	First	129	5A	Campfire
91	4A	Dish	130	5A	Dentist
92	4A	Feed	131	5A	Pocket
93	4A	Jeans	132	5A	Report
94	4A	Paint	133	5A	Sunshine
95	4A	Pond	134	5A	Traffic
96	4A	Toast	135	5A	Weekend
97	4A	Packet	136	5B	Milk

(continued)

(continued)

	Textbook	Real words		Textbook	Real words
98	4A	Canteen	137	5B	Sat
99	4A	Dolphin	138	5B	Stick
100	4A	Rubbish	139	5B	Keep
101	4A	Sketchbook	140	5B	Clock
102	4A	Visit	141	5B	Cloud
103	4A	Between	142	5B	Think
104	4A	Sixteen	143	5B	Bookshelf
105	4A	Thirteen	144	5B	Walk
106	4B	At	145	5B	Time
107	4B	While	146	5B	Outside
108	4B	Smile	147	5B	Princess
109	4B	Join	148	5B	Tidy
110	4B	Drum	149	5B	Loudly
111	4B	Knife	150	5B	Next

Appendix D
Codes for Classroom Observation Data

Code	Code definition	Examples
Activities used in phonics instruction		
Class asked to repeat-LS	The whole class was asked to say the letter sound again on their own	T: Let's read these words together. Skirt, skirt, purse, purse. Sorry. This way, /IR/ /IR/ skirt, skirt, ready? Go! SSS: /IR/ *(Class asked to repeat-LS)*, /IR/ *(Class asked to repeat-LS)*, skirt, skirt, /UR/ *(Class asked to repeat-LS)*, /UR/ *(Class asked to repeat-LS)*, purse, purse, /AU/ *(Class asked to repeat-LS)*, /AU/ *(Class asked to repeat-LS)*, Laura, Laura, /OOR/ *(Class asked to repeat-LS)*, /OOR/ *(Class asked to repeat-LS)*, floor, floor
Class asked to repeat-WS	The whole class was asked to say the word sound again on their own	T: Let's read these words together. Skirt, skirt, purse, purse. Sorry. This way, /IR/, /IR/, skirt, skirt, ready? Go! SSS: /IR/, /IR/, skirt *(Class asked to repeat-WS)*, skirt *(Class asked to repeat-WS)*, /UR/, /UR/, purse *(Class asked to repeat-WS)*, purse *(Class asked to repeat-WS)*, /AU/, /AU/, Laura *(Class asked to repeat-WS)*, Laura *(Class asked to repeat-WS)*, /OOR/, /OOR/, floor *(Class asked to repeat-WS)*, floor *(Class asked to repeat-WS)*
Class watch flash video-LSC/WS	The whole class watched the flash video for the letter-sound correspondence and word sound	⌈The whole class follow video to read "I-R, /IR/, skirt; U-R, /UR/, purse; A-U, /AU/, Laura; O-O-R, /OOR/, floor" and the rhyme.⌋

(continued)

K. Hua, *The Learning and Teaching of Phonological Decoding in Chinese EFL Children*, https://doi.org/10.1007/978-981-97-6891-2

(continued)

Code	Code definition	Examples
IS asked to repeat-LS	An individual student was asked to say the letter sound again on his/ her own	T: /AU/ SSS: /AU/ T: ## S: /AU/ *8 [8 pupils take turns to read it] *(IS asked to repeat-LS)*
IS asked to repeat-LSC	An individual student was asked to say the letter-sound correspondence again on his/her own	T: I-R, /IR/ SSS: I-R, /IR/ T: ##, you try S: I-R, /IR/ *6 [6 pupils take turns to read it] *(IS asked to repeat-LSC)*
IS asked to repeat-WS	An individual student was asked to say the word sound again on his/ her own	T: Purse SSS: Purse T: ##, you try. *(IS asked to repeat-WS)* S: Purse
T models and class repeats-LS	Teacher models the letter sound and the whole class repeats it after the teacher	T: Follow me, /IR/ *(T models and class repeats-LS)* SSS: /IR/
T models and class repeats-LSC	Teacher models the letter-sound correspondence and the whole class repeats it after the teacher	T: Follow me, I-R, /IR/ *(T models and class repeats-LSC)* SSS: I-R, /IR/
T models and class repeats-WS	Teacher models the word sound and the whole class repeats it after the teacher	T: Good. Follow me. Purse. *(T models and class repeats-WS)* SSS: Purse
T elicits-blending sounds	Teacher asks students to blend sounds	T: Good. Now, follow me, /PUR/ SSS: /PUR/ T: /SE/ SSS: /SE/ T: Together? *(T elicits-blending sounds)* SSV: Purse
T elicits-decoding word	Teacher asks students to decode words	T: Who can read this new word [purse]? ##. *(T elicits-decoding word)* S: /PUR/ T: Another try? ##. *(T elicits-decoding word)* S: /PUR/

(continued)

(continued)

Code	Code definition	Examples
T elicits-words of the same LS	Teacher asks students to say some words containing the target letter-sound relation	⌈T: T writes "ear, bear, /eə/" on the blackboard. ⌋ Follow me. E-A-R, /EAR/ SSS: E-A-R, /EAR/ T: Bear SSS: Bear T: Tell me other words with the same sound. *(T elicits-words of the same LS)* Ss (volunteers) Pear. Pear
T elicits-spelling word	Teacher asks students to spell words by converting phonemes to graphemes	T: Tell me other words with the same sound S (volunteer): Pear. Pear T: How to spell pear? *(T elicits-spelling word)* S (volunteer): P-E-A-R
T elicits-phoneme discrimination	Teacher asks students to discriminate phonemes	T: There. Hear <has a homophone> . H-E-R-E, so /hɪə/, not /heə/. /heə/ means <meaning of hair> . Follow me. Hair SSS: Hair T: Hear SSS: Hear T: Same or different? *(T elicits-phoneme discrimination)* Ss (volunteers): Different

Reading activities at text level

How (at the first encounter with the text)

Individual reading	Students are asked to read the text on their own, at the first encounter with the text	
Listening to teacher reading aloud	Students listen to the teacher reading the text aloud with the text in sight, at the first encounter with the text	
Watching flash videos	Students watch the flash videos for the text with scripts on, at the first encounter with the text	

(continued)

(continued)

Code	Code definition	Examples
Choral reading	Whole class or groups read aloud a piece of text in union, along with or without the teacher or the multimedia	
Finger-point reading while listening to the flash	Students finger-point read the text while listening to the flash, at the first encounter with the text	
How (after the first encounter with the text)		
Rereading	Students read aloud the text again, after the first encounter with the text	
In what		
Materials in the textbook		
Supplementary materials		

Appendix E
Questions for Teacher's Semi-structured Interview

Section one: Background information

1. How long have you been teaching English in primary schools?
2. Which grades have you taught before?

Section two: Teaching word reading

3. What methods do you use to teach students to sound out English words in different grades? Can you use examples to illustrate each type of method?
4. Do you have a preference for any method of teaching students to sound out English words in different grades? What are your reasons for this preference?

Section three: Teaching phonological decoding

5. Can you briefly describe how students are helped to develop the ability to sound out words using phonics rules?
6. How much time do you usually spend on the section "Learn the sounds"? Do you think it is sufficient? If yes, why? If not, why not?
7. What activities do you use to teach letters and sounds?
8. Do you provide any practice for children to apply taught letter-sound relations? If yes, in what forms? If not, why?
9. What do you think of the materials designed for teaching letters and sounds?
10. Do you think teaching letter sound relations helps your students learn to read in English? Why?
11. Have you met any challenges in helping children develop the ability to sound out words using phonics rules? If so, what are they?
12. Do you have anything you would like to ask or comment on that you don't think we have covered so far?

Appendix F
Questions for Textbook Writer's Semi-structured Interview

1. Can you briefly describe the main features of this textbook?
2. Can you describe which parts of the textbook are designed to help students develop the ability to sound out words by using phonics rules?
3. Can you describe the teaching objective of the section "Learn the letters" in the textbook 2A?
4. Can you describe the teaching objective of the section "Learn the sounds" in different grades?
5. What is the logic behind the decision on the scope of the letter-sound relations in the textbook?
6. What is the logic behind the sequence of introducing these letter sounds in the textbook?
7. What is the criterion for the choice of words in the section "Learn the sounds"?
8. What is the criterion for the choice of nursery rhymes in the section "Learn the sounds"?
9. Is there any other exercise provided in the textbook or students' workbook for children to practise the taught letter-sound relations?
10. Does the design of the textbook consider integrating the teaching of letter sounds with the teaching of other sections, such as vocabulary instruction and text-level reading? If yes, how? If not, why?
11. Is there any training in teaching letter sounds and word decoding to primary English teachers? If yes, what are they?
12. Do you have anything you would like to ask or comment on that you don't think we have covered so far?

K. Hua, *The Learning and Teaching of Phonological Decoding in Chinese EFL Children*, https://doi.org/10.1007/978-981-97-6891-2

Appendix G
Letter-Sound Relations in the Textbook Vocabulary

Letters	Sounds	Frequency of occurrence in OE vocabulary	Example	Covered in OE phonics or not
Single consonant letters				
t	/t/	224	Ten	√
n	/n/	222	No	√
m	/m/	134	My	√
d	/d/	117	Dog	√
l	/l/	112	Leg	√
p	/p/	109	Pen	√
b	/b/	106	Big	√
s	/s/	101	Sun	√
f	/f/	82	Face	√
r	/r/	71	Rain	√
c (except e/i/ y)	/k/	69	Cap	
h	/h/	58	Hair	√
v	/v/	54	Visit	√
w	/w/	52	We	
k	/k/	46	Kind	√
g	/g/	36	Good	√
s	/z/	27	Busy	
j	/dʒ/	17	Join	
g	/dʒ/	15	Gently	
c (e/i/y)	/s/	13	Centre	
y	/j/	13	Yes	

(continued)

K. Hua, *The Learning and Teaching of Phonological Decoding in Chinese EFL Children*, https://doi.org/10.1007/978-981-97-6891-2

(continued)

Letters	Sounds	Frequency of occurrence in OE vocabulary	Example	Covered in OE phonics or not
x	/ks/	8	Box	
z	/z/	4	Zoo	√
s	/ʒ/	3	Usually	
n	/ŋ/	2	Finger	
f	/v/	1	Of	
Single vowel letters				
i	/ɪ/	175	Sit	√
e	/ɛ/	111	Bed	√
a	/æ/	93	Bag	√
o	/ɒ/	75	Box	√
u	/ʌ/	57	Sun	√
y	/ɪ/	57	Gym	
a	/ə/	51	About	
e	/ə/	38	Open	
o	/əʊ/	37	Go	√
i	/aɪ/	34	Find	√
e	/ɪ/	34	Enjoy	
o	/ə/	32	Today	
a	/ɑː/	30	Ask	
a	/eɪ/	19	Baby	
o	/ʌ/	15	Other	
y	/aɪ/	13	My	
e	/iː/	11	He	√
u	/juː/	11	Music	√
a	/ɒ/	7	Want	
u	/ʊ/	7	Put	
i	/ə/	5	Pupil	
o	/uː/	5	Do	
i	/iː/	2	Ski	
a	/ɔː/	2	Water	
a	/ɛ/	2	Many	
o	/ʊ/	2	Into	
u	/ə/	2	Autumn	
u	/ɪ/	2	Busy	
u	/uː/	2	Ruler	
a	/ɪ/	1	Orange	

(continued)

(continued)

Letters	Sounds	Frequency of occurrence in OE vocabulary	Example	Covered in OE phonics or not
u	/jʊ/	1	January	
u	/jʊə/	1	During	
Consonant digraphs/trigraphs				
ng	/ŋ/	41	Long	
th	/θ/	36	Thin	√
sh	/ʃ/	36	She	√
ck	/k/	26	Back	√
th	/ð/	24	There	√
ch	/tʃ/	24	Chair	√
ll	/l/	22	Bell	√
ss	/s/	20	Class	√
pp	/p/	10	Happy	
rr	/r/	9	Worry	
tt	/t/	9	Better	
ph	/f/	8	Photo	
ff	/f/	7	Office	√
wh	/w/	6	What	√
bb	/b/	5	Rabbit	
tch	/tʃ/	5	Watch	
gg	/g/	4	Egg	
nn	/n/	4	Dinner	
gu	/g/	3	Guess	
mm	/m/	3	Summer	
zz	/z/	3	Pizza	
wh	/h/	2	Who	
dd	/d/	2	Middle	
kn	/n/	2	Knife	
mn	/m/	2	Autumn	
wr	/r/	2	Write	
th	/t/	1	Thailand	
ch	/k/	1	Toothache	
gn	/n/	1	Sign	
mb	/m/	1	Climb	
sc	/s/	1	Science	
Consonant clusters				
st	/st/	41	Stop	√

(continued)

(continued)

Letters	Sounds	Frequency of occurrence in OE vocabulary	Example	Covered in OE phonics or not
nd	/nd/	27	And	
nt	/nt/	24	Ant	
gr	/gr/	19	Green	√
tr	/tr/	16	Tree	√
dr	/dr/	14	Drink	√
br	/br/	13	Bring	√
cl	/kl/	13	Class	√
sk	/sk/	13	Ask	√
cr	/kr/	11	Cross	√
ld	/ld/	10	Old	
pl	/pl/	9	Play	√
bl	/bl/	7	Black	√
fr	/fr/	7	From	√
ft	/ft/	7	Soft	
pr	/pr/	7	Present	√
sm	/sm/	7	Small	√
sw	/sw/	7	Swim	√
lf	/lf/	6	Shelf	
nk	/ŋk/	6	Bank	
sp	/sp/	6	Spoon	√
ct	/kt/	5	Insect	
fl	/fl/	5	Fly	√
gl	/gl/	5	Glass	√
mp	/mp/	5	Jump	
str	/str/	5	Strong	
qu	/kw/	4	Quiet	
sl	/sl/	4	Sleep	√
st	/s/	4	Listen	
lk	/lk/	3	Milk	
sn	/sn/	3	Snow	√
thr	/θr/	3	Three	
tw	/tw/	3	Twelve	
lt	/lt/	2	Adult	
tw	/t/	1	Two	
chr	/kr/	1	Christmas	
ds	/dz/	1	Cards	

(continued)

(continued)

Letters	Sounds	Frequency of occurrence in OE vocabulary	Example	Covered in OE phonics or not
dw	/dw/	1	Dwarf	
lm	/lm/	1	Film	
lp	/lp/	1	Help	
sc	/sk/	1	Scarf	✓
sch	/sk/	1	School	
spr	/spr/	1	Spring	
squ	/skw/	1	Square	
tz	/ts/	1	Yangtze	
xt	/kst/	1	Next	
Letter combinations representing vowels				
er	/ə/	84	River	
i-e	/aɪ/	40	Like	✓
a-e	/eɪ/	38	Cake	✓
ee	/i:/	37	See	✓
ea	/i:/	27	Read	✓
oo	/u:/	27	Food	✓
ar	/ɑ:/	27	Card	✓
ay	/eɪ/	24	Day	✓
ou	/aʊ/	23	Out	✓
or	/ɔ:/	20	For	
o-e	/əʊ/	18	Rose	✓
ow	/əʊ/	14	Snow	
ai	/eɪ/	14	Rain	✓
o-e	/ʌ/	13	Love	
ir	/ɜ:/	12	Bird	✓
oo	/ʊ/	11	Book	
ow	/aʊ/	11	Now	✓
all	/ɔ:l/	11	Ball	
ea	/ɛ/	10	Head	
ur	/ɜ:/	10	Turn	✓
or	/ɜ:/	8	Firework	
our	/ɔ:/	8	Four	
igh	/aɪ/	7	Light	
ire	/aɪə/	7	Fire	
aw	/ɔ:/	6	Draw	
oa	/əʊ/	6	Coat	✓

(continued)

(continued)

Letters	Sounds	Frequency of occurrence in OE vocabulary	Example	Covered in OE phonics or not
i-e	/ɪ/	5	Live	
ou	/ʌ/	5	Touch	
or	/ə/	5	Doctor	
ear	/ɪə/	5	Near	√
ey	/ɪ/	5	Money	
oi	/ɔɪ/	5	Boil	√
air	/eə/	5	Hair	√
ou	/u:/	4	Soup	
ar	/ɔ:/	4	Warm	
al	/ɔ:l/	4	Always	
ui	/ɪ/	4	Build	
au	/ɔ:/	4	Autumn	√
u-e	/ju:/	4	Cute	√
are	/eə/	4	Square	√
a-e	/ɪ/	3	Cabbage	
ou	/ə/	3	Famous	
our	/aʊə/	3	Our	
ur	/ə/	3	Surprise	
ear	/eə/	3	Bear	√
e-e	/i:/	3	Eve	
ui	/u:/	3	Fruit	
ie	/aɪə/	3	Quiet	
oar	/ɔ:/	3	Blackboard	
oor	/ɔ:/	3	Door	√
ore	/ɔ:/	3	More	
oy	/ɔɪ/	3	Boy	√
ea	/eɪ/	2	Great	
ea	/ɪə/	2	Idea	
o-e	/u:/	2	Move	
ai	/ɪ/	2	Mountain	
our	/ə/	2	Colour	
ear	/ɜ:/	2	Heard	
al	/ɑ:/	2	Half	
al	/ɔ:/	2	Talk	
ey	/eɪ/	2	Grey	
ie	/aɪ/	2	Pie	√

(continued)

(continued)

Letters	Sounds	Frequency of occurrence in OE vocabulary	Example	Covered in OE phonics or not
ough	/ʌf/	2	Rough	
ia	/ɪə/	2	Aviary	
eau	/juː/	2	Beautiful	
oe	/uː/	2	Shoe	
ue	/uː/	2	Blue	✓
ere	/eə/	2	Where	
er	/əː/	1	Her	
a-e	/æ/	1	Have	
ee	/ɪ/	1	Coffee	
ou	/əʊ/	1	Shoulder	
ar	/ə/	1	Caterpillar	
ai	/aɪ/	1	Thailand	
our	/ɜː/	1	Journey	
ey	/iː/	1	Key	
au	/ɑː/	1	Aunt	
au	/ə/	1	Restaurant	
ie	/ɛ/	1	Friend	
oi	/ə/	1	Tortoise	
u-e	/uː/	1	June	
u-e	/ɪ/	1	Minute	
ough	/ɒf/	1	Cough	
ough	/ɔː/	1	Bought	
ough	/uː/	1	Through	
ei	/aɪ/	1	Either	
ei	/eɪ/	1	Beijing	
ei	/iː/	1	Receive	
ia	/aɪə/	1	Giant	
ew	/juː/	1	New	
ew	/uː/	1	Grew	
ae	/ɛ/	1	Aeroplane	
eer	/ɪə/	1	Deer	✓
eigh	/eɪ/	1	Eight	
eir	/eə/	1	Theirs	
eu	/ɪə/	1	Museum	
eye	/aɪ/	1	Eye	
iew	/juː/	1	Interview	

(continued)

(continued)

Letters	Sounds	Frequency of occurrence in OE vocabulary	Example	Covered in OE phonics or not
ure	/ʊə/	1	Sure	
uy	/aɪ/	1	Buy	
ere	/ɜ:/	1	Were	
ere	/ɪə/	1	Here	
Others				
-le	/l/	25	Apple	
-ce	/s/	18	Dance	
-ly	/lɪ/	17	Slowly	
-se	/z/	15	Nose	
-se	/s/	10	Mouse	
-ful	/fʊl/	6	Useful	
-tion	/ʃən/	5	Station	
-ture	/ʧə/	5	Picture	
-ve	/v/	5	Leave	
-es	/ɪz/	3	Glasses	
-es	/z/	3	Does	
-lly	/lɪ/	3	Really	
-able	/əbəl/	2	Vegetable	
un-	/ʌn/	2	Unhappy	
-shion	/ʃən/	1	Cushion	
-sion	/ʒən/	1	Television	
-sure	/ʒə/	1	Pleasure	

Appendix H
The Fully Decodable Words for Practising Target Letter-Sound Relations in OE (4B)

Modules	Units	Letters	Words for practising target letter sounds	No. of decodable words / Total No. of words	Decodable words (%)	No. of decodable monosyllables / No. of monosyllables	Decodable monosyllables (%)
Module 1	Unit 1	-ar	Car	0/1	0%	0/1	0%
		-ar-	Park, Mark, Yard	2/3	67%	2/3	67%
		-ue	Blue, Sue	2/2	100%	2/2	100%
		-oo-	School, Afternoon	0/2	0%	0/1	0%
	Unit 2	-ir-	Skirt, Girl	2/2	100%	2/2	100%
		-ur-	Purse	0/1	0%	0/1	0%
		-au-	Laura	0/1	0%	0/0	/
		-oor	Floor, Door	2/2	100%	2/2	100%
	Unit 3	-ee	Bee	1/1	100%	1/1	100%
		-ea	Tea	1/1	100%	1/1	100%
		-eer	Deer, Beer	2/2	100%	2/2	100%
		-ear	Tear, Fear	2/2	100%	2/2	100%
Module 2	Unit 1	-i-	Five, Mike, Line, Mine, Smile, Nice	0/6	0%	0/6	0%
		-ie-	Pie, Fries	2/2	100%	2/2	100%
	Unit 2	-oe	Joe, Toe	2/2	100%	2/2	100%
		-oa-	Goat, Toast, Boat, Coat	3/4	75%	3/4	75%
		-o	Flo, Hello, Go	2/3	67%	2/2	100%
	Unit 3	-oy	Toy, Boy, Joyce	2/3	67%	2/3	67%
		-oi-	Noise, Voice	0/2	0%	0/2	0%
Module 3	Unit 1	-are	Square, Clare	1/2	50%	1/2	50%
		-ear	Bear, Pear	2/2	100%	2/2	100%
		-air	Hair	1/1	100%	1/1	100%

(continued)

K. Hua, *The Learning and Teaching of Phonological Decoding in Chinese EFL Children*, https://doi.org/10.1007/978-981-97-6891-2

(continued)

Modules	Units	Letters	Words for practising target letter sounds	No. of decodable words / Total No. of words	Decodable words (%)	No. of decodable monosyllables / No. of monosyllables	Decodable monosyllables (%)
	Unit 2	-ou-	Mouse, <u>Cloud</u>, <u>Out</u>, <u>Ouch</u>, Aloud	3/5	60%	3/4	75%
		ow-	<u>Owl</u>, <u>Cow</u>, <u>Brown</u>	3/3	100%	3/3	100%
	Unit 3	-ay	<u>May</u>, Today, <u>Birthday</u>, Hurray, <u>Play</u>, <u>Day</u>	4/6	67%	3/3	100%
		-ai-	<u>Wait</u>	1/1	100%	1/1	100%
Module 4	/	/	/	/	/	/	/

Note The underlined words are the words that can be fully decoded based on the taught letter-sound relations

Appendix I
The Fully Decodable Words in the OE (4B) Vocabulary List

Grade	Module-unit	Vocabulary
4B	M1U1	A glass of, Cherry, Crunchy, Grape, Juice, <u>Not at</u> all, <u>Plum</u>, Strawberry, Vine, Want, Watermelon, Yum
4B	M1U2	All, Another, <u>Blind</u>, <u>Blunt</u>, Floor, <u>Hard</u>, Key, Knife, <u>Lost</u>-property, Office, Pencil, Case, Purse, Rough, <u>Sand</u>, <u>Sharp</u>, <u>Smooth</u>, <u>Soft</u>, Something, Take, Off, <u>Thick</u>, <u>Thin</u>, Whose
4B	M1U3	Again, Also, <u>At noon</u>, Away, <u>Back</u>, <u>Bench</u>, Bite, Deer, Follow, <u>Go</u>, Down, Grow, High, <u>Hill</u>, Lawn, Like, Path, Rise, Shadow, Stay, <u>Sun</u>, Tea, Tear, Wait
4B	M2U1	Ask, Before, <u>Club</u>, Enjoy, Exercise, <u>Fun</u>, Healthy, Join, Make, Notice, Play, Badminton, Basketball, Football, Table, Tennis, Volleyball, Poster, Remember, Sport, Sure, Swimming, Goggles, <u>Pool</u>, Swimsuit, <u>Too</u>, Warm <u>up</u>
4B	M2U2	Angry, Basket, Bone, Bowl, Cat <u>Food</u>, Catch, Cute, <u>Dog Food</u>, <u>Fish</u>, Goat, Hole, Large, Onto, Parrot, Shake, <u>Sleep</u>, Tortoise, Wake p
4B	M2U3	About, Bathroom, Bedroom, Bedtime, Chat, Cook, Dinner, Fairy, Tale, Go swimming, Have a holiday, Have a look, Homework, Interesting, Kitchen, Light, Living room, Make, Model, Plane, Noise, Star, Themselves, Turn off, Wash
4B	M3U1	Awake, <u>Bell</u>, Careful, Cry, <u>Doorbell</u>, Doze, Fly away, Have a bath, Have a <u>nap</u>, Loud, Noisy, Puzzled, Quiet, Ring, Sound, Square, Television, Unhappy, Watch, <u>Week</u>
4B	M3U2	A quarter past seven, A quarter to eight, All the way, Battery, <u>Brush</u> my <u>teeth</u>, Cartoon, <u>Finish</u>, <u>From</u>, <u>Get up</u>, Half past seven, Have breakfast, Have dinner, Last night, Late, Owl, Puzzle, Seven o'clock, Sofa, <u>Start</u>, Tomorrow, Wash my face
4B	M3U3	A little, Activity, Always, <u>At</u> weekends, <u>Bow</u>, Chinese, <u>Chess</u>, Clever, Friday, <u>Get</u>, Have a good time, <u>In</u> the middle of, <u>Kind</u>, Meeting, Monday, Never, Often, Really, Saturday, Show, Shy, Smile, Sometimes, Sunday, Thursday, Tuesday, Usually, Wednesday, While

(continued)

K. Hua, *The Learning and Teaching of Phonological Decoding in Chinese EFL Children*, https://doi.org/10.1007/978-981-97-6891-2

(continued)

Grade	Module-unit	Vocabulary
4B	M4U1	<u>Drum</u>, <u>Be</u> full of, <u>Gold</u>, Mouse, Mice, Music, <u>Piano</u>, Piper, Triangle, Violin
4B	M4U2	Colourful, Dragon boat, Race, Dumpling, During, Festival, Fireworks, Important, Money, New Year Eve, <u>Red</u> envelope, Relative, Rice dumpling, The Double <u>Ninth</u> Festival, The Dragon <u>Boat</u> Festival, The Mid-Autumn Festival, The Spring Festival, traditional
4B	M4U3	Drive away, Duckling, Fourth, Heavy, Lonely, <u>Nest</u>, Swan, Ugly, Worm

Note The underlined words are the words that can be fully decoded based on the taught letter-sound relations

Appendix J
Major and Minor GPCs for the Single Letters/ Letter Combinations Representing Vowels in the Monosyllabic Nonwords

Letters	Major GPCs (GPCs covered in the textbook phonics syllabus)	Minor GPCs	The number of textbook vocabulary that contain the GPCs
a	/ɛ/		2
	/æ/		98
	/ɑ:/		31
	/ɒ/		8
	/ə/		52
	/eɪ/		20
		/ɔ:/	2
		/ɪ/	1
e	/i:/		15
	/ɛ/		115
		/ə/	38
		/ɪ/	34
i	/ɪ/		184
	/aɪ/		77
		/ə/	6
		/i:/	2
o	/ʌ/		24
	/ɒ/		77
	/əʊ/		58
		/ə/	34
		/ʊ/	2
		/u:/	8
u	/ʌ/		57

(continued)

K. Hua, *The Learning and Teaching of Phonological Decoding in Chinese EFL Children*, https://doi.org/10.1007/978-981-97-6891-2

(continued)

Letters	Major GPCs (GPCs covered in the textbook phonics syllabus)	Minor GPCs	The number of textbook vocabulary that contain the GPCs
	/u:/		2
	/ʊ/		7
	/ju:/		16
		/ə/	2
		/ɪ/	2
		/jʊ/	2
		/jʊə/	1
ai	/eɪ/		14
		/aɪ/	1
		/ɪ/	2
oi	/ɔɪ/		5
		/ə/	1
igh	/aɪ/		7
al	/ɔ:/		6
		/ɑ:/	3
		/ɒl/	2
ea	/i:/		27
	/ɛ/		11
		/eɪ/	2
		/ɪə/	2
ou	/aʊ/		25
		/əʊ/	1
		/ə/	3
		/ɒ/	1
		/u:/	5
		/ʊ/	2
		/ʌ/	7
a-e	/eɪ/		40
		/ɪ/	2
o-e	/əʊ/		18
		/u:/	2
		/ʌ/	9
i-e	/aɪ/		40
		/ɪ/	5

Appendix K
The Vocabulary List of the Observed Unit and Supplementary Vocabulary in 4 Schools

School HL	Approaches to sounding out words	Taught/New	No. of syllables
Hard	PD*	Taught	1
Soft	WW*	Taught	1
Smooth	WW	Taught	1
Rough	WW	Taught	1
Sharp	PD	New	1
Blunt	PD	New	1
Thick	PD	New	1
Whose	PD	New	1
Blind	PD	New	1
Another	WW	New	>1
Lost	WW	New	1
Property	PD	New	>1
Key	WW	New	1
All	WW	New	1
Knife	WW	New	1
Pencil	WW	Taught	>1
Case	WW	New	1
Thin	WW	Taught	1
Floor	PD	Taught	1
Office	WW	Taught	>1
Purse	PD	New	1

Note PD represents phonological decoding approach; *WW* represents whole word approach

K. Hua, *The Learning and Teaching of Phonological Decoding in Chinese EFL Children*, https://doi.org/10.1007/978-981-97-6891-2

School JZ	Approaches of sounding out words	No. of syllables	Taught/New
Ask	WW	1	New
Club	PD	1	New
Fun	WW	1	Taught
Join	PD	1	New
Make	WW	1	Taught
Play	WW	1	Taught
Sport	PD	1	New
Sure	WW	1	Taught
Pool	WW	1	New
Too	WW	1	Taught
Warm	WW	1	Taught
Up	WW	1	Taught
Before	PD	>1	New
Enjoy	WW	>1	New
Exercise	WW	>1	New
Healthy	WW	>1	New
Notice	PD	>1	New
Badminton	PD	>1	New
Basketball	PD	>1	Taught
Football	WW	>1	Taught
Table	WW	>1	Taught
Tennis	PD	>1	New
Volleyball	PD	>1	New
Poster	PD	>1	New
Remember	WW	>1	New
Swimming	WW	>1	New
Goggles	PD	>1	New
Swimsuit	PD	>1	New
Supplementary words			
Favourtie	WW	>1	New
Would	WW	1	New
Talk	PD	1	New
Love	PD	1	New
Never	PD	>1	New
Spare	WW	1	New
Hobby	WW	>1	New
Will	WW	1	New
Body	PD	>1	Taught

School PM	Approaches of sounding out words	No. of syllables	Taught/New
Bell	PD	1	New
Cry	WW	1	New
Doze	PD	1	New
Fly	WW	1	Taught
Have	WW	1	Taught
Bath	PD	1	New
Nap	WW	1	New
Loud	PD	1	New
Quiet	PD	1	New
Ring	WW	1	New
Sound	WW	1	New
Square	PD	1	Taught
Watch	WW	1	Taught
Week	WW	1	New
Awake	WW	>1	New
Careful	WW	>1	New
Doorbell	WW	>1	New
Away	WW	>1	Taught
Noisy	PD	>1	New
Puzzled	PD	>1	New
Television	WW	>1	New
Unhappy	WW	>1	New
Supplementary words			
Voice	PD	1	New
Asleep	WW	>1	New
Baseball	WW	>1	New
Crayon	WW	>1	New
String	PD	1	New
Scissors	WW	>1	New
Different	WW	>1	New
Later	WW	>1	New

School SQ	Approaches of sounding out words	No. of syllables	Taught/New
Bell	PD	1	New
Cry	WW	1	New
Doze	PD	1	New
Fly	WW	1	Taught

(continued)

(continued)

School SQ	Approaches of sounding out words	No. of syllables	Taught/New
Have	WW	1	Taught
Bath	WW	1	New
Nap	PD	1	New
Loud	PD	1	New
Quiet	PD	1	New
Ring	WW	1	New
Sound	PD	1	New
Square	PD	1	Taught
Watch	WW	1	Taught
Week	WW	1	New
Awake	PD	>1	New
Careful	WW	>1	New
Doorbell	PD	>1	New
Away	WW	>1	Taught
Noisy	PD	>1	New
Puzzled	PD	>1	New
Television	WW	>1	New
Unhappy	PD	>1	New
Supplementary words			
Voice	PD	1	New
Asleep	WW	>1	New
Crayon	WW	>1	New
String	WW	1	New
Scissors	WW	>1	New
Lady	PD	>1	New
When	PD	1	New
Later	WW	>1	New

Appendix L
The Focal Sub-Word Units of Phonological Decoding in Vocabulary Instruction—4 Schools

School HL				
1. Monosyllabic words	Onset	Vowel	Coda	Rime (vowel + coda)
Hard	IC	V *	FC	Rime
Sharp	IC *	V *	FC	Rime
Blunt	IC *	V *	FC	Rime
Thick	IC *	V	FC *	Rime
Whose	IC *	V *	FC-e	Rime
Blind	IC *	V	FC	Rime *
Floor	IC	V *	/	/
Purse	IC	V *	FC-e*	Rime
Slim	IC *	V *	FC	Rime
The number of sub-word units that were decoded	6	7	2	1
2. Multisyllabic Words	1st syllable	2nd syllable	3rd syllable	1st vowel
Valentine	1st syllable*	2nd syllable*	3rd syllable*	1st vowel
Property	1st syllable*	2nd syllable*	3rd syllable	1st vowel
The number of sub-word units that were decoded	2	2	1	0

Notes IC initial consonant letter(s), *V* vowel, *FC* final consonant letter(s)
*means that the sub-word unit was decoded

School JZ						
1. Monosyllabic words	Onset	Vowel	Coda	Rime (vowel + coda)		
Club	IC	V *	FC	Rime		

(continued)

K. Hua, *The Learning and Teaching of Phonological Decoding in Chinese EFL Children*, https://doi.org/10.1007/978-981-97-6891-2

(continued)

School JZ						
Join	IC	V *	FC	Rime		
Sport	IC	V *	FC	Rime		
Talk	IC	V *	FC	Rime *		
Love	IC	V *(o)	FC	Rime		
The number of sub-word units that were decoded	0	5	0	1		
2. Multisyllabic Words	1st syllable	2nd syllable	3rd syllable	1st vowel	2nd vowel	3rd vowel
Before	1st syllable*	2nd syllable*	/	1st vowel	2nd vowel	/
Notice	1st syllable*	2nd syllable	/	1st vowel*	2nd vowel	/
Tennis	1st syllable	2nd syllable	/	1st vowel*	2nd vowel	/
Poster	1st syllable*	2nd syllable*	/	1st vowel	2nd vowel*	/
Goggles	1st syllable	2nd syllable	/	1st vowel*	2nd vowel	/
Swimsuit	1st syllable	2nd syllable	/	1st vowel	2nd vowel*	/
Never	1st syllable	2nd syllable	/	1st vowel*	2nd vowel	/
Body	1st syllable	2nd syllable	/	1st vowel*	2nd vowel	/
Badminton	1st syllable*	2nd syllable*	3rd syllable*	1st vowel*	2nd vowel*	3rd vowel
Basketball	1st syllable*	2nd syllable*	3rd syllable	1st vowel*	2nd vowel	3rd vowel
Volleyball	1st syllable*	2nd syllable	3rd syllable	1st vowel*	2nd vowel	3rd vowel
The number of sub-word units that were decoded	6	4	1	8	3	0

School PM				
1. Monosyllabic words	Onset	Vowel	Coda	Rime (vowel + coda)
Bell	IC	V *	FC	Rime*
Doze	IC	V * (o)	FC	Rime
Bath	IC	V *	FC	Rime
Loud	IC	V *	FC	Rime

(continued)

School PM				
Quiet	IC	V *	FC	Rime
Voice	IC	V *	FC	Rime
String	IC*	V	FC	Rime
The number of sub-word units that were decoded	1	6	0	1
2. Multisyllabic Words	1st syllable	2nd syllable	1st vowel	2nd vowel
Noisy	1st syllable*	2nd syllable	1st vowel*	2nd vowel
Puzzled	1st syllable	2nd syllable	1st vowel*	2nd vowel
The number of sub-word units that were decoded	1	0	2	0

School SQ						
1. Monosyllabic words	Onset	Vowel	Coda	Rime (vowel + coda)		
Bell	IC	V *	FC	Rime		
Doze	IC	V *(o)	FC	Rime		
Nap	IC	V *	FC	Rime		
Loud	IC	V *	FC	Rime		
Sound	IC	V *	FC	Rime		
Voice	IC	V *	FC	Rime		
When	IC	V *	FC	Rime		
The number of sub-word units that were decoded	0	7	0	0		
2. Multisyllabic Words	1st syllable	2nd syllable	3rd syllable	1st vowel	2nd vowel	3rd vowel
Awake	1st syllable*	2nd syllable	/	1st vowel	Rime*	/
Doorbell	1st syllable	2nd syllable*	/	1st vowel	2nd vowel*	/
Noisy	1st syllable*	2nd syllable	/	1st vowel*	2nd vowel	/
Puzzled	1st syllable*	2nd syllable*	/	1st vowel*	2nd vowel	/
Unhappy	1st syllable*	2nd syllable	3rd syllable	1st vowel	2nd vowel	3rd vowel
Lady	1st syllable*	2nd syllable	/	1st vowel*	2nd vowel	/

(continued)

(continued)

School SQ						
The number of sub-word units that were decoded	6	2	0	3	2	0

GPSR Compliance

*The European Union's (EU) General Product Safety Regulation (GPSR)
is a set of rules that requires consumer products to be safe and our
obligations to ensure this.*

*If you have any concerns about our products, you can contact us on
ProductSafety@springernature.com*

In case Publisher is established outside the EU, the EU authorized
representative is:

Springer Nature Customer Service Center GmbH
Europaplatz 3
69115 Heidelberg, Germany

Batch number: 08164799

Printed by Printforce, the Netherlands